Developing Zapatista Autonomy

DEVELOPING ZAPATISTA AUTONOMY

Conflict and NGO Involvement

in Rebel Chiapas

NIELS BARMEYER

UNIVERSITY OF NEW MEXICO PRESS ⬛ ALBUQUERQUE

15 14 13 12 11 10 09   1 2 3 4 5 6 7

Library of Congress Cataloging-in-Publication Data

Barmeyer, Niels, 1969–
Developing Zapatista autonomy : conflict and NGO
involvement in rebel Chiapas / Niels Barmeyer.
        p. cm.
Includes bibliographical references and index.
ISBN 978-0-8263-4584-4 (pbk. : alk. paper)
1. Chiapas (Mexico)—History—Peasant Uprising, 1994–
2. Mexico—Politics and government—1988–2000.
3. Mayas—Mexico—Chiapas—Government relations.
4. Non-governmental organizations—Mexico—Chiapas.
5. Conflict management—Mexico—Chiapas.
6. Ejército Zapatista de Liberación Nacional (Mexico)
I. Title.
        F1256.B36 2009
        972'.750835—dc22
                2008045276

Designed and typeset by Mina Yamashita
Composed in ITC Berkeley Oldstyle Std,
a typeface designed by Frederic W. Goudy.
Display text composed in Berthold City,
a typeface designed by Georg Trump.
Printed by Thomson-Shore, Inc. on 55# Natures Natural.

For Jannes

Contents

Preface

In spring 1995, I attended a congress in Berlin that had been organized by the remnants of the Autonomous Movement, an alliance of the undogmatic radical Left forged in West Germany in the 1980s. The meeting featured a vast array of panels ranging from gender politics to communal living, antifascist youth groups, political prisoners, and international solidarity. One of the panels had been organized by two Berlin-based solidarity groups and focused on the Zapatista rebellion in Chiapas, Mexico. They showed a documentary film made in the months after the uprising when large parts of Las Cañadas and Selva Lacandona were controlled by the Zapatista Army of National Liberation (Ejército Zapatista de Liberación Nacional, or EZLN).[1] The film featured an interview with the rebels' spokesperson and military commander Subcomandante Marcos, who was wearing a ski mask and taking the occasional puff from his pipe. His words were accompanied by images of Indígenas operating a roadblock in front of an impoverished-looking settlement situated in a breathtakingly beautiful landscape of mountains and jungle.[2] He spoke about the rebellion as having grown from the legitimate claims of the indigenous peasants of Chiapas to live in dignity. By organizing their liberation in the EZLN and by taking possession of the landholdings that had wrongfully been in the hands of a few, they had finally shaken off the yoke of exploitation and misery and taken control of their own lives. The film was followed by a captivating firsthand account by local activists who had just come back from Chiapas. With fervent enthusiasm, they told us about life in the liberated villages and spoke of the dreadful consequences a recent raid by the Mexican Federal Army had for the indigenous population.

I decided to join one of the groups and was exposed to more detailed information on the Zapatistas. Their communiqués and particularly Marcos's letters to national and international civil society read like poems and conveyed an urgent immediacy that was hard to resist. I perceived them as a call to action, feeling I was to miss something magnificent but fleeting if I was to ignore them. Our solidarity group was not particularly efficient, neither in raising money nor awareness, for being too preoccupied with clashing personalities and endless debates about things that had nothing to do with the Zapatistas. After six months, I took a break from the weekly meetings and flew to Mexico, where I wanted to see things for myself as a volunteer peace observer. After the devastating army raid into Zapatista territory, an alliance of NGOs and the Catholic diocese of San Cristóbal had organized peace camps in the affected villages with internationals and Mexicans acting as human shields against further incursions.

When I arrived in March 1996, there were about forty of these camps in Chiapas and anyone who had two weeks to spare and a basic knowledge of Spanish was welcome to have a go. Although the Human Rights Center in San Cristóbal gave us an introductory workshop, the reality of an indigenous community hit hard on first impact. There were severe communication problems, fleas, ticks, and diarrhea, as well as an absolute lack of privacy. For two weeks, I lived on a diet of nothing but tortilla and had to confront constant questions by indigenous men who crowded my hut every evening (Do you want more tortilla? Where is your family? How much did you pay for your flight? Would they let us in if we came to work in your country? Could I have one of your aspirins?). All this took place in San Emiliano, a small village in Las Cañadas that had been settled by indigenous peasants in the 1960s.[3] Located in the core area of the Zapatista uprising, the community was one of many raided by the federal army for supporting the rebels. By the time I came to visit, the locals were weary of weekly incursions by military convoys, which I had to keep at bay by running out onto the road with a camera whenever I heard the roar of approaching vehicles.

Figure 1: As seen from a peace camp in 1996, the convoys of the Mexican Federal Army have turned into an everyday menace along the roads through Las Cañadas, April 1996. Photo by author.

Three days before my plane was scheduled to return to Germany, I made my way back to San Cristóbal on the loading bay of an ailing truck along dusty dirt tracks. Once I got to Mexico City I realized that the past two weeks had been the best thing that had happened to me in a very long time. For once, I felt, I had not been appreciated for my money or for what people thought they might get from me but simply for my presence. I postponed my flight and three days later I was back in San Emiliano. The local population saw my spontaneous return as a sign of commitment and put me to use as a surrogate teacher for the fifty children in the community. I remained in Chiapas for another three months and the experience left its mark on me. I was touched and inspired by the dignified resistance with which the people I stayed with held out against the repression by the army, paramilitaries, and special police units.

Returning home, I rejoined my circle of Berlin-based activists to organize fund-raising parties and rallies in front of the Mexican embassy. We also took part in the coordination of the first *encuentro*

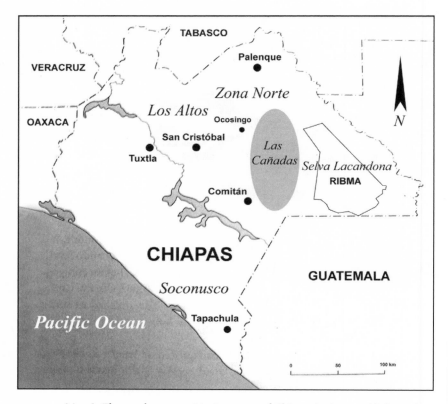

Map 1: The southernmost Mexican state of Chiapas is shown with its main towns and geographic regions. Las Cañadas and the Selva Lacandona are located in the eastern part of the state. The Montes Azules Biosphere Reserve (RIBMA) takes up much of the Selva Region. Map by author.

(meeting), Against Neoliberalism and for Humanity, which was held in Berlin in summer 1996 by pro-Zapatista solidarity groups from all over Europe.

THE PROBLEM OF ACCESS

Combining political activism with academia, I returned to the same village in winter 1996/97 to undertake fieldwork for an MA thesis at the Ethnological Institute at Freie Universität, Berlin. Four years later, in September 2000, research for my doctoral thesis led me back to Chiapas once more. The challenges I faced this time were tremendous.

Whereas I had been a solidarity activist with an interest in anthropology at my first visit, this time I had come as an anthropologist with a background in activism. In the years of my absence there had been considerable changes in the human rights infrastructure in San Cristóbal, and my activist acquaintances in town had left their nonprofit niche and moved on to greener pastures elsewhere. I myself was now an official researcher associated with the local Center for Research and Higher Studies in Social Anthropology (CIESAS) Sureste, and a host of friendly academics were eager to welcome me into their circle. I would have been in a perfect position to investigate the local intellectual elite but my actual target seemed more distant than ever before.

I somehow had to weave my way into the semiclandestine world of pro-Zapatista support structures, the only access route into the rebellious *pueblos de base* that I had come to study. In such a situation, contacts are everything. Anticipating a difficult start, I had come equipped with two e-mail addresses of people from a new generation of international activists. When I looked them up soon after my arrival I was warmly received and taken along to all manner of social occasions, where I once again mingled with that peculiar tribe of globalized utopians who had lost their hearts to someone else's revolution.

I got to know most of the people during these first weeks' work in Zapatista communities. The majority of men help install water systems in rebel villages while many of the women teach workshops aimed at the empowerment of indigenous women. There are various other groups in town involved with human rights, community health, teacher training, or the setting up of production collectives. My new social circle is made up of Mexicans and mostly Anglophone foreigners ranging from volunteers in their early twenties to salaried NGO workers in their midthirties. Most of the long-termers are either paid by an NGO or receive funding from charity stipends.

Whilst being rather upfront about proclaiming their identity as solidarity activists, everybody is terribly clandestine about what exactly they do here. Being part of the scene is everything and the men have a special handshake that takes months to master for a novice like me. Since most are out in Zapatista communities half of the time, where there is a ban on alcohol and people go to bed by nightfall, everyone is keen on partying when in San Cristóbal. Usually, people bring beer, gather at someone's house, and only go out to one of the town's bars in small groups. During the weekends, there are big private parties where everyone knows each other. New faces are almost always short-term volunteers from the United States or Europe and bringing along a tourist or even a local is an unspoken taboo.

(Field diary, October 2000)

It did not take long until Charlie, one of the local project workers, asked me to join his team to help build a water system in a rebel community.[4] In preparation, he made me memorize a set of security recommendations for pro-Zapatista activists: no mentioning of any names, times, and places on the phone, the Internet, or in public. E-mails had to be coded, and taxis were only to be used well away from the house. Work was not to be talked about to anyone who wasn't an insider; for everyone else a story had to be invented.

Although I received generous support and advice from CIESAS Sureste and particularly from my colleague Xochitl Leyva Solano, who is an expert on the Zapatistas, my affiliation with the research center quickly became an obstacle for my integration into the solidarity scene. Local activists regarded any institution remotely associated with mainstream politics with great suspicion. The repression and structural changes in the local NGO sector that marked the second half of the 1990s had turned this heterogeneous crowd into gatekeepers of the indigenous Zapatista communities, whose inhabitants generally tended to have surprisingly little qualms about inviting an outsider into their homes. In a small town such as San Cristóbal and a social circle as rife with gossip as the one I was trying to be part of, it was nearly impossible to discretely join the semiclandestine sphere of pro-Zapatista activists and the vivacious social world of local academics at the same time.

Charlie did not have a problem with me being an anthropologist in search of thesis material. Others did. Not feeling that I had to conceal anything, I spoke freely to my new acquaintances about my plans to write a book about the Zapatistas. The word eventually got round to a man called Bruce who was in charge of the NGO I was to work with and I ran into trouble. The following excerpt from my field notes hints at the type of difficulties that were a recurring issue during the two years of research that followed.

Two months after my arrival in Mexico, things are looking grim. After an early string of lucky encounters and excursions, I now feel as if a door has been slammed shut in my face. On the day we were scheduled to leave for Las Cañadas, I showed up at Charlie's house with ten kilos of vegetables for our weeklong outing. To my surprise, I met Bruce there and he told me we had to talk. When we sat down at the kitchen table, he broke the news to me that he would not allow me to join the water team as a volunteer. He has a big problem with me being an anthropologist and doesn't see how that will benefit anyone in the communities. On the contrary, he insists that a publication of my findings could only help their enemies. He even argues that the fact that I received an official visa for doing research in Chiapas is proof that the Mexican government expects to benefit from my study.

Bruce made it clear that he did not want any part in facilitating my access to rebel villages. Moreover, if anyone in the Zapatista authority structure were to ask him who I was, he would have to tell them he didn't know me, which apparently is enough to put me on a blacklist barring my access to rebel territory once and for all. I suggested that he read my research proposal and asked him how he had "got in" himself. He wouldn't tell me but mentioned that it took five long years earning the trust of the EZLN until he got to where he was now. To underscore his point, Bruce then told the story about the peace camper who was stopped and searched by police in the central square of San Cristóbal in 1998. They found some grass on him and threatened to throw him into prison for a year if he didn't give them names of foreigners involved with the Zapatistas. Apparently, half of the long-term activists in town came under surveillance by undercover police as a result. This is all very frustrating.

_____

(Field diary, November 2000)

Just as one door was slammed shut in my face, another one opened due to my developing friendship with an indigenous young man whom I had met during those first weeks. Cipriano had grown up in a Zapatista community in Las Cañadas and moved to San Cristóbal in the late 1990s, where he found work with an activist NGO. As he was looking for a housemate at the time of my arrival, I moved in to what turned out to be a prime research location. The houses we shared for the next two years not only became my base for trips to various Zapatista communities, but they were also the main sojourn for Cipriano's extended family while they stayed in town to attend to business, look for work, or take part in workshops offered by the local NGOs. As our visitors were from Zapatista base communities, I not only learned a lot about these places, but also enjoyed the unique opportunity to build social relations that eventually led me to some of the villages by way of personal invitation.[5] Despite my initial troubles, I eventually became immersed in the vibrant scene of pro-Zapatista activists in San Cristóbal, who enriched my research with their perspectives. The activists' narratives exchanged at private parties, before and after basketball games, or during reading groups were teeming with remarkable accounts of life in rebel territory and the various NGO projects implemented there. At the time of my research, this territory covered much of eastern Chiapas and comprised five zones, each associated with a Zapatista political and cultural center named Aguascalientes: Oventic in the Zona Altos, Morelia in the Zona Altamirano, Roberto Barrios in the Zona Norte, La Realidad in the Zona Selva Tojolabal and La Garrucha in the Zona Selva Tzeltal (see map 2).[6] They were the first port of call for solidarity activists.

The described difficulties of access linked to clandestinity and my ambiguous role were exacerbated by the methodological challenges

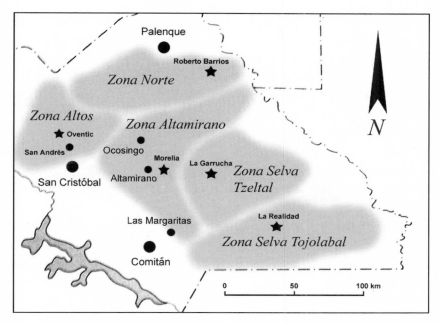

Map 2: The area referred to as "rebel territory" in this book is congruent with the five Zapatista regions. The stars mark the five regional Zapatista capitals formerly known as Aguascalientes. They were renamed Caracoles in August 2003. Map by author.

of participant observation under conditions of low-intensity warfare. Apart from the danger posed by soldiers and paramilitaries, none of whom were particularly keen on what they regarded as foreigners meddling in internal affairs, there was the constant worry of being deported by Mexican immigration officials. As a rule, any foreigner was barred from entering the "conflict zone." The visa identifying me as a researcher on autonomous municipalities, issued to me by the Mexican embassy in London, made me even more susceptible to scrutiny by local functionaries. On one occasion, I was summoned into a police post and questioned for half an hour by a migration officer who had seen my passport entry and was convinced that I was on my way to meet the subcomandante himself. Difficulties such as these have so far stood in the way of any substantial research in the conflict zone and to my knowledge, no empirical work comparable to the one this publication is based on has been carried out in Chiapas.

Structure of the Book

The introduction gives an overview of the literature on the Zapatistas with a focus on those texts that share themes covered in this book. To situate my own study in the debate on the rebels' relations with the Mexican State and the role of alternative development to advance their autonomy project, I provide a background on key concepts such as political action, the state, transnational activism, and the ambivalent implications of development.

The first chapter highlights the nexus between the emergence of the EZLN and the historical experience of the settler communities in Las Cañadas and La Selva Lacandona. For the greater part of the twentieth century, these remote indigenous regions have been marked by an absence of state institutions. This is in stark contrast to the neighboring Chiapas Highlands where the Mexican government's attempts to get a foothold were more successful. After outlining the role of power brokers and government programs for the consolidation of hegemony in indigenous rural communities, I discuss the developments at the periphery of state influence that led to the 1994 rebellion. This is followed by a summary of key events in Chiapas in the fourteen years that have passed since the uprising. The chapter concludes by putting Zapatista autonomy into the historical context of the struggle for indigenous autonomy in Mexico and by emphasizing the more tangible aspects that the concept has had for Zapatistas on the ground.

In chapter 2, narratives from the Zapatista villages I visited during my fieldwork provide indigenous perspectives on the guerrilla movement's emergence in its core area. They emphasize the strong ties between the organization and its base manifested in all aspects of village life. The topics range from the administration of "recuperated terrains," as Zapatistas call the *finca* lands, occupied in the course of their uprising, to local attitudes toward collective work and private enterprise.[7]

After an outline of traditional village hierarchies, chapter 3 covers the organizational aspects of Zapatista communities and autonomous districts. Particular attention is given to the parallel existence of a civilian setup operating side by side with a strict military command structure. An assessment of patriarchal practice and the role of women in rebel communities, and a discussion of Zapatista claims to base democracy conclude the chapter.

The fourth chapter links the political division that beset many former Zapatista strongholds at the end of the 1990s to a shift in EZLN policy regarding the acceptance of state aid. Case studies from San Emiliano and La Gardenia illustrate the broader conflict over this issue. While San Emiliano lost most of its rebel support base in the process, La Gardenia's Zapatistas emerged having the upper hand and the new autonomous institutions were employed to broker an agreement between the opposing groups.

Subsequent chapters put the Zapatista autonomy project into the context of recent NGO involvement in Chiapas and outline the historical developments that have allowed marginalized communities to equip themselves with a social and material infrastructure independently from the Mexican State. Chapter 5 retraces the process whereby only NGOs that actively supported the consolidation of Zapatista autonomy have remained operative in the region controlled by the rebels. These groups have dedicated themselves to addressing the most pressing needs, as by providing water systems to new settlements founded on land occupied in the course of the rebellion. The funding for such projects came primarily from solidarity groups and international NGOs in North America and Europe, but local communities have increasingly gained control over the actual project management.

Chapter 6 introduces a series of Zapatista initiatives in the areas of education, production, and health that turned what had been a selection of relatively isolated ventures into centrally coordinated development programs. Narratives by Zapatista community teachers proved to be particularly rich sources for local experiences of *educación autónoma* (autonomous education) on which large parts of the chapter are based. It concludes with a discussion of the wider implications the presence of both Zapatista and government schools in indigenous villages have had with regard to local hegemony.

To elucidate the implications of development projects in Zapatista communities, chapter 7 draws on my experiences as a volunteer installing gravity-flow water systems. Using examples from project work in these villages, I discuss partisan NGO involvement, issues of sustainability, and the allegation that development projects in rebel territory accelerate the process of capitalist transformation.

Chapter 8 investigates the local impact of NGO involvement with regard to mobility and culture change. Using the cases of two indigenous NGO employees, I address the consequences of imported values, cash remuneration, and cronyism. The last part of the chapter focuses on the 2003 administrative restructuring by which the Zapatistas hoped to bring the negative side effects of outside involvement under control.

The final chapter focuses on the implications of what I identify as the EZLN's double role. I argue that, since its public appearance in 1994, the guerrilla movement has become a campaign engine for its various civil society supporters. For its indigenous base in Chiapas, however, it has served classic functions of a counterstate by providing protection and ensuring the continued flow of international aid. After an overview of the factors facilitating the EZLN's efforts to mobilize civil society, I argue that the EZLN's success has also been due to its ability to address a yearning for utopian notions that its urban and international supporters associate with "the indigenous community." Using my own accounts of the 2001 caravan to Mexico City that brought together a wide array of EZLN supporters, I illustrate both their concrete practical use for the Zapatistas as well as the contradictions brought about by their presence. The chapter concludes with an analysis of loyalty, hegemony, and the broader implications of alternative development in rebel territory.

Acknowledgments

As the bulk of the research for this book was conducted in the context of a PhD course at the University of Manchester, England, I want to address my gratitude to the German Academic Exchange Service (DAAD), the Economic and Social Research Council (ESRC), and the Department of Anthropology in Manchester, which have all contributed to the financing of this project.

During the field research I have had help from more people than I can remember. The following, however, I will never forget. I want to thank Cipriano and Sergio, who have become my *valedores*, for our countless conversations. Their football team of brothers deserves my gratitude for always coming round with the latest news, and so does Miriam, who gave me a much-needed glimpse at a woman's perspective, as well as Griselda and Santos, for having put me up under difficult circumstances. I thank Yasmin for astounding me with her knowledge, Blas for giving me a teacher's take on things, Fausto for his hospitality, and Espártaco for his breathtaking stories. To not forget anyone, I send an all-inclusive *abrazo* to the people of San Emiliano, La Gardenia, 29 de Febrero, La Utopía, Tierra Nueva, and Arcadia.

For welcoming me into their exclusive circle in San Cristóbal, I am greatly indebted to the people whom—for anonymity's sake—I'll just refer to as *la banda*; many of them have shared their stories with me. Special thanks to Charlie, Gem, Lalo, and the others who took me along to work in the communities. I also want to thank Donatella, Moshe, Joshua, Joscha, and Yoshi, as well as Nina, Ina, Esther, Anne, Aida, Magaña, Thomas, and a bunch of Catalans and Basques who have enriched my research with their narratives.

I am also grateful to Xochitl Leyva Solano for supplying me with academic advice and for putting up with my decision to shun San Cristóbal academics in favor of a shady existence among outlaws in the shantytowns; to José Luis Escalona and his wife, Vero, for giving me shelter, for feeding me, and for lending their ears to my grievances; to Axel Köhler for giving me an opportunity to show my documentary about the 2001 "Zapatour" at a San Cristóbal film forum; and to Florian Walter for his friendship and his advice. Much data on the unfolding conflict in San Emiliano is owed to my reliable friend Barney Rübe, who accompanied me to the village under difficult circumstances in times of communal strife.

The writing would not have been possible without the people of my very own solidarity group who were there for me when I needed them. My special thanks goes to John Gledhill, who prepared me for my time in Chiapas. During the research he was there for me with his advice that was fast, challenging, and helpful all at once. I am grateful to my sister Mareike, my companion Alice, and my parents Gudrun and Eike for providing encouragement and for being there when I needed them.

Finally I thank my partner, Anja, who came to join me in rebel Chiapas whenever she could, and my son Jannes, who was born during the writing of this book, for being so patient with me.

Abbreviations

ANIPA: Asamblea Nacional Indígena Plural por la Autonomía / National Assembly of Indigenous People for Autonomy

ARIC: Asociación Rural de Interés Colectivo / Rural Collective Interest Association

AT: Appropriate Technology

BANRURAL: Banco de Desarrollo Rural / Bank of Rural Development

CCRI: Comité Clandestino Revolucionario Indígena / Indigenous Clandestine Revolutionary Committee

CCRI-CG: Comité Clandestino Revolucionario Indígena-Comandancia General / Indigenous Clandestine Revolutionary Committee—General Command

CEOIC: Consejo Estatal de Organizaciones Indígenas y Campesinas / State Council of Indigenous and Peasant Organizations

CGH: Comité General de Huelga / General Strike Committee

CIEPAC: Centro de Investigaciones Económicas y Políticas de Acción Comunitaria / Center for Economic and Political Research of Community Action

CIESAS: Centro de Investigaciones y Estudios Superiores en Antropología Social / Center for Research and Higher Studies in Social Anthropology

CIOAC: Central Independiente de Obreros Agrícolas y Campesinos / Independent Union of Agricultural Workers and Peasants

CNC: Confederación Nacional de Campesinos / National Peasant Confederation

CND: Convención Nacional Democrática / National Democratic Convention

CNI: Congreso Nacional Indígena / National Indigenous Congress

COCOPA: Comisión de Concordia y Pacificación / Commission for Concord and Pacification

COLEM: Colectivo de Mujeres / Women's Collective

COMPITCH: Consejo de Organizaciones de Médicos y Parteras Indígenas Tradicionales de Chiapas / Council of Organizations of Indigenous Traditional Healers and Midwives of Chiapas

CONASUPO: Compañía Nacional de Subsistencias Populares / National Company for the People's Subsistence

CONPAZ: Coordinadora de Organizaciones No-Gubernamentales por la Paz / Coordination of Nongovernmental Organizations for Peace

CORSAM: Coordinación Suiza de Acompañamiento en México / Swiss Coordination of Accompaniment in Mexico

DESMU: Desarrollo Mujeres / Women's Development

DICONSA: Programa de Abasto Rural / Program of Rural Provisions

DPI: Departamento de Protección Indígena / Department for the Protection of the Indigenous

ESPAZ: Espacio por la Paz / Space for Peace

ETA: Euzkadi Ta Askatasuna / Basque Homeland and Freedom (Militant Basque Nationalist Separatist organization)

EZLN: Ejército Zapatista de Liberación Nacional / Zapatista Army of National Liberation

FAC-MLN: Frente Amplio para la Construcción del Movimiento de Liberación Nacional / Broad Front for the Construction of a National Liberation Movement

FIPI: Frente Independiente de Pueblos Indígenas / Independent Front of Indigenous Peoples

FLN: Fuerzas de Liberación Nacional / National Liberation Forces

FZLN: Frente Zapatista de Liberación Nacional / Zapatista Front of National Liberation

GE: Global Exchange

ILO: International Labor Organization

INGO: International Nongovernmental Organization

INI: Instituto Nacional Indigenista / National Indigenist Institute

JBG: Junta de Buen Gobierno / Good Government Council

LP: Línea Proletaria / Proletarian Line

MAREZ: Municipios Autónomos Rebeldes Zapatistas / Autonomous Zapatista Rebel Municipalities

NAFTA: North American Free Trade Agreement

NGO: Nongovernmental Organization

ORCAO: Organización de Caficultores de Altamirano y Ocosingo / Organization of Coffee Growers from Altamirano and Ocosingo

PAN: Partido de Acción Nacional / Party of National Action

PCM: Partido Comunista Mexicano / Mexican Communist Party

PEMEX: Petróleos Mexicanos / Mexican Petroleum Corporation

PGR: Procuraduría General de la República / Attorney General's Office

PPP: Plan Puebla Panamá

PRD: Partido de la Revolución Democrática / Party of Democratic Revolution

PRI: Partido Revolucionario Institucional / Institutional Revolutionary Party

PROCAMPO: Programa de Apoyo Directo al Campo / Direct Rural Support Program

PROCEDE: Programa de Certificación de Derechos Ejidales y Titulación de Solares Urbanos / Program for the Certification of Ejido Land Rights and the Titling of Urban House Plots

PROGRESA: Programa de Educación, Salud, y Alimentación / Program for Education, Health, and Nutrition

PRONASOL: Programa Nacional de Solidaridad / National Solidarity Program

RAP: Región Autónoma Pluriétnica / Autonomous Pluriethnic Region

RIBMA: Reserva Integral de la Biosfera de Montes Azules / Montes Azules Biosphere Reserve

SEDESOL: Secretaría de Desarrollo Social / Secretariat for Social Development

SFC: Schools for Chiapas

SME: Sindicato Mexicano de Electricistas / Union of Mexican Electricians

SOLIDARIDAD: Government Program for Rural Development (see also PRONASOL)

TAN: Transnational Activist Network

UNAM: Universidad Nacional Autónoma de México / National Autonomous University of Mexico

UU: Unión de Uniones y Grupos Campesinos Solidarios de Chiapas / Union of Ejido Unions and Solidary Peasant Organizations of Chiapas

WTO: World Trade Organization

Introduction

Making Sense of the Zapatistas

Since the Zapatista uprising shook not only the Mexican public and political elites but also international financial markets and an increasingly globalized civil society, a lot has been written about the insurrection. The first publications, often emerging from within the Mexican and international pro-Zapatista support network, were based on the EZLN's own portrayal of events and celebrated the Chiapas uprising as the first postmodern rebellion against neoliberal globalization (Burbach 1994; Ross 1995; Katzenberger 1995). Particularly in the early communiqués, laden with myth and metaphor, the guerrilla movement's spokesperson Subcomandante Marcos portrayed the insurrection as a popular uprising by exploited indigenous peasants fighting for land that was rightfully theirs and freedom that had long been denied them (EZLN 1994c). Other early articles contested that the Chiapas rebellion was an indigenous revolt. Authors such as Enrique Krauze (1994), Arturo Warman (1994), or Octavio Paz (1994) imputed a parasitic and even racist nature into the relationship between a supposedly *ladino* guerrilla command and its indigenous base, failing to account for the powerful support the EZLN had achieved among broad sectors of the indigenous population in Chiapas.[1]

More thoroughly researched studies placed an emphasis on the historical emergence of the rebel movement at the periphery of modern Mexico (Collier and Quaratiello 1999; Benjamin 1996; Harvey 1998; García de León 2002). Others sought to discredit the movement by depicting the EZLN's indigenous base as having been misled by outsiders, who pitted them against their own kin with false hopes and Maoist propaganda (Tello Díaz 1995; De la Grange and Rico 1997), or by likening its methods of garnering global support to terrorist organizations (Ronfeldt and Arquilla 1998). More recent books analyzed the Zapatistas from a broader perspective on the relation Mexico's indigenous populations have had with the state (Stephen 2002; Higgins 2004) or explored issues relating to the Zapatista campaigns for the promotion of indigenous autonomy (Díaz Polanco 1997; Nash 2001; Mattiace 2003). With a focus on the Zapatistas' transnational support network, Olesen (2005) and Bob (2005) investigated the rebels' achievements to win widespread appeal, and Earle and Simonelli (2005) celebrated the apparent successes of community-run development projects in Chiapas. As some of these studies share themes covered in this book, I will introduce them as I develop an outline of my key arguments.

The following pages provide a frame of reference with regard to the theoretical backdrop informing the lines of argumentation employed throughout this book. After a brief tour through what appear to me the most useful contributions to explain political action, I arrive at what I have termed a project-based perspective with which to contemplate the developments in Zapatista territory over the past decade. This is followed by a discussion of the state and my argument that the EZLN has taken on state functions in the remote regions of Chiapas. The chapter concludes with a discussion of NGOs and development aid and their side effects in Zapatista communities.

Understanding Political Action

The case studies in this book emphasize the importance of agency on the part of the indigenous communities who, I argue, created the EZLN as their "project," a point backed by examples throughout all chapters. Whereas individual action has had a role-model effect in some cases described here (as in chapter 8), I found *collective* action, following informal debates and those in the formal setting of village assemblies, to be decisive for the events that have shaped eastern Chiapas. The very existence of the EZLN is owed to such collective action—developed over the course of more than a decade—and so is the recent and still unfolding history in the region.

Max Weber already argued at the beginning of the twentieth century that "social structure does not exist over and above actors, whose interactions in terms of meanings and expectations shape the structures (regularities) of social life" (Weber 1978, 4). The so-called structure-agency debate—albeit under various guises—has been central with regard to the analysis of social action, from the assessment of revolutionary potential to the effects of migration. As different takes on this theme have been used to justify policies and political action, from the Russian Revolution to the free market policies of NAFTA, it is important to note that none of them is free of ideological charge. The list of proponents and their lines of argumentation in this debate are too long to be included here but I will briefly touch on a selection, which I regard as relevant to my study.

In *Power and Its Disguises*, a textbook on political anthropology, John Gledhill (1994, 131–35) provides a comprehensive overview of the structure-agency debate. Accordingly, the functionalist perspective on social behavior as the simple enactment of fixed norms by actors who are assigned equally fixed roles was prominently challenged by the "transactionalist theory" of Frederic Barth (1966), which explains the regularities of social organization in terms of the strategizing behavior of social agents interacting to maximize value. Developing this perspective of "economic man" into a concept of "political man," Gledhill brings in F. G. Bailey's (1969) analysis of politics based on the metaphor of a competitive game. Bailey argues that all political systems can be analyzed in terms of a rule-governed game, whether or not the participants are fully conscious of the codes, which regulate their actions. He distinguishes between culturally determined rules and pragmatic ones, operating in a political field where teams of political players compete with each other. Bailey distinguishes between "contract teams," whose internal relationships are based on material benefits alone and "moral teams" based on a shared ideology, the latter tending to be more stable when things go badly (Gledhill 1994, 132–33). I found this differentiation useful when contemplating the motivations found among the diverse Zapatista base in the light of the question why a considerable number left the EZLN in the late 1990s (see chapter 4).

The other line of analysis of political process in terms of a game traced by Gledhill is that of Pierre Bourdieu (1991), whose theory of political representation is not unlike those of Barth and Bailey in the extensive use of the economic metaphor of capital. Thus, all practices, including those that are not outwardly "economic," are about increasing financial, political, cultural, or symbolic capital (as in the form of prestige). Class is a key concept for Bourdieu as is his focus on the symbolic practices surrounding power relations. He introduces the concept of the "habitus" whereby "social agents are imbued with dispositions to think and behave in certain ways by the action of historical social forces. They are like musicians whose improvisations are neither predictable in advance, a product of conscious intent, nor simply a 'realization' of a structure which already exists in the unconsciousness" (Gledhill 1994, 137). Bourdieu's theory explains the reproduction of systems of domination as the collective practices brought about by the habitus reproducing the historical conditions, which shape the cognitive and meaning structures making up the habitus itself.

With relevance to the Zapatista movement "Bourdieu concludes that the primary problem facing political organizations designed to subvert the established orders is that, given the cultural and economic deprivation of those they represent, they tend to become more and more apparatuses of mobilization and less and less means for expressing the will of their 'base'" (Gledhill 1994, 141). I will return to this argument in chapter 4 when discussing the mass exit from guerrilla ranks toward the end of the 1990s. To make sense of it, I focus on the notions of progress prevalent in the remote rural communities of eastern Chiapas. Although these may be temporarily compatible with the EZLN's agendas, they are not invariably latched to a political ideology. Autonomy in the sense of being in control over their own lives and being independent from the manipulation of government agencies they regard as inimical has been a historical goal of the colonists of Las Cañadas and the Selva Lacandona. At times, however, these aspirations were eclipsed in importance by their yearning to take part in the development and economic prosperity that other parts of Mexico seemed to be experiencing. Particularly as guerrilla membership lost its appeal due to the hardships it came to entail in the late 1990s, many former Zapatistas sought alliances that resonated with their notions of developmental progress and drove some of them back into the abominated embrace of the Mexican State.

Contemplating the State on the Periphery of Its Reaches

Back at the beginning of the twentieth century, Max Weber (1978) defined the state as an institution that possesses a monopoly on the legitimate use of force. In a discussion on the particularities of the modern nation-state's penetration into everyday social life, Gledhill (1994, 17–20) introduces Giddens's (1985) contention that Weber's statement pertains only to the modern Western state, as premodern states lacked the administrative, communicative, and military infrastructures to exert such total control over their population. Inspired by Foucault (1980), Giddens contends that internal control moved away from military repression and was increasingly based on surveillance techniques and administrative institutions that proved particularly effective under conditions of industrialized capitalism where "dull economic compulsion" forced the workers to accept the disciplines of wage labor and the workplace itself turned into a site of surveillance. It is no coincidence that the Zapatista challenge to state control and hegemony has come from the rural periphery where the type of surveillance characteristic for industrialized urban regions has largely been absent.[2] However, as multinational development schemes for the entire region—such as the Plan Puebla Panamá (see chapter 1)—envision the large-scale allocation of people from remote border areas in Chiapas around assembly plants for export production (*maquiladoras*), this situation may well change in the not too distant future.

Giddens (1985) goes on to say that nationalism became an important element for consolidating unity in the territory that the modern state had come to control administratively. This ideology relies on a symbolic sense of shared history, culture, and language, much of which is based on invented traditions. Florencia Mallon (1995, 10–12) regards the view of the nation as an imagined community (Anderson 1983) and a project for collective identity as equally crucial for organizing society. In her analysis of the state, she emphasizes the importance of decentralized sites of struggle where hegemony is both contested and reproduced.

Gledhill (1994, 20) notes that nationalism can also be used by disadvantaged groups and oppositional movements who claim administrative sovereignty and autonomy. Indeed, since their 1994 rebellion, the Zapatistas have engaged the Mexican State also on a symbolic level by using some of its icons and by taking recourse to nationalist ideology. This ranges from ubiquitous references to the Mexican Revolution and Emiliano Zapata in their communiqués to the pervasive use of the Mexican flag and a host of other symbols in ceremonies, which bear every characteristic of invented traditions in the sense of Hobsbawm and Ranger (1983).

An approach I found particularly useful in explaining the effectiveness of the Zapatista movement comes from Michael Gilsenan (1977), who studied the emergence of the Sicilian Mafia in the nineteenth century. He found that the armed guards of the old farming estates had taken advantage of drastic changes in the agrarian structure to insert themselves as intermediaries between the peasantry and the wider society (quoted in Gledhill 1994, 125). Gilsenan's thesis traces the existence of mediators between local communities and the state to a gap caused by weak horizontal linkages between these communities and the limited reach of the state. He argues that the existence of a set of relations and structures ensures that this gap is always filled. The present study documents how the EZLN has reached into this gap to replace a whole set of mediators or mediating agencies with its own people and institutions and a host of specially recruited NGOs taking on the role of service providers.

In her 2002 book *Zapata Lives!* Lynn Stephen uses the cases of four indigenous communities in Chiapas and Oaxaca to trace their involvement with the Mexican State over forty years of interaction with agrarian officials, not least to arrive at an explanation why they engaged in the struggle for indigenous autonomy in the 1980s and 1990s, some of them by joining the EZLN. Focusing on the figure of Emiliano Zapata and the meaning of the Mexican Revolution, the author illustrates the multiple senses of citizenship and loyalties that people in the studied villages have had through time and shows that local views of the nation are filters for how national policy is given meaning.

Stephen's detailed and informative study describes how the inhabitants of two Oaxacan villages developed an ambiguous relationship with the state, regarding it as either a good or a bad father, whereas the colonists of the Zapatista strongholds of Guadalupe Tepeyac and La Realidad came to identify the state as the "*mal gobierno*" (bad government). Stephen shows that the different views of the nation in the four communities she studied are linked to historical differences in the relationships of their inhabitants with agents of the state. The book also convincingly demonstrates that the way national policy is interpreted at the margins of the state where its legitimacy is in dispute—as it is in rural Chiapas—affects how such policy is redeployed back at the center. Thus, the Zapatista rebellion and land invasions forced the state to renegotiate the supposed end of land reform in the mid-1990s (82).

I found Stephen's analysis particularly useful for understanding how the Mexican State attempted to consolidate a national identity and establish its institutions at the periphery of its influence in the 1930s and again in the 1990s. As Stephen focuses on the issues of education and agrarian reform that are especially relevant to my study, I take recourse to her analysis in the following chapter when describing efforts of the state to get a foothold in rural Chiapas. In this regard, the strategies of various Mexican governments were rather successful in the highlands around San Cristóbal (see chapter 1). However, at the very margins of Mexican territory, where indigenous colonists were pushing the frontier of human habitation ever farther into the roadless Chiapas jungle by slashing and burning plots of land to grow their maize, the state hardly had a presence. Nevertheless, attempts were made, particularly from the late 1980s onward, to gain influence by way of building schools and development schemes in the context of the National Solidarity Program (Programa Nacional de Solidaridad, or PRONASOL).

Often, teachers, doctors, and engineers measuring the land and building basic infrastructure were the only contact that inhabitants of these remote areas had with government agents. After the uprising, however, tens of thousands of federal soldiers and special police units flooded into the region in several waves. From the military offensive in February 1995 onward, hitherto rather inaccessible mountain and jungle areas were developed by building roads, bridges, and power lines. Along the roads, army camps were set up and a service infrastructure grew around them. As part of a counterinsurgency strategy and to split local support for the guerrillas, a lot of state money was spent on basic infrastructure projects and to finance cattle farming in those villages that were not unanimously supporting the EZLN.

My study illustrates how the Zapatistas countered by consolidating existing autonomous organizational structures and by enlisting outside support to develop their infrastructure independently from government agents. Despite the military siege from the mid-1990s onward, the EZLN created and consolidated—and in many instances replaced—institutions and structures typically supplied by the state, such as those pertaining to justice, law enforcement, education, health care, and social security, with its own. It thereby not only challenged the Mexican State but took on its role as the guarantor of rule of law, supplier of education and health care, and—last but not least—as the provider of a quasinationalist identity project. Although "being Zapatista" became an important factor for the self-confidence of the EZLN's base communities, and the ethnic identity of "being indigenous" was employed profusely in the guerrilla movement's political campaigns, local realities in the communities where I undertook research were often characterized by fluctuating political affiliations.

A Project-Based Perspective on Zapatista Affiliation

But what exactly is a modern-day Zapatista? Given that the general knowledge on the rebel movement is far from uniform and seldom does justice to the complexities on the ground, the term is generally rather vague when used by people who are not from rural Chiapas. Inside the indigenous villages, on the other hand, there is nothing vague about guerrilla membership, as it is highly regulated. You are either a *compa* or in some way associated with the government.[3] However, this does not mean that political affiliation is static. On the contrary, local fluctuation between the various factions in a given village is high, and

Figure 2: Following the 1995 army raid, heavy machinery was used to plow access routes into reaches of the Lacandon jungle that had hitherto been inaccessible to motor vehicles, January 1997. Photo by author.

a visitor to a base community might well find the situation changed when returning a few years later.[4] As will be shown in chapter 4, both communal and individual membership in the EZLN is often temporary and motivated by pragmatic considerations.

In this book, I use the term Zapatista for those among the indigenous population of Chiapas who are members of the EZLN as either insurgents, militias, or support base (for details, see chapter 2). However, some authors have used the term to include the guerrilla movement's nonindigenous supporters. Thus, Leyva Solano (1998, 45–47) distinguishes between the guerrillas and the "New Zapatista Movement" (NMZ), an "imagined community" in the sense of Anderson (1983). Accordingly, the NMZ consists of diverse political actors who share certain symbolic references, general political goals, and the feeling of belonging to the collective of *Zapatismo*. Leyva Solano (1998, 46) describes the NMZ as consisting of different levels, ranging from the diocese of San Cristóbal and local NGOs to international solidarity groups,

Amnesty International, and even the Latin America Commission of the European Parliament.

Indeed, over the years since the uprising, numerous actors have approached the Zapatistas for a variety of reasons. The following paragraph gives an overview of the broad spectrum of groups that sought Zapatista affiliation to advance their projects. The founding of the settlement 29 de Febrero (see chapter 2) shows how—on the local level—some made use of the momentum the rebellion had caused by occupying land and then becoming Zapatistas themselves. Collier (1997) describes a similar development for the case of Zinacantán, where the dominant political faction adopted parts of the Zapatista discourse, albeit for an interim period, to remain in power. On the national level, many representatives of Mexico's indigenous peoples organized in the National Indigenous Congress (Congreso Nacional Indígena, or CNI) after their comrades in Chiapas had put indigenous issues on the agenda. Internationally, references to the Chiapas rebellion have been widely used by anarchists, communists, and even nationalists (as in the case of many Basques and Catalans) to promote their own respective agendas. Many of them have converged in a broad movement against capitalist globalization. At mass events such as the 1999 protests in Seattle or the 2001 demonstrations in Genoa, the Zapatista struggle was ubiquitously referred to as a role model for "globalizing the resistance" (see also Olesen 2005, 45–47).

I believe any model that serves to help us understand the wider Zapatista phenomenon has to do away with notions of static interest groups to take into account the fluidity of affiliations, and possibly also of identities, prevalent among many individuals and groups involved with the rebels. To do justice to the polycentric networks and shifting affiliations found among indigenous communities as well as among national and international civil societies, I therefore prefer a model that centers on bounded projects that can be defined with regard to purpose, beginning and end. Such a model accommodates personal projects as well as those of a family, a political faction, a village, an *ejido* union, or even an imagined community of international supporters.[5] Such bounded projects can be specific ventures such as attaining a plot of land to live off, enabling a son or daughter to go to school, or getting a drinking water supply built in the village, but also gaining symbolic capital as international activists. They can also constitute wider aims such as achieving higher living standards for indigenous Mexicans and partaking, as a group, in the progress that the rest of the country seems to be experiencing. I believe a project-based perspective does justice to the apparent fluidity in the way alliances are forged and events are made to happen by the individuals and groups who have shaped the Zapatista movement. Many of these alliances are strategic in the way that they are entered into with personal motives by all of those involved. By definition, such linkages are temporary and can be uncoupled as the people who conceive and manage their projects seek other alliances to better meet their needs.

This book covers the wider developments, propelled by a multitude of such bounded projects. In the following chapters I aim to show how the indigenous communities that make up the EZLN's base have achieved autonomous control of key social processes such as law enforcement, education, health care, and production against a strong opposition of the state. The case studies outline the difficulties that have accompanied efforts to set up a local infrastructure for these functions and document attempts at resolving them, including attaining material independence from the Mexican State. From 1998 onward and through to the period of my research in 2000–2002, this area saw important achievements that came about by employing outside actors, particularly NGOs and solidarity groups.

Transnational Activism in Rebel Territory

In their book *Activists beyond Borders*, Margaret Keck and Kathryn Sikkink (1998) investigate the role of what they have termed "transnational activist networks" (TANs) of NGOs, social movements but also churches, trade unions, intellectuals, and the media, who are all "motivated by values rather than by material concerns or professional norms" (2). The various actors associated with the Zapatistas exemplify such transnational advocacy networks and I will briefly introduce their characteristics here.

With their ability to mobilize information strategically, to create new issues, and to put pressure on governments, as Keck and Sikkink argue, TANs have become significant for groups and individuals world-wide who are engaged in domestic political and social struggles. With the aim to change the behavior of states and international organiza-tions, TANs bring new ideas, norms, and discourses into policy debates by "framing" issues to make them comprehensible to target audiences.[6] Linked by numerous formal and informal connections, the groups making up a TAN share values and information as well as funds, ser-vices, and personnel (9).

The authors also describe a "boomerang pattern of influence" that can occur when channels between the state and domestic NGOs are blocked and the NGOs seek out international allies organized in a TAN to bring outside pressure on their government (12). I see this effect as being behind the Mexican government's tolerance toward the rebels, which has contributed to an atmosphere of relative calm since the late 1990s that has made development in the region possible and ensured the physical survival of many EZLN militants. With regard to Chiapas, the Mexican government experienced its most palpable boomerang moment after the Acteal massacre in 1998. After a lobbying campaign by pro-Zapatista TANs in the aftermath of the massacre, parliamentar-ians from several European Union countries made the ratification of an important trade treaty with Mexico conditional to the improvement of the human rights situation there and even demanded the resumption of the San Andrés talks (see also Olesen 2005, 84, 92; Petrich 1998).[7]

Keck and Sikkink note that the cultural milieu of internationalism characterizing advocacy networks in the north is often in stark contrast to "the ingrained nationalism common to many political groups in the developing world" as well as to their memories of colonial relations (16), which represent a considerable obstacle for cooperation; this can be overcome only by high levels of trust and existential necessity. This ties in with my argument that the cooperation and the dependency on outside support characteristic of the situation in Chiapas a decade after the uprising developed in a process of mutual attunement (see chapter 5) and was driven by the sheer need of the Zapatistas to survive as a broad-based and largely civilian movement.

The 2005 study *International Zapatismo* by Thomas Olesen sets out to investigate the creation, infrastructure, and activities of what he calls the "transnational Zapatista solidarity network." Although the study is heavy on rather abstract terminology and lacks firsthand empirical data on Chiapas, it does provide a convincing analysis of the EZLN's efforts to bridge the gap between its different constituencies. According to Olesen, the movement does this by universalizing its appeal and by invoking "a global consciousness enabling people to recognize their own situations in settings far removed in terms of physical, cultural and social distance" (9). The author attempts to show how, facilitated by new information technologies like the Internet, the EZLN has referred to the global spread of neoliberal policies along with ideas of human rights and democracy to construct a set of frames within which to situate its struggle in order to form a transnational solidarity network.

To make his theory of transnational framing plausible, Olesen takes recourse to the notion of a recently developed global consciousness. I doubt whether this consciousness is new, though, as the need for utopian visions that the Zapatista communiqués appeal to has existed for a long time and so have those doing the work of cultural translation, as utopian prose such as that of More (*Utopia*), Swift (*Gulliver's Travels*), or Defoe (*Robinson Crusoe*) testifies. Whereas I believe the concept of transnational framing to be useful for understanding the Zapatistas' success in garnering global support, I also see the need to explicitly anchor any analysis to the motivations of the individual actors involved. These are driven not only by economic and security needs but by the strife to accumulate social, symbolic, and cultural capital (in the sense of Bourdieu 1991).

In his work, Olesen introduces the concept of "mutual solidarity," which he defines as emphasizing similarities between physically, socially, and culturally distant actors, while at the same time respecting and acknowledging local and national differences. However, only in passing does the author touch on arguments that, if elaborated, would critically challenge his rosy portrayal of an essentially new "mutual solidarity paradigm," as when he considers the possibility that "the solidarity dialogue takes place almost exclusively between the educated leadership of the EZLN and network activists" (2005, 124). I consider this to be a key point that any analysis needs to take into account and that has been addressed by the Zapatistas themselves in administrative changes announced at the inauguration of their Good Government Councils in August 2003 (see chapter 8).

In *The Marketing of Rebellion*, Clifford Bob (2005) compares the Zapatista experience of garnering the support of international NGO networks with that of the Ogoni in the Niger Delta regarding both their domestic and overseas strategies. The two groups framed distinct aspects of their causes and employed contrasting means to alert the world to their needs. Although factors such as institutional setting, dominant ideologies, technological development, state structures, societal groupings, and attitudes are almost the same for the two sets of movements, the Ogoni have differed from the Zapatistas not only by exclusively employing peaceful protest but also by making use of direct lobbying. The Zapatista rebellion of course had been an armed insurrection and relied on diffuse international consciousness raising by orchestrating media and Internet reports. Although it took the Ogoni a long time to gain assistance, the Zapatistas' initial success meant that their main problem was retaining activist interest (11–13).

Bob not only differentiates between NGOs as "foreign organizations giving aid" and the domestic social movements receiving it, but also distinguishes solidarity groups that take sides with social movements from those NGOs that champion principles rather than parties. But what about those homegrown NGOs that act as intermediaries between international donor organizations and indigenous communities? I believe that the small project-oriented groups I have worked with during my research constitute another distinct category. Although they were taking sides, they have remained ideologically and organizationally separate from the Zapatista guerrilla movement. With increasing local control over project management and a possible rise in revenues from autonomous export production, they may only be a fleeting phenomenon. For the period covered by this study, however, these NGOs were important precisely for bridging the gap between the world of international donors and the indigenous Zapatistas in Chiapas.

I agree with Bob's emphasis on the Zapatistas' action, innovation, and skill, over their strategically important location or the intervention of third parties, to explain their international success. However, I also attribute this to processes whereby the most effective images, slogans, and utopias are amplified, replicated, and modified by a variety of actors. This includes indigenous Zapatistas but also NGOs, journalists, and the bulk of global civil society, who reads the EZLN's communiqués, buys Zapatista coffee, donates money, writes background articles, staffs peace camps, and engages in volunteer work. I thus regard the marketing situation to be more complex for the case of Chiapas than Bob has described it. Apart from the Zapatistas' own marketing efforts, I have found there to be a host of secondary framers who are working away in the wings. For one, the activists themselves engage in the proliferation of particular images. These may well be replicating those issued in EZLN communiqués but often are new creations adapted to the discourses of a particular subculture (see chapter 9). Other framing processes occur under the direct influence of economic considerations or even commercial interests. In these, the Zapatistas are either turned into a label, or may be depoliticized and transformed into less conspicuous and more palpable candidates for charitable endowments (such as "Mayan communities") to maximize the spectrum of donors (see chapter 5).

In their book *Uprising of Hope*, Duncan Earle and Jeanne Simonelli (2005), present "a dissenting view of community development potential" by sketching out various projects that have been implemented in regions under Zapatista control. The narrative style of the book is a hybrid between novel and ethnography, laced with a mix of Mayaphile folklore and hair-raising esotericism. That said, the study also provides a host of useful data on alternative development projects in the Tojolabal area of Chiapas. The thought-out analysis thereof is both sincere and refreshing, if stunningly uncritical of the rebels' politics. The key message of the authors, however, resonates with some of what I am trying to convey in the following pages, namely that "for the poor of Chiapas, autonomy means local and regional control of governance, resource extraction, development processes and projects, education, and health care, in a system that runs largely independent from the official Mexican model" (8).

The authors describe Zapatista autonomy rather optimistically as "the restraint on the hegemonic appetites of international development"

(16) while painting the future for autonomous municipalities in bright colors. But is this really what is happening in Chiapas? While attempting to highlight the achievements of more than a decade of increasingly community-run development, my own analysis also hopes to point out drawbacks and smokescreens that have come into being under a diverse and changing set of circumstances. In an attempt to extrapolate their analysis onto a broader scale, Earle and Simonelli contend that the successes of "social capitalism" in Chiapas have created an alternative to migration by allowing people to maintain a milpa-based mode of production while increasing global participation, "an adaptation especially suited to the uncertain times and high market flux that the future is likely to visit on us all" (21).

I am afraid that my own findings are more ambiguous. The biography of my indigenous friend Cipriano (chapter 8) shows that the inclusion of local Indígenas into the running and administration of development projects have at least encouraged some Zapatistas to leave their communities and migrate northward while others have begun to use their improved positions in the villages for personal gain. Furthermore, I doubt that Earle and Simonelli's interpretation of Zapatista aims, or even their interpretation of what the Zapatista revolution should reasonably achieve, does justice to the shifting agendas created by a diverse set of actors with what are in fact often rather disparate projects.

Development and Its Side Effects

Reflecting on the political performance of nongovernmental organizations in Chiapas, García Aguilar (1997) describes a "new" type of NGO, displaying elements characteristic of New Social Movements, such as an organizational paradigm based on the invocation of civil society.[8] Most of these groups directed their activities toward the alleviation of poverty among the indigenous and peasant population by promoting organic agriculture, communal development and education, human rights work, or women's organizations. While García Aguilar has given an overview of the broad spectrum of NGOs operating in Chiapas in the mid-1990s, lacking concrete case studies, her analysis unfortunately does not offer any deeper insights into what exactly these groups do on the ground. Bob (2005) and Olesen (2005) have described some aspects of the international activist scene in Chiapas, and Earle and Simonelli (2005) have outlined some concrete projects, but information on the micropolitics involved in their implementation as well as data on project conceptualization, management, and financing is still rather thin.

Most NGOs rely on fund-raising schemes in North America and Europe that sell the story of those the respective projects are to benefit to charity-minded segments of the population. Middleton and O'Keefe (2001) differentiate between larger International NGOs (INGOs) with an operational base in both the "developed" and the "developing" worlds and indigenous NGOs with strong ties to local communities. The authors describe the relationship between the two types of organization as unequal because "indigenous groups do not control the purse strings, [and] they are usually unable to take part in the planning and deliberations in the headquarters of INGOs. . . . An INGO's choice of local NGO partners is often made managerially and the relationship is frequently one of patronage" (148). I found that things were hardly ever this clear-cut. Thus, the groups I worked with during my research were crossbreeds. They were local NGOs that received funding from INGOs and were partly staffed by internationals sympathetic to the Zapatista cause who, I argue, managed to significantly contribute to the Zapatista project of community development by setting up NGOs, attracting INGO funds, and shaping local projects in cooperation with the EZLN command and Zapatista-run autonomous municipalities (see chapter 5).

The need for outside assistance by NGOs became particularly pressing for the EZLN's base communities when the guerrilla movement proscribed the acceptance of rural development programs offered by the Mexican State (see chapter 4). A significant number of Zapatista villages had been beneficiaries of such programs until the broad implementation of measures related to what is locally known as the *resistencia* in 1996. I contend that the principal reason for the EZLN's hard-line manifested in these measures is the open competition with the Mexican State into which the guerrilla movement has entered since its spectacular coming out in January 1994. The EZLN challenged the state not only by replacing the few institutions with which it had been present in the remote communities, but also by legitimating its own existence with regard to grievances the local population associated with the government. The struggle for hegemony in the communities was exacerbated over the past decade as the state sought to boost its presence by building roads and deploying the army and special police units, but also by using development programs as a measure to incite communal strife. Faced with the state's double strategy, the EZLN hardened its ideological stance toward the acceptance of "alms," and used disciplinary measures in sanctioning deviance. This study outlines how, spurred on by this development, a new phase of cooperation between the autonomous communities and nongovernmental aid and solidarity groups began, by which outside actors gradually took on the role of service providers that had hitherto been assumed by the state. For this, new NGOs were created, in some cases in response to a direct request by the guerrilla movement.

While some groups became the favored partners of the Zapatistas, some of the original activist NGOs either phased out their operations in rebel territory on their own accord or were boldly rejected by the EZLN. Employing examples from my fieldwork and from evaluation reports by solidarity groups, chapter 5 demonstrates how the cooperation between the guerrilla movement, its base communities, and local NGOs evolved to leave the base communities and the EZLN in a position of greater control. This finds its expression in a more even distribution and a deeper integration of locals into development projects. By the end of 2003, a set of programs relating to production, health, and education had been conceived and implemented in twenty-nine autonomous municipalities under Zapatista control. In its aim to achieve both economic and educational independence from governmental institutions, this large-scale integrated approach was part of the realization of what local Zapatistas have called "the second phase of the revolution" (see chapter 6).[9]

The establishment of Zapatista autonomy was accompanied by a conflict of interests between the guerrilla movement and local communities. In their endeavor to provide assistance, nongovernmental groups ran the risk of getting caught up in this conflict. While the EZLN sought to strengthen its local power base by using NGO-provided development as an incentive for its base to remain in the guerrilla movement, local communities were intent upon establishing ties to outsiders on their own terms to attain privileged access to goods and services. A graphic example of this conflict was an incident that took place in Las Cañadas in the mid-1990s, related to me by a local NGO project coordinator.[10] After making arrangements with both the autonomous municipal authorities and the community in question, the NGO construction team drove a truckload of material to the prospective building site. Shortly before arriving at their destination, the team was intercepted at a roadblock set up by inhabitants of a neighboring rebel community. These people felt ignored by the Zapatista authorities and took direct action, insisting that the system be built in their village. For three days the NGO truck was held up until the EZLN's regional major "came down from the mountains" to settle the matter. In the end, both villages got a water system and, due to the competition between neighbors, the building work is said to have progressed extra fast.

Earle and Simonelli (2005, 140–44) use the case of the Chiapas-based NGO Women's Development (Desarrollo Mujeres, or DESMU) to demonstrate what they call the "fast-food model of community involvement." DESMU offered indigenous women's groups a limited menu of possible projects, such as the promotion of horticulture or the breeding of hens, rabbits, or bees. The women would discuss these options and choose one of them. The authors criticize that this created the illusion of grassroots decision making for everyone involved. They also point out the stark differences between what the NGO intended the projects to achieve and what the local population was interested in. Thus, the communities would have preferred to convert production projects, which DESMU had implemented to improve the immediate nutrition of women and children, into something that could be commercialized for the long-term benefit of all villagers. They still agreed to DESMU's plans, however, as the continued cooperation with the NGO guaranteed access to resources, information, and outside contacts. The example of Semillita del Sol, presented in chapter 5 of this book, illustrates this discrepancy between NGO plans and the perceived needs of the communities and shows how locals were able to change the project during its implementation period into something they themselves regarded as more sustainable.

Earle and Simonelli continue their account of the DESMU experience outlining the dilemma NGO workers faced after realizing that they needed to make their programs both more inclusive and to limit the duration of engagement in any one particular community (see Duran Duran 2001, 6). They realized that, to continue to receive funding from their donor organization, they had to write reports that veiled the complex and often ambiguous results of their project. The need to do this was even more pressing as the employment of NGO workers hinged on the continued payments from abroad. The limited sources of funding available to local NGOs also created an atmosphere of competition that prevented the sharing of information with other groups engaged in similar projects. Thus, NGOs working in the same region "sometimes replicated each other's failed projects since to make this information public might undermine their efforts to sustain funding" (Earle and Simonelli 2005, 141). DESMU eventually had to quit as the donors realized that the organization worked with families in politically divided villages rather than with all women and children of a particular community.

A charge against NGOs in Zapatista territory, frequently brought forth by some of the more radical activists, was that their operations played into the hands of counterinsurgency. They argued that the Mexican government had its reasons to allow NGOs, whose agendas it did not control, to work in the politically volatile regions that had slipped from its grip. The potentially divisive effects of a few development projects in a region where demand vastly exceeds supply were indeed palpable and it looked as if the state undertook measures to aggravate this situation. In fact, rather than preventing NGOs from engagement in Zapatista territory, the Mexican government increasingly offered similar projects to those run by independent NGOs, particularly in regions with a Zapatista presence. In the first years of the Fox presidency, it looked as though the new government's strategic approach toward the Zapatistas replaced classic counterinsurgency measures with private investment. Government agencies were indeed preferred by some communities because of their incomparably greater capacity to deliver the goods. The limitations of nongovernmental development only slowly dawned on local communities. When NGOs told a regional assembly in 2001 that they would be able to install new water systems in only about six rebel communities per year, they faced genuine surprise and disappointment.

Middleton and O'Keefe (2000, 16) recognize indigenous NGOs as the new political vehicles of class struggle, but they contend that the bulk of international NGOs are dedicated to the perpetuation of capitalism in spite of their claims to sustainability. Are NGOs preparing indigenous communities for their integration into the world market in workshops on export production taught in the context of supposed empowerment schemes? It could be argued that NGO involvement renders a potential workforce for transnational capital in the hitherto inaccessible periphery of rural Chiapas fit to participate on the world market both as producers and consumers. Moreover, by taking on the role as providers of basic infrastructure in rural areas, NGOs relieve the state of its duty for social welfare.

A compatibility with an increasingly globalized market may be an unavoidable by-product of the type of development that international NGOs are able to deliver, but they also promote empowerment, particularly if there are strong organizational structures in place that emphasize local autonomy. Before assessing an inevitable causal relation between international NGOs and the perpetuation of capitalism, it is therefore important to consider that things on the ground are often more complex than the dichotomy between all-powerful INGOs and impotent indigenous NGOs that Middleton and O'Keefe presuppose. In the course of the emerging work division among NGOs described in chapter 5, networks of interdependent NGOs have formed that differ both with regard to specialization and ideological approach. It is therefore possible that an INGO that is at best reformist provides funding for a local NGO dedicated to the advancement of radical social revolutionary goals.

CHAPTER ONE

Roots of Zapatista Autonomy

The emerging picture of the attempts made over the twentieth century to anchor the Mexican State in the indigenous areas of Chiapas shows stark regional differences both with regard to the depth of state involvement and the local reception to it. Most of these differences can be explained by the recent colonization of eastern Chiapas. From the 1940s onward, the formerly sparsely inhabited Las Cañadas and Selva Lacandona regions were settled by indigenous campesinos, many of whom had received ejido titles for mostly inhospitable and remote terrains in steep valleys overgrown by jungle.[1] It was there, in the absence of state agents and institutions, that autonomous forms of organization emerged, which the descendants of the first settlers are defending to this day. This is in contrast to the traditional indigenous areas in the Chiapas Highlands where the postrevolutionary Mexican State established itself more successfully. With much insight, Jan Rus (1994) describes how indigenous bilingual scribes and teachers recruited by the Cárdenas government (1934–1940) transformed into power brokers within a few years. After a summary of his findings, I outline more recent attempts by the Mexican State to gain influence in Chiapas—including in the hitherto isolated Las Cañadas/Selva Lacandona regions—by way of the National Solidarity Program (PRONASOL) introduced in the late 1980s.

To provide historical depth to the case studies and analyses making up the remainder of this book, the following sections also outline the events that have accompanied the colonization of Las Cañadas and Selva Lacandona, particularly the increasing organization of the inhabitants in ejido unions, which contributed to the eventual emergence of the EZLN. To illustrate this history as well as the local implications of

PRONASOL, I have chosen Womack's portrayal (1999) of the Tzeltal settler community La Sultana, not far from where I undertook some of the research for this book. This is followed by a discussion of the EZLN's roots and the mobilization for the uprising as presented by various authors. The chapter goes on to outline the events that have marked the time since the rebellion and concludes by providing the regional contexts to efforts at indigenous autonomy, a demand that soon became a key feature of the post-1994 Zapatista project.

Institutionalizing the Indigenous Community in Los Altos

In Mexico, and particularly in rural areas, the relationship between the state and its citizens has long been characterized by the mediation of party officials and the figure of the cacique. Gledhill describes the cacique as "a local (male) leader linked to political patrons at a higher level, who maintains his own power by winning resources from above for the communities he represents" (Gledhill 1994, 109). Lomnitz-Adler (1992) sees the caciques as providing inroads for the state to regionally specific "intimate cultures" to establish a bureaucratized institutional structure for their management. While the cacique becomes absorbed into the apparatus, the local population loses touch with the state. The regions of Las Cañadas and Selva Lacandona that were to become the EZLN's areas of key support in the late 1980s were characterized by a relative absence of *caciquismo* and established institutional structures, a prerequisite for the Zapatistas to take root there.

In his astute study of the Comunidad Revolucionaria Institucional, Jan Rus (1994) illustrates how reforms that Mexican President Lázaro Cárdenas initiated in the late 1930s to improve conditions for indigenous highland communities eventually led to their domination by the Institutional Revolutionary Party (PRI). "Cardenistas and their successors reached inside the native communities, not only changing leaders but rearranging the governments, creating new offices to deal with labor and agrarian matters at the same time that they were granting vast new powers to the officials charged with maintaining relations with the party and state" (267). A certain Erasto Urbina, director of the newly created Department for the Protection of the Indigenous (DPI), played a key role in this transition as he was put in charge of forming an indigenous workers union. The new department proved to be particularly disruptive to traditional authority structures because it would deal only with municipal presidents who were bilingual. At first, traditional elders managed to hold on to their power positions to a degree, but authority structures were definitely changing.

Rus describes the situation in the highland town of Chamula in 1937, where two people were sharing the key office of municipal president. These were a traditional but illiterate elder who had passed through the ladder of ceremonial and political offices (*cargos*) and spoke only Tzotzil and a bilingual young man who—within the community— held the position of municipal scribe but represented the town before the government as municipal president (278). Within a few years, such young indigenous scribes took on positions in the apparatus of the state party PRI. They became labor union officials and representatives of the National Peasants Confederation (CNC), and headed municipal agrarian committees; soon they eclipsed traditional elders with regard to the power they wielded. As a concession to what was considered traditional practice, the new power holders took on costly religious cargos, which they financed by the sale of liquor—timely legalized by the government after years of prohibition. After a period during which the municipal scribes derived much of their influence from covert opposition to the government, many of them became bilingual teachers for the National Indigenist Institute (Instituto Nacional Indígenista, or INI). In the early 1950s, the INI implemented a regional development program in the Chiapas Highlands that centered on the building of community schools, health clinics, and cooperative community stores (287). It is noteworthy that both the Mexican government and the EZLN focused on providing these same key facilities for the building and maintenance of local hegemony in the regions of Las Cañadas and Selva Lacandona some forty years later.

Lynn Stephen (2002, 40–41) describes rural schools as part of an endeavor to civilize the indigenous population by training them in rationality and modern market behavior. Before the INI's recruitment of the bilingual scribes as teachers, the impact of schooling on indigenous highland populations in Chiapas had been negligible due to opposition by local ladino elites who regarded education as a threat to their dominant position (58). The strong link between the government and the new indigenous power brokers in the highland villages led to the implementation of projects that were not in the interest of their inhabitants. Thus, in the 1950s scribes-turned-caciques pressured their communities to accept the building of telecommunication towers on sacred mountains, which are still visible to anyone visiting San Cristóbal today. Parallel to this, they gained both influence and wealth as they forged alliances with ladinos to acquire land, becoming truck operators and beer and soft drink distributors. In return, the bilingual agents blocked land reform petitions, arranged for the building of roads, and granted wholesalers access to their villages. Still in the 1970s, the same individuals made way for the Mexican oil company PEMEX to drill on indigenous lands (Rus 1994, 291–92). With such measures the state had "managed to co-opt not only the native leaders who were their direct collaborators but also, ironically, the very community structures previously identified with resistance to outside intervention and exploitation—independent self-government, strictly enforced community solidarity, and religious legitimation of political power" (267). The absurd situation of the state enforcing supposed local traditions against indigenous campesinos to stay in control led many to look beyond their communities, joining evangelical sects, opposition parties, labor unions, and new agrarian cooperatives—in a sincere search for alternative ways to be "Indian" (Higgins 2004, 132–33). This is in stark contrast to what happened at the periphery of state control down in the valleys where the colonist communities were mostly left alone by the government and developed their own organizing structures—albeit not without integrating the contributions of various outsiders.

Neoliberal Intervention

In his book, *Understanding the Chiapas Rebellion*, Nicholas Higgins analyzes governmentality as a historical process effecting changes in the self-understanding of individuals and—on a larger scale—in institutional and political structures. He argues that the late twentieth century project of neoliberalism is but the latest—if the most pervasive—of three distinct Mexican governmentalities that the country's indigenous population has experienced (Higgins 2004, 178). Higgins sees a deep-seated conflict in Mexico taking place between different historical and cultural self-understandings and the power embodied within each. He argues that the Zapatista uprising led to a reorientation of the Mexican national and cultural constitution as it brought to light an Indian populace that had both political opinions and sociocultural visions. Higgins also suggests that "the Zapatistas' lack of a clearly discernible large-scale governmental strategy or policy was not a failure of political vision on their part but rather the result of an alternative historical and political perspective that clashes with the modernist governmentalities of the orthodox political elite" (185–86). With Higgins, I believe this perspective to be rooted in the organizational history of the colonists. However, I argue that this seeming lack of governmental strategy along with a perceived absence of authoritarianism has become the Zapatistas' hallmark, as the indigenous rebels' survival is linked to the image of a "guerrilla light" that is more conducive to the support of transnational activists.

Apart from individual power brokers such as the bilingual scribes described by Rus (1994), the Mexican State also relied on a set of institutions and development programs to secure its influence in indigenous communities. This is particularly salient in the context of the large-scale government initiatives introduced by president Carlos Salinas in the late 1980s. Womack (1999, 209–10) notes that when Salinas took office in 1988, his first official act was the creation of PRONASOL. From an impressive initial 32 percent of the federal budget, social spending within the program annually increased to reach 55 percent at the end of his presidential term in 1994. The bulk of the funds went into the development of infrastructure such as water and sewage systems, electricity, farm roads, and the building of hospitals, clinics, and schools but also into the provision of nutrition, housing, scholarships, and credits to ruined farmers. The individual projects were proposed by voluntary associations constituted by inhabitants of poor and mostly rural communities. By 1994, 250,000 of such "solidarity committees" had formed, with 6,400 of them in indigenous communities (210).

Higgins (2004, 140) points out that PRONASOL constituted a social component of Salinas's neoliberal agenda. Whereas previous administrations had introduced similar programs, PRONASOL was the first to feature direct credit to individuals or groups. This was not only a way to incorporate popular groups into a newly structured party machine (Dresser 1994), but also what Higgins calls an "apolitical political project." He argues that by way of providing independent expertise, with technical and business advisors counseling small farmers on scientific farming practice and the best way to commercialize their products, the relation between them and the state was transformed according to the neoliberal paradigm: "expertise both among the political elite and among the 'independent' advisors who help institute its programs should come to be the central means through which citizens relate to the state, to their society, and to themselves" (Higgins 2004, 140).

Throughout Mexico, PRI party officials frequently used PRONASOL funds and the allocation of projects to ensure their reelection. Womack (1999, 210) estimates that 75 percent of the almost 9,000 solidarity committees in Chiapas were "PRI-creatures." That state had received a disproportionately large amount of funding, much of which was spent on "regional development" grants administered by the National Indigenist Institute. In all, indigenous councils pertaining to six hundred organizations and representing more than two thousand indigenous communities realized some nine hundred local development projects under the Salinas presidency (211). However, federal funding for regional development in Chiapas fell against the national trend of increasing budgets and independent solidarity committees increasingly met with official obstructions. In response, many highland villages raised bitter complaints and some communities in Las Cañadas gave their PRONASOL grants to the EZLN, which was clandestinely preparing the rebellion. In the year before the Zapatista uprising, Salinas committed an extra US$50 million to the state, and particularly to Las Cañadas, to regain ground. Womack suggests that the prospect of an increase in (counterinsurgent) development aid not only prompted the EZLN to plan their uprising rather sooner than later but also made the revolt less extensive than it might otherwise have been (213).

The use of government programs as a means of state control in the rural periphery did not end with Salinas's term in office. In fact, the ejido privatization and crop subsidy programs PROCEDE and PROCAMPO, introduced as part of neoliberal reform policies toward the end of the Salinas presidency, were still relevant at the time of my fieldwork in 2000. Stephen (2002) describes the process of state formation—the penetration of state ideologies and institutions—in Chiapas throughout the twentieth century as decentered and uneven (see also Joseph and Nugent 1994). This began with the agrarian reform and federal education under Cárdenas in the 1930s and again showed up in the PROCEDE campaign of the 1990s, which aimed at the liberalization of land tenure in Mexico's 27,410 ejidos. This massive outreach and education campaign linked each ejidatario to the state by way of an individual certificate designating the respective plot as mapped and measured, thereby opening the way for its possible sale (Stephen 2002, 65–73). Once a community decided to take part in PROCEDE, a privatization process was initiated that could lead to the breakup of the previously inalienable, communally held ejido land.

As a part of the federal government's strategy of "modernizing" the countryside, the PROCAMPO program paralleled these measures. It offered more than 3 million Mexican "farmers of corn, beans, wheat, rice, soy beans, sorghum, and cotton a subsidy of about 100 US$ per hectare over fifteen years. Guaranteed price supports for these crops were phased out in the autumn and winter seasons of 1994–95 (in line with NAFTA policies), pitting Mexican producers against cheaper U.S. imports and aligning Mexican crop prices with international prices" (66, 297).

Los Olvidados: On the Periphery of the State's Reach

The first colonists of Las Cañadas and Selva Lacandona were landless laborers who had worked in debt peonage on fincas, cattle ranches, and coffee plantations close to the towns of Ocosingo, Altamirano, Comitán, and Las Margaritas. They first settled the steep river valleys in the late 1930s and 1940s, petitioning the government for title to the land as ejidos. The idea behind the ejido goes back to the agrarian proponents of the Mexican Revolution, in particular Emiliano Zapata, and became a central element of the agrarian reform that was laid down in the 1917 constitution. Until a 1991 change in legislation, the term referred to a common land owned and used by ejidatarios forming an association of independent producers with use rights over individual plots (Chevalier and Buckles 1995; Schüren 1997, 33–65). As a formal organization with officially recognized members, resources, and responsibilities, the ejido is composed of a general assembly of all its members who come together in monthly meetings and make decisions by majority vote. For daily management and negotiations with the state the ejidatarios elect an unsalaried executive committee for a term of three years (Nuijten 2003, 48–54). Apart from overseeing individual and communal plots, this committee is also in charge of various government programs that have come to rely on the ejido to channel resources to the countryside. Although the Agrarian Law allowed the individual possession and the inheritance of ejido plots, it also stressed that ejidatarios had use rights to only one plot and were not allowed to divide or sell their land. Use rights could be taken away in the case of misconduct and be transferred to someone else by the general assembly (71–74).

Since the agrarian reform was laid down in the Mexican Constitution it took almost two decades for ejido land to be distributed on a large scale. President Cárdenas, who is also remembered for the nationalization of the largely U.S.-owned oil industry, stands for a massive redistribution of land in many Mexican states. In Chiapas, however, the property and interests of large landowners were mostly left intact and exploitative social relations in rural areas were generally preserved (Gilly 2005). This changed only in the 1950s when the federal government canceled existing titles to large tracts of uninhabited forest that dated back to the times of Porfirio Díaz. More land was expropriated in the 1960s and early 1970s and granted to the colonists for whom the region served as a "safety valve" (Benjamin 1996, 228). Due to several waves of colonizations, many of them from overcrowded highland communities, the population in the Selva Lacandona rose from 1,000 in 1950 to 10,000 in 1960, to 40,000 in 1970, to 100,000 in 1980, and to 150,000 in 1990 (De Vos 1995, 348–55; Stephen 2002, 102).

The granting of land petitions was the only state assistance the colonists received in more than four decades, the reason why some locals referred to themselves as *los olvidados*, "the forgotten ones"

(Stephen 2002, 111). In the 1970s, the region remained marginalized and excluded from national development programs. This is in marked contrast to other parts of the country that received developmental aid from the federal government during this time.[2] There are a variety of probable causes for this disparity. From early on, there was a nonagricultural agenda for Lacandon resources (timber, oil, mineral deposits, and, more recently, patentable genetic material) to which the state gained access through the creation of the Montes Azules Biosphere Reserve (RIBMA). Moreover, the indigenous settler communities were not regarded as particularly important to the overall maintenance of state control. Their inhabitants were left to grow maize for subsistence on what were usually low quality plots. When there was a surplus, they fed it to their pigs and sold them and sometimes small quantities of coffee to the *coyotes* (intermediary merchants). Between 1989 and 1993 coffee prices fell drastically and economic hardships increased as many lost their only source of cash. In addition to a high population growth, there were grave infrastructural shortages, such as a lack of clean water, electricity, roads, sewage systems, health care, or schooling. But it was in this absence of the state that autonomous forms of organization flourished. In the 1970s, this culminated in the creation of the ARIC Unión de Uniones (Rural Collective Interest Association Union of Unions), which Stephen (2002, 124) describes as the "de facto subterranean government of the region."[3] This federation of ejido unions worked by way of communal assemblies who elected their own officials and staffed their own police as well as committees for health and education (see Leyva Solano 1995, 382), the seeds of the autonomous institutions that became key features of the Zapatista project some twenty years later.

La Sultana: A Case in Point

Based on Womack's (1999, 219–22) account, the following section introduces the indigenous settlement and early Zapatista stronghold of La Sultana. The history of this Tzeltal colonist community emphasizes the difference between the situation in the highlands and that of the villages in Las Cañadas/Selva Lacandona, where agents of the state hardly had a presence and extralegal practices such as the

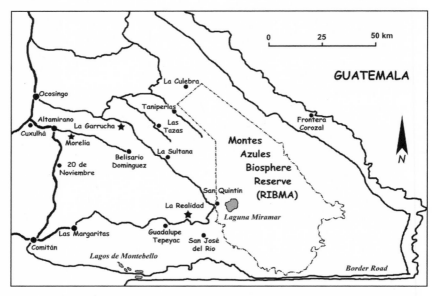

Map 3: The heartland of Zapatista organization consists of Las Cañadas and the Selva Lacandona regions, which border Guatemala to the northeast and to the south. Depicted are the main thoroughfares that link the towns of Ocosingo, Altamirano, Las Margaritas, and Comitán to the three Zapatista capitals of La Garrucha, Morelia, and La Realidad. Map by author.

occupation of land were the order of the day. La Sultana shares many characteristics with two of the communities featured in this book, San Emiliano and La Gardenia, the exact location of which I regrettably can not reveal.

La Sultana is located at the lower end of one of the river valleys that locally go by the name of Las Cañadas. Here, at the confluence of the Játaté and Tzaconejá, the climate is wet and warm from May until October, and dry and increasingly hot for the rest of the year. It does get even hotter downriver to the east, toward Laguna Miramar and beyond. Today, the gravel road that joins Ocosingo with the lagoon is lined by milpas (maize fields) and cow pastures with only patches of big trees left, but when the first people came here in search of mahogany, fur, and *chicle*, this was all jungle.[4] Sultana's thirty founding families had worked on the finca El Porvenir—way up the valley toward the town of Ocosingo—and settled at the joining of rivers in 1960. The settlers cleared the jungle and prepared their milpas only with the aid of fire and sowing sticks and then sent a petition for legal land recognition to the state capital Tuxtla Guiterrez. It was granted to them five years later. They raised chicken and pigs with the maize surplus and eventually bought some cattle. Within a decade, the population had doubled and the young men without ejido titles began preparing their milpas on *territorio nacional*. With eighteen other villages in the region, the community founded the ejido union Quiptic ta Lecubtesel (Tzeltal for Strength from Unity) in 1975 and five years later the Unión de Uniones. The organization enabled the villagers to resist government relocation plans and secure the construction of a road that linked their village with the rest of the country. As the government rejected further ejido claims in 1983, extralegal land occupation by the younger generation resumed and in 1986 the first villagers, among them the local *tuhunel* (indigenous deacon) and the secretary of Unión de Uniones, clandestinely joined the Zapatista guerrilla movement. Although in 1989 the government finally granted the longed-for ejidal expansion, the 1991 change of constitutional article 27 put an end to the hopes of landless youngsters and compelled many of them to join the EZLN as militias and insurgents.

Higgins (2004, 149) notes that Salinas removed subsidies and credit for traditional crops such as coffee and maize while cattle was increasingly subsidized. This is a clear example of the Mexican State strategically making use of subsidies to pursue a particular agenda; in this case the transformation from subsistence to export production, in line with wider neoliberal policies. However, it is often overlooked that the indigenous campesinos themselves make strategic use of state aid that can be diametrically opposite of the intended purpose; in this case, the colonist communities used the cattle credits for arming the insurrection (see chapter 2).

PRONASOL, too, had its impact on La Sultana. Solidarity committees were created and in the context of a federal census, government officials attempted to measure the index of poverty in the community. By the time of the Zapatista uprising, PRONASOL had provided a drinking water system, a clinic, a schoolhouse, two trucks for public transport, and a store selling subsidized goods. The youngsters had a basketball court built in the center of the village and those who joined a solidarity committee received credits to pay back their investments in cattle. The government-funded projects contributed to political division in La Sultana as in other EZLN's base communities and when it became clear that the uprising was imminent, those not wanting to take part in the uprising left the village, some in fear of the coming war and some because the Zapatista majority made them leave (Womack 1999, 219–22).

A String of Visitors: Perspectives on the EZLN's Origins

In an armed rebellion during which it briefly occupied San Cristóbal and other strategically important towns in eastern Chiapas, the Zapatista Army of National Liberation went public on January 1, 1994. Images of gun-toting Indígenas wearing ski masks and *pallacate* bandanas disrupted the post–Cold War calm, stunning TV audiences in Mexico and the world over.[5] As the day of the uprising coincided with the taking effect of the North American Free Trade Agreement (NAFTA), the rebels' spokesperson Subcomandante Marcos used his first media appearances to point out its devastating effects on the livelihoods of Mexican workers and peasants. In a declaration of war against the Mexican government and its army, the EZLN also issued a set of basic demands for work, land, housing, food, health care, education, independence, freedom, democracy, justice, and peace; only in the months and years to come did the Zapatistas increasingly shift their focus onto indigenous autonomy (EZLN 1993b).

Among the authors who have presented a differentiated analysis of the EZLN's origins are Benjamin (1996), Leyva Solano (1998, 2003b), Harvey (1998), Collier and Quaratiello (1999), and García de León (2002). According to their interpretations, it was a combination of circumstances that allowed the guerrilla movement, which had grown clandestinely through a network of social relations in the indigenous communities, to become a key actor in Mexican politics. The economic crisis of the 1980s had seen a drastic deterioration in the quality of life for Mexicans inhabiting peripheral areas such as the remoter parts of eastern Chiapas. The unwillingness of the ruling party to change traditional mechanisms of political control, along with the fragmentation of the Left following its inability to successfully contest electoral fraud in 1988, contributed to a situation in which large parts of the population identified with the EZLN (Harvey 1998, 196–98; Leyva Solano 1998, 38; Collier and Quaratiello 1999, 83–87). An investigation into the origins of the guerrilla movement also necessitates a closer look both at living conditions and the intercommunal organization in Las Cañadas and parts of the Lacandon jungle. Thus, Harvey (1998, 8–9) regards the combination of ecological crisis, a lack of available productive land, and the dwindling of other sources of income, combined with the political and religious reorganization of the indigenous communities since the 1960s, as decisive for the emergence of the EZLN.

Since the late 1960s, catholic priests and *catequistas* influenced by liberation theology had tried in their missionary work in Las Cañadas and Selva Lacandona to focus on indigenous practices and traditions as well as to further the foundation of local cooperatives.[6] This was in line with the grassroots principle the diocese of San Cristóbal had adopted after its bishop, Samuel Ruiz, had attended the conference of Latin American bishops in Medellín in 1968. In the peripheral and dispersed settlements of the region, the diocese succeeded in building a support base for autonomous forms of popular representation. The common social and religious identification of the colonists facilitated the intense learning process that accompanied this organization (27–28).[7] Crucial for this development was the Indigenous Congress held in San Cristóbal in 1974, called by the state governor but organized by the San Cristóbal diocese. In the preparation of the delegations, the diocese initiated courses in agrarian law, history, and economics, providing political education for local community leaders. With the participation of over a thousand Indígenas representing more than three hundred communities, the delegates attacked corruption, the practice of land title distribution, and the encroachment of ranchers. Their demands included a minimum wage for plantation workers, greater access to markets, education in indigenous languages, and medical care (77–79). It was at the Indigenous Congress that progressive indigenous catequistas met activists of the organized Left (García de León 2002, 174–76).

The engagement of Mexico's independent Left played an important role in the emergence of the EZLN and its predecessor organizations. The meetings of the Indigenous Congress between 1974 and 1977 served as a catalyst for grassroots organization in the highlands of Chiapas, Las Cañadas, and Selva Lacandona. Throughout the 1970s the region was visited by student activists from the Mexican metropoles in the North who had survived the 1968 repression.[8] The National Forces of Liberation (FLN), a revolutionary group from urban Mexico, installed a guerrilla camp in the Lacandon as early as 1970. The FLN was founded by students on August 6, 1969, in the northern city of Monterrey. However, by 1974, most of its guerrillas had been killed by police and the army before getting a foothold in the indigenous communities. Drawing heavily on confidential army material, the investigative journalist Tello Díaz (1995, 62–85) has provided an extensive but questionable account of this period.[9]

Upon an invitation by Bishop Samuel Ruiz, who had met them on a visit a year earlier, a group of unarmed Maoists from Torreón arrived in Chiapas in 1977. They were student activists inspired by the Marxist professor Adolfo Orive Berlinguer of the National Autonomous University of Mexico (UNAM), and they intended to build a popular front with the "working masses" in the periphery. The members of this group, who are still remembered as the *asesores* (advisors) by the older people in the villages where I undertook research, were part of a nationwide movement to build new forms of popular organization along Maoist lines that went by the name of Línea Proletaria (LP). In an effort to undermine centralized decision making, they promoted the division of community meetings into *asambleas chicas* (small assemblies) to discuss issues that were then forwarded to the community assembly. They also organized commissions that traveled between individual communities to establish links and build up broader alliances of villages (Harvey 1998, 81–83). Making use of new agrarian legislation introduced by President Echeverría in 1971, many colonist communities formed so-called ejidal unions to counter the official politics of exclusion and to heighten their chances of obtaining support from the government. This mainly concerned funds for regional development, credits and resources for agricultural production, and most importantly the assignment of new ejido land titles.

Another important factor for uniting the indigenous communities of eastern Chiapas was the launch of resettlement programs in the 1970s. Some seven thousand Tzeltal and Ch'ol colonists faced the threat of expulsion after the Chiapas government had given an enormous area of 614,000 hectares of jungle to the Lacandon Indígenas in 1972, who consisted of a mere seventy families and were subsequently paid by a government-owned foresting company to let it exploit rare woods in the region (Benjamin 1996, 236; Harvey 1998, 80; De Vos 2003, 26). The necessity for joint resistance against forced resettlement spawned the founding of the ejidal union Quiptic ta Lecubtesel near Laguna Miramar. When another 400,000 hectares were declared a biosphere reserve (RIBMA) in 1978, the menace of resettlement loomed once more. Further cooperation among the affected peasant population brought about the large Unión de Uniones. This umbrella organization, made up of three independent ejidal unions in the Selva/Cañadas region and comprising more than one hundred individual villages, was to become an important organizational factor in the emergence of the EZLN (Benjamin 1996, 236; Leyva Solano and Ascencio Franco 1996; Gledhill 1999, 19). Leyva Solano (2003b) argues that the unchallenged position of the Unión de Uniones turned Las Cañadas into a de facto autonomous region with its own forms of government and its indigenous regional authorities that were able to control the provision of services to the population.[10] In 1982, the Unión de Uniones split up. Six of the participating ejidal unions and two rural production associations eventually were constituted as the ARIC Unión de Uniones in March 1988 (Harvey 1998, 256).

The Makings of a Counterstate

In 1983, members of the FLN returned to Chiapas and managed to build contacts with local campesino organizations, notably Quiptic ta Lecubtesel, and created a base for the construction of the EZLN. As is conveyed in the accounts by Subcomandante Marcos, which Harvey (1998) and Collier and Quaratiello (1999) use as a source on the issue, the guerrillas soon learned that their survival and success depended on adapting to local forms of organization and decision making (Leyva Solano 1998, 42; Harvey 1998, 164–66; Collier and Quaratiello 1999, 83–90). According to Harvey (1998, 167), the EZLN merits a "complex, culturally sensitive and multistranded analysis" that investigates the convergence that took place between the FLN activists' critical interpretation of Mexican history and the indigenous peoples' own stories of being subjected to humiliation, exploitation, and racism. As Harvey puts it, by gaining political direction over the movement, the Indígenas "inverted the traditional leader-masses relationship and provided a distinctive model of popular and democratic organization" (167).

Due to these organizational processes, there already was a substantial network of politically allied villages in eastern Chiapas when the FLN activists arrived in 1983. Unlike a decade earlier, conditions were more favorable for the formation of a guerrilla movement. Land claims had received a definite rejection from the government and established independent campesino organizations were searching for a new approach. The option of lending force to their demands by military means must have appealed to the people in the colonist villages.

Although Wickham-Crowley (1991) and Wolf (1969) both undertook their studies on rebellion before the Zapatista uprising, I consider some of their findings to be applicable for its further analysis. The main prerequisites for the success of guerrilla activity, as set out by Wickham-Crowley (1991, 35), were fulfilled in the case of Chiapas: the social contract had not been met and the colonist communities perceived government officials as "predatory authorities." The existing organizational community structures and the relative absence of state authority were an ideal breeding ground for an organization promising to provide a "counter state or alternative government." Similarly, in his analysis of peasant revolutions, Wolf (1969) stresses that a peripheral location with regard to the center of state control constitutes a crucial factor for a peasant uprising. If there is an ethnic differentiation as in the Las Cañadas/Selva Lacandona regions of eastern Chiapas, this enhances the solidarity among the rebels, and a language distinct from the one used by state officials can provide an autonomous system of communication (292–93).

Higgins (2004, 159–61) places particular importance on what Subcomandante Marcos has called the "Indianization" of the EZLN (Le Bot 1997, 150). This took place as the mestizo FLN activists realized that if they were to be successful in their attempt to win the local population over to their cause, they had to understand not only their language but also their culture. Thus, tales of indigenous mythical characters such as the Sombreron, Votan, and Ik'al, as well as stories about exploitation, humiliation, and racism became the primary means through which the mestizos became aware of the cultural richness and otherness of their indigenous compañeros. This experience of oral history became the base for the language of Zapatismo, which immediately strikes anyone reading the communiqués and declarations from the Selva Lacandona for its peculiarity and richness in metaphor (Higgins 2004, 162–63).

According to Subcomandante Marcos, the beginnings of the EZLN were motivated by the colonist communities' need for self-defense in the face of the repression by landowners and judicial police (see also García de León 1994, 26–28). The group of armed students from the city, among them Marcos himself, were eventually received in some of the villages organized in the Unión de Uniones and the project of an armed guerrilla was brought to life in the indigenous communities (see also Barmeyer 2003). This process did not constitute a mobilization in the style of Latin American revolutionary groups of the 1970s, but was rather initiated by the indigenous colonist communities and the guerrillas alike (Le Bot 1997, 142–52; Harvey 1998, 165–67). My own interviews with inhabitants of Zapatista base communities also reveal that the gradual involvement of indigenous communities in guerrilla activities was a lengthy process. It took until the early 1990s for a substantial part of the villages in Las Cañadas to join the ranks of the EZLN.[11] Sometimes, those who refused to join were expelled from their villages in the run-up to the rebellion (also see Womack 1999, 222). The cases I know of (La Gardenia, San Emiliano, and Amador Hernández) involved up to a dozen families per village who had to move to Ocosingo, where they were compensated by the regional PRI government for the land they had left behind.[12] The fact that it took eight years (in La Gardenia) until these terrains were distributed among landless Zapatistas shows that the maintenance of cohesion rather than the land issue had been the motivating factor for the expulsions. Indeed, at the time of the uprising most of the EZLN's core communities were collectively behind what they considered to be their project. However, it was often only a matter of years until this unanimity gave way to communal division (see chapter 4).

According to my own analysis, the economic aspirations of the people on the ground were a crucial mobilizing factor for the uprising itself as well as for the later consolidation of the Zapatista autonomy project described in this book. For the remote rural villages this meant access to an infrastructure of roads, electricity, and fresh water, as well as the means to transport goods in and out of the region. Most of all, the inhabitants of Las Cañadas's settler communities longed for the fertile lands farther up the valley that their grandparents had worked on as serfs and that were usually much larger and more productive than their own meager plots. Another important motivation for local communities to choose membership in an armed organization was to end the repression by district police and the landowners' private armies. It is against the backdrop of such material and security considerations by the Zapatista base that aims such as cultural, legal, and economic autonomy can be properly understood. This is also in line with Wickham-Crowley's assertion (1991, 35) that the authority of a guerrilla movement builds on "the three classic contributions of government": defending the populace, maintaining police and administrative functions, and providing material security.

Rus (1994) describes indigenous highland communities in the immediate postrevolutionary period of the 1920s and early 1930s as having been closed to the outside world. As outlined in the first section, this soon changed and various initiatives and government programs "integrated" them into a regime of state control, in stark contrast to what one can observe in contemporary indigenous villages organized in the EZLN, be it in the formerly inaccessible Las Cañadas/ Selva Lacandona regions or in the highlands. Have those communities actually performed a circular movement over the course of the century and reverted back to a closed state? Or have they rather become "globalized" in their own chosen manner and turned into something that is actually much more open to the outside? The chapters on NGO involvement show that there has indeed been an opening but outside involvement has increasingly been brought under the control of state-independent institutions, such as the Juntas de Buen Gobierno (Good Government Councils). These chapters also demonstrate that it is possible to sell innovations in a conservative guise. Thus, the reversal to *usos y costumbres* (customs and traditions) within the framework of EZLN organization actually served to bind individual communities to the strictly hierarchical (and vanguardist) structures of the guerrilla movement.

Fourteen Years of Movement: The Time Since the Uprising

After several thousand Zapatista fighters had taken over important municipal seats like Ocosingo, Las Margaritas, Altamirano, and San Cristóbal on New Year's Day 1994, the Salinas government sent federal troops to Chiapas, reinforcing existing contingents, to recapture the towns. The guerrillas withdrew from all towns except Ocosingo, where large numbers of poorly armed rebels were trapped in the market and more than a hundred of them died in a hail of bullets.[13] Media coverage of the massacre contributed to a rapid mobilization of civil society in the capital and other large cities, culminating in a peace demonstration of two hundred thousand in Mexico City's main square. The pressure from the street and the fear that reports of human rights abuses committed by the army would further damage the investment climate in Mexico led President Salinas to declare a cease-fire after twelve days of war (García de León 2002, 253).

On February 1, 1994, the EZLN's command faxed a call for help directly to NGO offices throughout Mexico (EZLN 1994d). In it, the guerrilla movement issued a request for civil society organizations to gather together to form a "belt of peace," a buffer zone with the objective of minimizing friction between the EZLN and federal troops while the first dialogues between the EZLN and the government representative Camacho Solis took place in San Cristóbal. Addressing the neutrality of the NGOs, the guerrilla movement stated that it did not require any commitment or even sympathy with their struggle. As shown in chapter 5, in the decade to come this policy underwent a decisive change in the way that the EZLN came to expect partisanship of any organization operating in the territory under its control. In its early communiqués, however, the EZLN emphasized the need to promote alliances between a broad range of popular organizations to create an alternative national project and to avoid ending up in a dialogue with only the government and political parties (EZLN 1994b; 1994d).

In their book on The Zapatista "Social Netwar" in Mexico, David Ronfeldt and John Arquilla focus on the Zapatista movement and the multitude of NGOs and civil society activists involved with them. They portray the struggle for democratic change as one in which the protagonists use networked forms of organization, strategies, and technologies attuned to the information age. Describing "dispersed small groups who communicate, coordinate and conduct their campaigns in an internetted manner, without a precise central command" (1998, 9), the authors use the NGOs in Chiapas as an example for the protagonists of such a netwar. They recount how (reacting to the EZLN's request) national and international NGOs physically and electronically "swarmed" into Chiapas in the months following the uprising and joined forces once they got there, voicing sympathy and support for the guerrilla movement's demands.[14] Although I appreciate the authors' description of the NGO network formation in Chiapas as well as their attempts at differentiating the various groups (see chapter 5), I strongly disagree with the ubiquitous analogy of warfare in their analysis because it completely disregards that the principal motivation for the 1994 convergence of social actors on Chiapas was peace.[15] I prefer Leyva Solano's analysis (2003a, 1), which contends that the "neo-Zapatista networks" that came about after the 1994 uprising were not the product of a strategic plan devised by the guerrilla movement. She regards the networks as a heterogeneous political convergence of individuals, organizations, and movements that came together to support the EZLN's demands, but transformed and redefined their content in the process.

A first round of negotiations between the rebels and the government took place in the cathedral of San Cristóbal under the mediation of Bishop Samuel Ruiz at the end of February 1994. In a first agreement, the government recognized the rebels as a fighting force and guaranteed them a protected territory; the EZLN commenced a discussion with its bases whether to continue the war or whether to turn into a political movement. In a climate of mistrust exacerbated by the assassination of the PRI's presidential candidate Donaldo Colosio on March 23, the Zapatista delegation postponed the mandate to seek a "peace with dignity and justice" that it had received from its support base. In May, the presidential candidate for the left-of-center Party of Democratic Revolution (PRD) Cuauhtémoc Cárdenas, who hoped to capitalize on the rebellion in the upcoming elections, visited the rebels in their jungle stronghold but was received coolly (García de León 2002, 254–55).

To demonstrate the EZLN's isolation, the state government called on the indigenous and campesino organizations in Chiapas to form a broad front that would reject both the violence and the guerrillas. Thus, the State Council of Indigenous and Peasant Organizations (Consejo Estatal de Organizaciones Indígenas y Campesinas, or CEOIC) was constituted by 280 different groups but, while rejecting the EZLN's methods, they declared themselves to be in agreement with the rebels' demands (248). In the following six months, CEOIC members alone took over 50,000 hectares belonging to 340 private farms (Harvey 1998, 211).[16] Governmental distribution, in an apparent reaction to the seizures, amounted to 180,000 hectares (Castro and Hidalgo 1998).

Just before the presidential elections in August 1994, the EZLN convoked the National Democratic Convention (Convención Nacional Democrática, or CND), mobilizing a broad spectrum of social actors and opening a space for dialogue between them that led to further meetings and national and international forums for years to come. Thus, social movements such as the debtor organization El Barzón became established on a wave of pro-Zapatista sentiment. About five thousand people came to the Aguascalientes of Guadalupe Tepeyac, where hardworking Zapatistas had created the infrastructure for the conference in record time. What had been conceived as the beginning of a broad opposition, however, soon turned into sectarianism instigated by the group that had been put in charge by the rebels to promote their cause outside of Chiapas. This was the FAC-MLN (Broad Front for the Construction of a National Liberation Movement), the leadership of which had belonged to the same FLN that had sent its militants to Chiapas in the early 1980s. At their initiative and with the hope to build an alternative opposition to the newly elected PRI government, a broad spectrum of intellectuals and civil society organizations came together at the second CND meeting in Tuxtla Guiterrez in October 1994. To the incomprehension of most participants, however, the meeting turned into a battlefield between two factions of former FLN members (García de León 2002, 256–57).

On August 21, 1994, the PRI candidate Ernesto Zedillo was voted into office for the Mexican presidency while the contender for Mexico's Left, Cuauhtémoc Cárdenas (PRD), finished a distant third. In the Chiapas state election, however, things were less clear-cut. Here, the Zapatistas endorsed Amado Avendaño, a San Cristóbal newspaper editor, as a candidate for civil society; he ran for the PRD and actually won in the area controlled by the EZLN. Demanding that the PRI governor renounce, Avendaño set up a "transition government in rebellion" with the backing of the EZLN. The official governor Robledo Rincón was replaced by another PRIista, Ruiz Ferro, in the process (257). On December 19, two weeks after the Chiapas state elections, the EZLN officially declared the first autonomous municipalities in an attempt to break the military encirclement. Roadblocks were set up by the rebels, and Zapatista communities inside and outside of the area hitherto controlled by the EZLN announced their independence from the Mexican government. The stated aim was to create a space where the indigenous communities could govern themselves according to their own social and political customs and without state intervention.[17]

Seven weeks later, the Mexican Federal Army raided Zapatista territory in an attempt to capture the guerrilla command. According to García de León (257), the supposed territorial gains made by the EZLN had allowed the hardliners in the new Zedillo administration to make their case for a military solution. The rebels perceived the attack on their villages as a breach of the cease-fire agreements, and members of the affected communities still referred to it as the *traición* (treason) years later. Although the army failed to capture the EZLN's commanders, the raid resulted in the displacement of thousands of people who fled into the mountains as the federal soldiers raped and pillaged their way into Las Cañadas.[18] The army stayed on, setting up a string of military bases along the main access routes into the Selva Lacandona, drastically increasing its presence in the region to more than thirty thousand, and reducing the area controlled by the Zapatistas to jungle and mountains.[19] After a mobilization of civil society by the NGO network CONPAZ and the San Cristóbal diocese, peace camps were set up, enabling most of the refugees to return to their looted villages (see chapter 5).

As large numbers of federal troops installed themselves in or close to Zapatista villages in Las Cañadas and Selva Lacandona, both the San Cristóbal diocese and the rebels had an interest to resume peace negotiations (261–63). Under renewed mediation of the diocese, a new round of dialogues was begun in the village of San Miguel in Las Cañadas in May 1995. At the end of 1995, the talks between delegates of the EZLN and a commission from the Mexican Congress (Comisión de Concordia y Pacificación, or COCOPA) were moved to the highland town of San Andrés Larrainzar, which subsequently turned into a focus for civil society mobilizations. The themes to be covered in the negotiations were Indigenous Rights and Culture, Democracy and Justice, Living Standards and Development, Women's Rights, and Peace with Justice and Dignity. From its situation of military siege, the EZLN was able to capitalize on the negotiations by inviting indigenous leaders and experts and by issuing frequent communiqués that kept the guerrilla movement's demands in public discourse. Only in the first topic, indigenous rights and culture, was an agreement reached and signed in February 1996. When the next round of negotiations started a month later, the government sent a low-level delegation whose only aim seemed to be the stalling of the talks; within a few sessions, negotiations were suspended on September 1, 1996 (261–63).

This time saw a flurry of activity in the way of pro-Zapatista mobilization. In a fulfillment of the decision to promote the civic, nonpartisan front that had been arrived at in the 1995 referendum in Zapatista base communities, local assemblies all over the Mexican Republic founded the Zapatista Front of National Liberation (FZLN) (Harvey 1998, 208). At the National Indigenous Congress (CNI) convoked in the same year, the FZLN represented the guerrilla movement. On the international

Figure 3: Since the 1980s, thousands of indigenous Zapatistas have regularly been mobilized for political rallies around particular issues. This 1996 march through San Cristóbal demanded an end to the occupation by the Mexican Federal Army. The pasamontañas have been widely used by Zapatistas to protect their identity, March 8, 1996. Photo courtesy of an anonymous solidarity activist.

level, there was a first European Meeting against Neoliberalism and for Humanity in Berlin in summer 1996. It was organized by pro-Zapatista solidarity groups that had developed in North America and Europe. A few weeks later, delegates from all these groups converged in Chiapas for the Intergalactic Meeting against Neoliberalism and for Humanity held in five Zapatista strongholds. When President Zedillo refused to present the "COCOPA law" on indigenous rights and culture to the Congress for ratification in December of the same year, the EZLN reacted with deep indignation, calling an end to the dialogue with the government and entering a period marked by an absence of communiqués and heightened alert in the base communities.

As a supporter turned critic, García de León (2002, 266–69) attests severe tactical mistakes to the guerrilla movement. By focusing too much on the San Andrés negotiations, the EZLN had allowed the PRI government to isolate the rebels from their original demand for land and thereby from a broad support base among the campesino organizations that had originally shared their demands. By limiting the negotiations to the "conflict zone" and an abstract debate on autonomy, the author argues, the dominant political system had expelled the rebels from national all-party discussions about democratic transition and electoral reform that were to bring about the first legitimate elections in 2000 (271). Obviously beset by deep disappointment regarding the EZLN's strategy since 1996, García de León contends that, by concentrating on international solidarity and a change in national legislation, the guerrilla movement lost sight of communal conflicts, which became crucial for further developments.

Whereas much of the land seized by campesinos from large estates in the course of the uprising was retaken by the landowners with the help of the Mexican army in February 1995, many terrains of small and medium-size ranches remained occupied by both the Zapatistas and independent peasant organizations. This was important for the Mexican government's counterinsurgency campaign, because the farmers who were deprived of their lands turned into fierce supporters of paramilitary groups that emerged in the region in the mid-1990s (see also Gledhill 1999). Many of these organizations were involved with the PRI and received funds from federal programs. Their recruits were often from the same poor and landless families that had supported the Zapatistas. The new role of gunman offered the young men prestige they could not otherwise acquire because they were excluded from the hierarchy of public offices in the community due to their landlessness (Aubry and Inda 1997, 1998). At the height of paramilitary activity in 1997 and 1998, there were massive expulsions in which paramilitary groups were able to dispose of the plots of the expelled families, selling their harvest and possessions. Particularly in Los Altos and La Zona Norte of Chiapas this resulted in many thousands mainly Zapatista, internal refugees, ten thousand of them in the Chenalhó area alone (Hidalgo 1997a, 1997b, 1998).[20]

The most effective counterinsurgency, however, was far more insidious. Soon after the insurrection, both federal and Chiapas politicians had made promises for peace and prosperity in the region. Along with

Figure 4: As part of the Mexican government's counterinsurgency strategy, federal soldiers regularly stopped their convoys in rebel communities to hand out food packages to people from neighboring villages who were not organized in the guerrilla movement, March 1997. Photo by author.

the deployment of troops a wave of development money was issued for the "conflict zone" in the east of the state. A 2000 report by the secretary for social development (Jarque 2000) describes the large-scale development scheme Programa Cañadas (Cañadas Program).[21] Within the first five years of its operation, Mex$386 million (approximately US$38 million) were transferred from state and federal budgets to realize some 4,381 projects. More than half of this money went into the building of roads and power lines, which had the principal purpose of supplying the new army camps.

Two programs that became particularly crucial both for the Zapatista's internal policies and their relation with the Mexican State were DICONSA and PROGRESA. The secretary of social development's Program of Rural Provisions (Programa de Abasto Rural, or DICONSA) was aimed at providing for the nutritional needs of the population living in the remote and marginalized rural areas of the Mexican Republic.

This was to be achieved by delivering nonperishable products such as maize, sugar, beans, rice, and powdered milk to 22,866 stores of the National Company for the People's Subsistence (Compañía Nacional de Subsistencias Populares, or CONASUPO), about a third of which were located in indigenous areas. The purchase of the goods sold at competitive prices was reserved to those receiving less than two minimum wages per family household (Jarque 2000, 26–28). This applied to most of the population in the settler communities of Las Cañadas and Selva Lacandona, and many Zapatistas bought their basic goods in these stores until 1997.

The Program for Education, Health, and Nutrition (Programa de Educación, Salud y Alimentación, or PROGRESA) was initiated by president Zedillo in 1997 and renamed Oportunidades during the Fox presidency in 2002. Aimed at breaking the intergenerational transmission of poverty by improving levels of education, nutrition, and health of both children and adults, the program provided cash transfers, preventative health care, and food donations to the families of children who regularly attended school. The amount of money per enrolled child ranged from Mex$90 in the third grade of primary school to Mex$290 in the third grade of secondary school (eighth grade) for boys and up to Mex$335 for girls. School attendance was closely monitored and missing more than five days per month led to the suspension of the payments. In 1999–2000 PROGRESA provided stipends to 2.4 million Mexican children. In 2000 Chiapas contributed the second largest group of PROGRESA beneficiaries, which amounted to 288,570. An additional Mex$135 of monthly cash depended on the conscientious fulfillment of a family health scheme, which included consultancies, inoculations, and a family planning program (Jarque 2000, 38–45). With its special focus on rural women and their integration into medical and income-generating projects, PROGRESA came to be in direct competition with the Zapatistas' own health and production collectives that were characterized by a high degree of female participation.

The late 1990s saw a fortification of the Zapatista autonomous municipalities through the founding of new population centers (*nuevos centros de población*) on land that had been occupied in the course of the uprising. This period also stands for the systematic integration of independent NGOs into the project of communal autonomy through the provision of infrastructure and training (see chapters 5 and 6). In their expansion onto "recuperated terrains," the Zapatistas increasingly found themselves in confrontations with other social organizations that occupied the same territory. Into this situation, and from 1997 onward, Chiapas state governor Albores imposed new administrative structures in the context of a remunicipalization scheme. This exacerbated existing tensions both among the people living in the concerned areas and between autonomous municipalities and the Mexican State (García de León 2002, 277–79). As a reaction to an increasing consolidation of the independent institutions in 1998 there were brutal attempts by the government to dismantle the new administrative structures. As the government stepped up its counterinsurgency campaign by way of repression, inducements, and the financing of paramilitary groups, the EZLN too tightened the rules that their base communities had to abide by. In an effort to secure both the dignity and the allegiance of its supporters as well as its own outward credibility, the guerrilla movement proscribed the acceptance of "alms" from the state, be it money, subsidized foodstuffs, teachers, or medical aid. As I argue in chapter 4, these measures resulted in desertions of factions and even entire villages from Zapatista ranks.

In a renewed and internationally publicized effort to exert pressure on the Zedillo government, the Zapatistas convoked the 1999 Consulta, a referendum for indigenous autonomy held all over Mexico, which yielded more than 3 million votes demanding an implementation of the San Andrés Accords (Collier and Quaratiello 1999, 162). Not all of the EZLN's attempts at publicity were this successful. Thus, soon after the Consulta, the guerrilla movement supported a student strike against the introduction of tuition fees at Mexico City's largest university, the Universidad Nacional Autónoma de México, which lasted for a year. As the strike turned increasingly sectarian and unpopular among the wider population, the EZLN's unwavering loyalty with the remaining hard core of students organized in the General Strike Committee (CGH) met with incomprehension across the Mexican Left.

In summer 2000, the Mexican political system that had been dominated by the PRI for the greater part of a century was shaken up by the victory of Vicente Fox from the rightist Party of National Action (PAN) in presidential elections. Fox had promised to "solve the Chiapas problem in fifteen minutes" and adapted the strategy to deal with Chiapas by promoting large-scale private investment within the Plan Puebla Panamá (PPP). The megaproject aims at making both human and natural resources in the region accessible to globalized capital. The main constituents are an expansion of infrastructure between the Pacific and Gulf Coast, from central Mexico to Panama City and from Central America's Caribbean coast to Texas. Apart from the construction of roads and the upgrade of electrical grids to supply power for the U.S. market (much of it hydroelectricity from Chiapas), the plan envisions new ports, airports, and bridges, as well as the creation of biological reserve corridors for exploitation by pharmaceutical and seed companies, a practice also referred to as biopiracy (Barreda 2001; Pickard 2002). None of the PPP's policies address the roots of structural poverty that afflicts the majority of the 65 million people who live in the area. Instead, the projects were designed in collaboration with multinational companies to optimize the exploitation of natural and human resources for corporate profit. This is most salient in the construction of maquiladoras, assemblage plants operating preferably in the depressed border areas where people need work and wages are low.

After what was possibly the first democratic election in Chiapas, Pablo Salazar Mendiguchía was voted into office as governor on a PAD-PRI ticket in 2000. He was expected to approach the conflict in Chiapas with mediation rather than repression. Salazar had represented the PRI in the COCOPA delegation during the San Andrés negotiations and had always championed the implementation of the Law on Indigenous Rights and Culture. As a reaction to the changes in government both at federal and state levels, the EZLN began another large mobilization that was to culminate in a motorized march on Mexico City to advocate the implementation of the San Andrés Accords (see chapter 9). In an apparent concession to the rebels, President Fox not only ordered the removal of army roadblocks in Chiapas but also fulfilled some of the EZLN's demands, such as the largely symbolic dismantling of seven out of more than three hundred military bases in the state and the freeing of about one hundred political prisoners. The motorcade by twenty-four rebel commanders and several thousand indigenous and international activists through the southern and central states of the Mexican Republic drew massive crowds in the towns and cities along the route. Before entering the capital, the comandantes participated in the third National Indigenous Congress in Nurío, Michoacán, integrating most delegates into their ranks. Once in the capital, the participants of the march besieged the political establishment for three weeks until the Zapatista commanders and CNI delegates were allowed to speak before Congress to make the case for the stonewalled Law on Indigenous Rights and Culture.

After the rebels had returned to the jungle, the PRI- and PAN-dominated Congress rejected the COCOPA law and ratified an emaciated version of the bill that was lacking crucial elements such as indigenous control over their resources and the right to self-determination. Both the CNI and the EZLN strongly condemned the new law and the guerrilla movement commenced another period of silence that lasted for over a year. The EZLN could be criticized for failing to capitalize on the momentum it had achieved through the mobilization for the march on Mexico City. Thus, possibly due to its self-imposed silence, the guerrilla movement did not join ongoing popular campaigns such as the one against the privatization of electricity or the mobilizations against the Plan Puebla Panamá. On the other hand, and particularly through its control of Mexico's main television channels, the Fox government was able to portray itself before wide parts of the general public as supporting the demands for indigenous rights articulated during the march, although it had in fact appropriated the "indigenous issue" by introducing an inadequate piece of legislation.

In Chiapas, several peasant organizations that had been shunned by former PRI administrations started to receive development aid from the new state government; locally, particularly the credits for cattle led to a drastic increase in the demand for land that could be used as pasture. The bulk of terrains "recuperated" in the course of the uprising had been used for raising cattle prior to 1994 and many of the Zapatista new population centers had in the meantime been built on former cow pastures. The stage was set for a series of communal conflicts. While paramilitary groups still operated in Chiapas, the occurrence of rural violence increasingly involved Zapatista communities and members of peasant organizations competing for territory that they had often jointly squatted on in 1994.[22]

In December 2002, as the EZLN broke its silence after more than a year with a string of communiqués, Subcomandante Marcos addressed the issue of regional autonomy from yet another angle. To the puzzlement of many observers, he challenged the prominent Spanish judge Balthasar Garzón in an attempt at mediating in the conflict between the Basque population and the Spanish State. While the project that received a stiff rejection from ETA could be interpreted as a further indication of the EZLN's command having lost touch with local issues, (of which there were plenty at the time) the rebels had made a comeback.[23] The communiqués issued by the guerrilla movement in the following months announced a restructuring of the autonomous municipalities that was to culminate in an inaugural ceremony of the Juntas de Buen Gobierno in August 2003. The resulting consolidation of governance that entailed the local administration of all NGO projects shows how much self-sufficiency in Zapatista territory had advanced over the past ten years.

According to SIPAZ, or the International Service for Peace (2006), the new regional councils excelled in the mediation and resolution of community conflicts, reducing their incidence both among Zapatistas and other factions despite the continued tensions caused by the constant army presence. Such conflicts often revolved around infrastructure projects and public services such as water and electricity but were also caused by the existence of parallel institutions regarding justice and law enforcement in villages marked by factional splits. Thus, in April 2004 the highland town of Zinacantán became the scene of violent attacks by militants of the PRD against local Zapatistas who had refused to take on traditional community cargos and the financial obligations that go with them (SIPAZ 2006). The Montes Azules Biosphere Reserve continued to be another cause for conflict as the Mexican government threatened to evict predominantly Zapatista villages located in the conservation zone. The EZLN displayed a disposition for compromise by relocating some of the villages in question on its own accord.

The year of the 2006 presidential elections in Mexico brought the culmination of a new campaign by the Zapatistas that represented both a shift in strategy and a renewed effort to extend their influence at the national level. La Otra Campaña (The Other Campaign), devised to run in parallel to the electoral campaigns of Mexico's established political parties, was initiated with the sixth declaration (la Sexta) from the Selva Lacandona (EZLN 2005), which hits a distinctly different tone than its predecessors. La Sexta proposes the creation of a broad popular front, made up of civil society actors, with the aim of creating a new constitution. In a move away from indigenous issues, the document emphasizes the importance of anticapitalist ideology and puts a focus on mobilizing workers and campesinos. This latest campaign to build a class-based national movement—potentially more encompassing than one based on ethnicity could ever aspire to be—testifies to the unflagging flexibility of the EZLN to reinvent itself to not only persevere as an organization but to advance the interests of its base in Chiapas.

Zapatista Autonomy in Context

Autonomy is the concrete expression of exercising the right to self-determination, expressed within the framework of the Nation State. As a consequence, the indigenous peoples can decide on their form of internal government as well as on their ways of political, social, economic, and cultural organization. . . . The indigenous peoples' exercise of autonomy should contribute to the unity and democratization of national life and should strengthen the country's sovereignty.[24]

(*San Andrés Accords on Indigenous Rights and Culture* 1996, quoted in Hernández Navarro and Vera Herrera 1998, 68)

The anthropologist June Nash (2001, 197) notes that autonomy and the desire to govern themselves have been integral to the strategies of Latin America's indigenous peoples since the conquest. Land as a territorial base was of prime importance for this conception of autonomy. In colonial times, the Spanish Crown granted the rights of *pueblos indios* (indigenous peoples) over water, woods, and communal lands.

Although these rights were abolished under Porfirio Díaz, they reappeared in the revolutionary Mexican Constitution of 1917. Under the Salinas presidency, changes to the land reform article 27 again called these territorial rights into question by making way for the privatization of ejido land. Although the Zapatistas have taken great care to emphasize their aim of democratic coexistence within the Mexican nation, both in their communiqués and in public acts such as the ceremonial display of the Mexican flag, claims to land and the collective rights to it—including the subsoil riches beneath their territory—have been among their most salient demands (197).

Héctor Díaz Polanco, one of the EZLN's advisors during the San Andrés negotiations on indigenous rights and culture in 1996, regards the Zapatista insistence on *autonomy* to be the key for fulfilling all other claims by the indigenous peoples of Chiapas, such as cultural recognition, bilingual education, or a guaranteed representation in elected office (1998, 216–17). Whereas Collier and Quaratiello (1999, 161) contend that "autonomy" hardly existed as a concept in rural Chiapas before 1994, Mattiace, Hernández Castillo, and Rus (2002, 27) argue that the organizational initiatives taken at the indigenous congress in San Cristóbal in 1974 were already based on factual autonomy, that is, on the communal practices of indigenous people. Indeed, Leyva Solano (2003b, 174–75) asserts that the indigenous communities organized in the Unión de Uniones had achieved a degree of de facto autonomy in the 1980s that was again lost in the aftermath of the 1994 uprising.

The concepts of autonomy prevalent among Mexico's indigenous groups that have voiced their demands since the Zapatista uprising are diverse. However, their demands are often shaped by a common history. Mattiace (2003, 90) sees important antecedents to current demands in the experiences of earlier decades when peasant organizations claimed greater political and economic autonomy from the government under President Echeverría (1970–1976). As part of that nationwide effort, ejido unions and Rural Collective Interest Associations (ARICs) were created to encourage local producer groups to join together. Again, during the Salinas presidency PRONASOL monies initially boosted autonomous peasant organizations, as a substantial proportion of funds went directly to municipal governments or to local solidarity committees, thus bypassing state governments and regional bosses (Fox and Gordillo 1989, 141–42; Mattiace 2003, 91–92).

One of the first organizations in Chiapas to raise the claim for autonomy was the Independent Front of Indigenous Peoples (Frente Independiente de Pueblos Indígenas, or FIPI). It emerged in the late 1980s from within the nationwide framework of the Independent Union of Agricultural Workers and Peasants (Central Independiente de Obreros Agrícolas y Campesinos, or CIOAC). Founded in 1975, CIOAC had been conceived by the Mexican Communist Party (Partido Comunista Mexicano, or PCM) in an effort to organize the campesinos to fight for higher salaries and better working conditions. CIOAC and PCM militants saw indigenous peasants primarily as an agricultural proletariat and regarded the struggle for land ownership as secondary. Only in response to nationwide campesino mobilizations in 1980 did the CIOAC refocus on agrarian reform and land invasions. In the mid-1980s, Chiapas's indigenous leaders such as Auldárico Hérnandez, Margarito Ruíz, and Antonio Hérnandez all organized in the CIOAC, along with the anthropologists Héctor Díaz Polanco and Gilberto López y Rivas, and instigated a debate about indigenous autonomy that led to the formation of the FIPI in 1988 (Hernández Castillo 2006, 120). The organization focused on self-determination, indigenous identity, culture, education, and last but not least political representation (Ruiz and Burguete 2003, 36–38). FIPI's participation in international forums and the contact with advisors of Nicaraguan regional autonomy as well as with Indígenas from other parts of the continent inspired its activists to reformulate their cultural and political demands in terms of a discourse on regional autonomy (Stephen and Collier 1997, 11).

Along with the Union of Tojolabal Ejidos and Villages, the FIPI launched an experiment in indigenous self-government in the municipality of Las Margaritas in the late 1980s. In a ceremony held in the ejido Plan de Ayala, leaders of the two organizations declared the first autonomous regional government in Chiapas. This act formalized activities such as mediation and conflict resolution, the operation of a bus service, and the administration of small development projects that were already being carried out by the ejido union. Although this parallel Tojolabal government did not survive the early 1990s, the experience prepared the ground for the later founding of the Autonomous Pluriethnic Regions (Regiones Autónomas Pluriétnicas, or RAPs) (Díaz Polanco 1997; Stephen and Collier 1997, 11; Mattiace 2001, 83–84).

Four years before the Zapatista uprising, key figures of FIPI took part in the founding of the National Assembly of Indigenous People for Autonomy (Asamblea Nacional Indígena Plural por la Autonomía, or ANIPA). The movement developed out of the mobilization for the quincentennial celebration of indigenous resistance in 1992 and soon became a key actor in defining and promoting autonomy throughout Mexico (Nash 2001, 198). FIPI also became part of CEOIC, the broad alliance of indigenous and campesino groups that emulated the EZLN's land invasions throughout Chiapas right after the uprising and that was instrumental in devising the Autonomous Pluriethnic Regions.

From a perspective, the development of the Zapatista autonomy project and the creation of the RAPs resulted from a dialectical relationship between two autonomist currents, which was fertile at first but later became increasingly competitive. The National Democratic Convention (CND), which the Zapatistas convoked in August 1994, was attended by indigenous groups organized in ANIPA who used the event to revise their proposal for a new pact between indigenous peoples and the Mexican State. They envisioned three levels of government that would operate simultaneously: the community, the municipality, and the region (Ruiz and Burguete 2003, 23–115). Parallel to the developments in Zapatista territory, the proposal for the creation of Autonomous Pluriethnic Regions was presented at a meeting in the central plaza of San Cristóbal as early as October 12, 1994. The proclamation was taken up by communities and organizations in Los Altos, Las Cañadas, and other parts of the state that pronounced seven Autonomous Pluriethnic Regions on January 21, 1995 (Nash 2001, 199; Mattiace 2001, 85).

Meanwhile the Zapatistas had also declared thirty-eight municipalities in rebellion in December 1994, many of them in Los Altos and the Zona Norte, not only outside of the region besieged by the federal army but also outside of the heartland where their rebellion had originated. All communities within the new Zapatista municipalities heeded the EZLN's call to boycott the municipal elections in October 1995, which resulted in the PRI winning in Zapatista strongholds. The EZLN did not recognize the electoral results and declared "parallel governments" in the communities under its control. In the state elections a year earlier, ANIPA and the Zapatistas had both backed the PRD candidate Amado Avendaño as the governor in rebellion who took his office at the occupied grounds of the National Indigenist Institute in San Cristóbal, which had been squatted on by ANIPA activists and also housed the headquarters of the Autonomous Pluriethnic Regions in Chiapas.

The declaration of the RAPs was accompanied by takeovers of governmental buildings by indigenous activists who demanded the removal of the PRI municipal presidents. In several Chiapas municipalities, ANIPA militants were able to remove public officials and establish their own municipal councils, which based their activities on a consensus established at a community level. Both the Zapatistas and RAP activists engaged in various acts of civil disobedience, such as the refusal to pay their electricity and water bills and impeding the free movement of governmental officials (Burguete 2003, 198–201). Neither the Zapatista municipalities nor the Autonomous Pluriethnic Regions comprised all inhabitants of a certain territory, as many of them remained loyal to the official administration. The juridical and territorial boundaries of the autonomous entities were therefore virtual in the sense that they depended on the respective affiliation of the people who lived there.

In the months and years to come, ANIPA organized numerous national assemblies and engaged in designing a legal foundation for the establishment of a pluriethnic autonomous system. The Zapatistas, too, were struggling for legal recognition of the very practices that were already part of everyday life in their base communities. These efforts found their focus during the 1995 negotiations between delegates of the EZLN and the COCOPA in San Andrés. Interestingly, the Zapatistas based their proposals for the negotiations on autonomy on the CEOIC drafts that had been devised to govern the Autonomous Pluriethnic Regions (Nash 2001, 145–46). The pluriethnic entities were to consist of all ejidos, villages, and communities in a given region and were to be run by a council of representatives, an executive coordination, a municipal indigenous council, a general assembly, and an executive commission of all the communities involved. The proposal envisioned the participation of the indigenous peoples on state and federal levels as well as the presence of deputies of pluriethnic regions in the Congress of the Union. However, the government rejected regional representation and proposed to limit autonomy to the jurisdiction of the community (200).

The Accords on Indigenous Rights and Culture were agreed on by both parties and were signed in February 1996. If adopted into the Mexican Constitution, they would guarantee the recognition of indigenous communities as entities of public law and the right of communities and municipalities to freely constitute themselves. They would also guarantee the recognition of indigenous normative systems and their own forms of government as well as the cultural recognition of indigenous migrants and defendants in court (Esteva 2003, 256–57). Cabedo Mallol (2004) notes the emphasis that the San Andrés Accords place on the sovereignty and national unity of the Mexican State, which must not be damaged by indigenous autonomy and self-government. This indicates the efforts made by the negotiating parties to disentangle the concept of self-determination (*libre determinación*) from any secessionist connotations. Within that context, however, indigenous normative systems were recognized, by which indigenous authorities are able to exercise jurisdictional activities, such as the resolution of intracommunal conflicts. Along with this recognition of judicial pluralism goes the endorsement of access for Indígenas to use state jurisdiction to guarantee the use of their own languages in judicial processes or to take recourse to experts in customary indigenous law (197–98).

Although the federal government praised the agreements, President Zedillo refused to present the constitutional amendments to Congress and increased the presence of the army in Chiapas (Nash 2001, 201). In December 1996, he issued a counterproposal, which deviated from the original regarding the rights to access and operation of mass media (especially radio stations) and the development of educational institutions (such as autonomous schools) as well as the use of natural resources on indigenous land (López Bárcenas 1999, 208–9). Angry and disappointed, the EZLN withdrew from further negotiations and concentrated on expanding Zapatista autonomy on the ground by building up local administrative structures and by making use of public relations. In a November 1998 communiqué, Enlace Civil, the EZLN's coordinating organization for national and international solidarity, declares the Autonomous Zapatista Rebel Municipalities (Municipios Autónomos Rebeldes Zapatistas, or MAREZ) to be a manifestation of resistance and a way of forcing the ratification of the San Andrés Accords.[25] As a consequence of being "abandoned by the state" and in need of basic services, the indigenous communities of Chiapas have thus opted to resolve their problems by way of self-organization. The document announces that some of the new districts opened their own public registries for weddings, births, and deaths, at times taking over existing offices, as in the town of San Andrés. The new administrative entities justify their existence with the recognition of municipal autonomy in article 15 of the Mexican Constitution and the right of indigenous peoples to live according to their customs and practices laid down in convention 169 of the International Labor Organization (ILO), which Mexico signed (Enlace Civil 1998).[26]

Crucially, the San Andrés Accords and more recent attempts to include indigenous rights into federal legislation, such as the 2001 campaign, are part of a long-term effort to end the de jure state of illegality of what has become a way of life for tens of thousands of indigenous people living en resistencia.[27] Most importantly, this would strip the legal base for the menacing presence of massive police and military contingents in the region. At the end of the twentieth century, the EZLN was present in 40 of the 111 constitutional municipalities in Chiapas. Well over 30 MAREZ had been formed since the uprising, totaling over 1,000 individual communities.[28] The number of rebel municipalities had dropped by 2002 when Enlace Civil listed 23 municipalities belonging to five zones in eastern Chiapas: Altos, Norte, Altamirano, Selva Tzeltal, and Selva Tojolabal.[29] At the inauguration of the five Juntas de Buen Gobierno, each constituting the new government of a region that was congruent with one of the five zones, the associated MAREZ amounted to 29, indicating a recent increase in

Zapatista affiliation (Marcos 2003). Each of these regions was associated with a civilian guerrilla base that included a cultural and political convergence center with the facilities to provide for large meetings. There were assembly halls, sleeping quarters, and also a number of workshops and machines, such as tractors or coffee roasters, used by all Zapatista communities pertaining to the respective region. From their inception in 1996, they went by the name of Aguascalientes, until August 2003 when they were rechristened Caracoles to mark the introduction of the new regional administrative structures. They hosted large meetings between the EZLN and civil society such as the Intergalactic Meeting in 1996, as well as countless smaller conventions, councils, workshops, and celebrations complete with dances and basketball tournaments.

Although representatives of the RAPs had still taken part in the Intergalactic Meeting against Neoliberalism and for Humanity in summer 1996, ANIPA increasingly differentiated itself from the Zapatistas, first by seeking recognition as a national political association, and then by participating in the electoral process and eventually accepting government aid (Burguete 2003, 203). By 2001, Zapatistas and FIPI militants in the Autonomous Pluriethnic Region of Tumbalá had even engaged in violent confrontations over conflicting land claims (Hidalgo 2006). Although the proposal for regional representation, originating from FIPI's experiences with the Tojolabal government and the drafts of the CEOIC, was not incorporated into the San Andrés Accords, the Zapatistas notably implemented regional autonomy themselves at the inauguration of five regional Good Government Councils in August 2003.

At the time of my research, the Zapatista rebel municipalities were alliances of villages with a variety of historical backgrounds. Whereas some had been the cradle of the guerrilla movement, others had joined the EZLN only after the uprising. Zapatista-dominated communities regularly bordered villages under governmental control, where a majority of inhabitants supported the PRI. Almost the only villages whose inhabitants were unanimously Zapatista were "new population centers" settled on land occupied in the course of the 1994 uprising (see chapter 2). More often, Zapatistas lived together with one or two other political factions of PRI loyalists or members of a peasant organization such as the ARIC *independiente*.[30] Each group usually had their own administrative structure, so that in some larger villages there were two or three sets of municipal councils. Relations among the factions were heterogeneous for they often shared family ties but also competed for resources. Moreover, there was a high fluctuation of group membership among individual families.

In contrast to many of their neighbors who were members of various political factions, the Zapatista base did not recognize any state authorities. Instead, the compas elected their own councils and authorities in general assemblies at intervals of one to three years—with the possibility of instant recall in case of misconduct in office. They also elected delegates who represented them on a municipal and—from 2003 onward—on a regional level. The delegates carried out their work in their respective indigenous languages and in adherence to a canon of Zapatista revolutionary laws based on social, economic, and gender equality among the diverse ethnic groups making up the Zapatista base.[31] Crucially in the light of factional divisions in the late 1990s, Zapatista autonomy implied the refusal of state assistance of any kind (see chapter 4). Property taxes and electrical energy fees were not paid and official institutions were not permitted to enter the communities. Alcohol was banned to prevent violence against women and children and to ensure the safety of clandestine organization. The practice was also part of an effort to remain independent from caciques who often sold liquor to build their clientelistic networks.

In all Zapatista communities, a group of young men (and sometimes women) took on the duty of policing the village, the first rung on a ladder of posts in a hierarchy of cargos.[32] Autonomous communal and municipal councils convened to impart justice over those who had transgressed local norms, particularly those laid down in the Zapatista revolutionary laws, including the Revolutionary Women's Law (see chapter 3). To this end, all villages were equipped with a wooden shack serving as a short-term jail and in many autonomous municipal seats there were concrete prisons reserved for more serious offenders. Most punishments, however, consisted of paying a fine (*multa*) or of obligatory labor such as the mending of facilities on communal lands.

That the autonomous legal practice was portrayed as a threat to the official Mexican justice system comes across in an episode described by Speed and Collier (2000, 896–98). The authors relate the events that led to the dismantling of the autonomous municipal seat of Tierra y Libertad located in the Tojolabal town of Amparo Aguatinta. On May 1, 1998, about one thousand police, soldiers, and immigration agents raided the town and detained fifty-three people, among them the Autonomous Council's president, its secretary of agrarian affairs, and its vice-minister of justice. The pretext for the raid had been a conflict about non-Zapatista inhabitants of a neighboring village illegally cutting wood on the territory of the autonomous municipalities. When the accused failed to appear before the autonomous council, one of them was detained and jailed while the indigenous authorities unsuccessfully attempted to negotiate a settlement between him and his accusers. After a week he was relieved by the other accused, who happened to be his brother. State officials used the jailing of the brothers as their justification for the raid and the arrest of Tierra y Libertad's autonomous authorities. They were charged with "kidnapping, assault, and usurping the functions of legitimate municipal authorities" (896–98). That the charges against the council members had less to do with the detention than with the community's assertion of political autonomy and its affiliation with the EZLN is propounded by the fact that the incident was preceded by the dismantling of the autonomous town hall in Taniperlas (Zapatista municipality of Ricardo Flores Magón) a few weeks earlier. More raids were to follow. At least ten people lost their lives during a similar attack on the autonomous town hall in the Zapatista town of El Bosque (autonomous municipality of San Juan de la Libertad) just a month later.

In the light of the efforts by NGOs and solidarity groups detailed in later chapters, it could be argued that Zapatista autonomy and the de facto independence from the Mexican State came at the cost of new dependencies on outside actors and to the resources they provided. Also, most Zapatista communities were subject to regular incursions by federal soldiers and special police. However, the inhabitants of such communities in resistance still considered themselves to be autonomous. What exactly that meant to individuals and communities may have differed from case to case, but usually I had the notion of autonomy explained to me by locals in very tangible terms. "We've got educación autónoma," a father would proudly say to me. "Our community teacher is not paid by the government. He teaches our children what we want them to learn." This local hands-on attitude toward autonomy is also exemplified by an episode I witnessed during a Zapatista holiday on April 10, 2003, in the Aguascalientes of Morelia. Youngsters from all over the region had gathered to present textiles, vegetables, soap, coffee, honey, and herbal medicine that had been produced by Zapatista collectives in their respective communities. On the occasion, the EZLN's regional delegate was speaking to the congregation of two hundred teenagers from Tzeltal and Tojolabal communities, explaining the importance of the work they all were doing. At the end of his speech he held up a glass of honey made by a local apicultural collective and exclaimed, "This is our autonomy!"

CHAPTER TWO

Pueblos de Base

The following chapters are primarily based on the narratives of indigenous Zapatistas and on the observations I made when living and working in their communities. One of them is San Emiliano, where I first came as a *campamentista* and worked as a stand-in teacher for the local children over a period of three months in 1996. In that position, I got to know several families who shared their stories with me. When I returned to San Emiliano in 1997, I approached my research more methodically, arranging interviews in various settings: at home and while working in the field, alone and in the company of others, with men and women, the young and the old. In open interviews I worked through a premeditated set of questions—in addition to the daily conversations I was having with the people who lived there. Most data on the village presented in this chapter was obtained during that time, but I also use narratives further on in the book that were related to me several years later and from when I visited the village again in June 2001 (see chapter 4).

Although I had met people from neighboring Gardenia during my first visits to Las Cañadas, I really only got to know the community through my friend Cipriano with whom I shared a house in San Cristóbal between 2000 and 2002. His brothers, some of whom held important posts in the village hierarchy, came to stay at our home on a regular basis, sometimes with their spouses, friends, and members of their extended family. I was invited to stay with them, too, and I sporadically joined Cipriano as he traveled to his village of origin when he had a couple of days off work and felt like seeing his parents. The fact that Zapatista regulations proscribe such spontaneous private visits meant that these sojourns were not entirely unproblematic (see chapter 8).

The first part of this chapter is made up of accounts from San Emiliano and La Gardenia that tell of the joint efforts to build the guerrilla organization during the early years of its clandestine existence. After an outline of practices concerning the private and collective use of ejido land, the second half of the chapter concentrates on the social mechanisms that integrated the EZLN into everyday village life. The chapter concludes with accounts from the new Zapatista settlements of Tierra Nueva, Arcadia, and 29 de Febrero, the villages where I helped to build water systems as a volunteer. They are based on field observations and conversations with community members undertaken between January 2001 and April 2002. All three villages were founded only after 1994 and on land occupied during the uprising. Whereas the first two were settled by a select group of insurgents and their families at the order of the EZLN command, 29 de Febrero's inhabitants joined the guerrilla movement only after they had taken possession of their terrains in the wake of the uprising by way of direct action.

Oral History from the Core

Geographically, the villages of La Gardenia and San Emiliano are situated in the subregion of Las Cañadas (see map 1). They lie in one of the long river valleys winding down from the Chiapas Highlands into the Lacandon jungle and toward the Guatemalan border.[1] This is Zapatista heartland, where the FLN once made its first contact with local communities. La Gardenia and San Emiliano are among the villages where the EZLN originated in the early 1980s, when these remote parts were accessible only on foot or by plane. It was here that the 1994 uprising was debated and planned in communal assemblies by a local population who had, after a lengthy process of mobilization and sometimes violent expulsion, closed their ranks as rebels years before the modern-day Zapatistas became known to the general public. Originally settled by Tzeltal Indígenas who had worked as *peones* farther up the valley, La Gardenia was founded on the slopes of a forested mountain range.[2] Over the years, the government had allotted more and more ejido land to the growing population in *ampliaciones*; but what the men and women of La Gardenia were really after were the accessible and fertile lands of the adjacent finca where their grandparents had once toiled.[3]

In a joint effort with their neighbors, they finally took over the desired terrains in January 1994 and appropriated them, cattle and all.

While staying in La Gardenia in January 2001, I learned the following details about the origins of the village in conversations with Santos and Griselda, a married couple in their late fifties. According to their narrative, the first colonists had come to this particular spot from an older village farther up the valley after the Carrancista war in the 1920s. The original settlers were all dead now and had worked on the nearby finca before moving to La Gardenia. By the turn of the millennium, two hundred families lived in the community, which amounts to about one thousand inhabitants. The village, which had continuously grown since its founding, was big enough for its inhabitants to distinguish between five distinct barrios, largely inhabited by male relatives and their wives and children. The latest extension had been built only a couple of years prior to my first visit in 2000. With pride, Santos pointed out "where once there had been nothing but *monte* [underbrush], forest, and fallow milpas, there are now *solares* [urban plots]." These spaces of forty by twenty meters accommodated several small wooden houses, thatched with *zacate* (a type of reed) or corrugated iron, surrounded by a vegetable garden where chickens and the occasional pig roamed among banana trees.

In their narratives, Santos and Griselda gave special attention to the events following February 9, 1995, when the Mexican Federal Army raided Las Cañadas and all the inhabitants of Zapatista base communities fled into the mountains. When the soldiers entered the deserted villages, they broke into the houses, stole tools, and destroyed the furniture. An army unit that set up camp in La Gardenia for eight days slaughtered and ate the cows, pigs, and chickens the villagers had left behind. Houses where the soldiers found military clothing or "books by Che Guevara" were burned by the federal soldiers. When they moved on, they destroyed the maize granaries and roaming pigs and horses, and finished off the community's entire food reserves.

While the army was camped out in the village, the story continues, Gardenia's bravest men came down from the mountains to hide in the nearby woods. As night fell and they saw how the soldiers lit big fires and feasted on the stolen animals, they snuck into the village to retrieve some of their belongings. Upon returning to the makeshift camp that the community had set up in the mountains high above the village, they told their comrades about the havoc the army had wrought. At that time, there were daily overflights by military helicopters and reconnaissance airplanes. With growing outrage and frustration, the villagers waited for a week without daring to even make a fire to cook or keep warm at night. When the soldiers still had not left their village, Gardenia's Zapatista insurgents fired machine gun rounds from a nearby hill in the night to scare them away. To the relief of the villagers, the measure turned out to be effective, as the occupants broke off their camp the next morning, moving on to a safer spot farther down the valley. Despite this success, it took another three weeks until the community deemed the situation safe enough to move back into their village.

In their mountain hideout there was not enough food for everyone and several children and old people died of disease and exposure. Babies were born under difficult circumstances but with everyone's support. When Gardenia's inhabitants eventually returned in mid-March 1995, a host of journalists and human rights workers awaited them. Homes had been destroyed, anything of value had been stolen, and all animals were gone. Along with the army, the cowboys of the *finqueros* who had lost their land in the course of the uprising had entered Las Cañadas and rounded up all cattle they could find regardless of whom it had originally belonged to. Santos lost more than a dozen cows that way which had been his since before the uprising.

Sharing the Land

Situated farther down the valley, San Emiliano had only a third of Gardenia's population.[4] Having been founded in the 1950s, the village was also more than twenty years younger than its neighbor. Like the other settler communities of Las Cañadas, San Emiliano shares a history of relative isolation from the rest of the country, which was only occasionally pierced by Catholic missionaries and various waves of political activists (see chapter 1). The Mexican State made its presence felt only at rare occasions, in the shape of *ingenieros*, official surveyors who came to measure out new ejidal plots, which had been solicited

Figure 5: Incursions by federal soldiers were part of the everyday reality in Las Cañadas. The sign reads, "The trafficking, cultivation, and consumption of drugs and alcohol are prohibited in this community. Soldiers and drugs: No. Maize and Peace: Yes," April 1997. Photo by author.

by a generation of aspiring smallholders (*solicitantes*) in the village for years. Along with many of their neighbors, the people of San Emiliano cofounded the ejidal union Quiptic ta Lecubtesel in 1975 to bolster their position toward the state with regard to the ever-pressing land issue. The community joined the Unión de Uniones in 1980 and profited from state credit programs while the Ocosingo diocese trained local catequistas with the aim of raising political consciousness. The growing networks of politically sensitized campesinos coincided with the arrival of FLN activists in the region, who were soon welcomed into the homes of local villagers. After key figures in the community got organized in the EZLN, representatives from the guerrilla movement openly spoke at village assemblies, drawing more and more local support. By the late 1980s, almost everyone in San Emiliano had become integrated into the structures of the guerrilla movement. Amid growing pressure from what had become the village majority, those families unwilling to join the armed struggle became a focus of conflict at the Sunday assemblies. They eventually left the village a few months before the 1994 uprising in fear of the government's response and the prospect of getting caught up between the lines.

As in most other colonist villages in Las Cañadas, the people of San Emiliano relied almost entirely on subsistence agriculture for their survival. For growing maize, the local staple food, eight hundred hectares of land would seem sufficient for a small community of three hundred inhabitants. Much of the terrain, however, consisted of steep forested mountainside several walking hours away from the village. It was used for hunting, gathering firewood, and the occasional felling of a tree for house construction. However, the old growth was slowly disappearing due to the annual clearing of new plots for the growing population. In 1997, one third of the San Emiliano's total ejidal area still consisted of relatively intact rain forest, whereas the other two thirds were used for making milpa. Maize, beans, and pumpkin gourds grew on the slopes adjacent to the thick underbrush covering the fallow milpas that had been prepared and harvested in past years. In 1975, when San Emiliano had only half the population as at the end of the twentieth century, the amount of arable land around the village was sufficient to produce enough maize to ensure the subsistence of all community members, even taking into account five to seven years of fallow time necessary for the regeneration of the fields. The preparation of the milpas was achieved by swidden cultivation, that is, the roots of the trees and bushes on the milpas were left in the soil and only the vegetation above ground was slashed and burned. Thus, the soil was kept together by the roots and protected against erosion. Furthermore, this practice allowed bushes to grow, which in times of fallow were used by the villagers as a source of food and firewood.

Since the founding of San Emiliano there had been irregular ampliaciones to the solicitantes (title applicants), most of them young local men ready to have a family of their own who applied for a plot of ejido land with the government agencies in the state capital. In the late 1970s, however, land allotments to the colonist communities in Chiapas were stopped (see chapter 1). Due to a rapid population growth in the following two decades, there were substantial changes with regard to the land situation so that, by 1997, sixty of San Emiliano's mostly older male ejidatarios or *capacitados*, as they are locally known, faced a growing number of young men without a material base for survival of their own. At the time, they amounted to about forty young campesinos, many of whom already had a family. That they were able to survive in San Emiliano was due to an agreement made in the late 1980s at the height of guerrilla organization. In a move toward more collectivism, the Zapatista village assembly decided to make land held by capacitados available to villagers without an ejido title. Annually, the *comisariado ejidal*, a body representing all official titleholders in the community, allotted 1–1.5 hectares of milpa to each campesino without an official land title, often taking into account familial ties.[5] Under local conditions and in the absence of machinery, pesticides, or fertilizers, that amount of turf was about as much as an individual farmer could cultivate. It allowed for the subsistence of a family and, at the time of a good harvest, yielded a surplus of grains to fatten pigs that could be sold for cash at the Ocosingo market.

Since the government had stopped land distributions, the rapidly growing villages in the Las Cañadas/Selva Lacandona regions were forced to make do with ever less arable land per capita. By the time of the uprising, the survival of the community as a whole had come to depend on the practice of ejidatarios sharing their land with titleless youngsters. Because of shorter fallow times, intensive cultivation led to a degradation of soil quality. Because all surpluses were invested in building up the EZLN, there was no cash left over for chemical fertilizers, which could have balanced out the ensuing decrease in maize yields. Wood was also a crucial resource as it was required for the processing of maize into tortilla and *pozól*, the basic staple food of Chiapas's Indígenas.[6] In the absence of other fuels, large quantities of wood were necessary to boil the grains and to prepare the lime needed for the process of turning the gruel into supple dough.[7] To keep the kitchen fires ablaze, women and children with heavy bundles on their backs walked back and forth between the forest and the village all day. As building material for houses there was also no local alternative to wood: this contributed to it being regarded as a precious resource, the exploitation of which was regulated by the comisariado ejidal.

In the course of the Zapatista uprising, the finca lands, which Gardenia's original settlers had still worked on as peons, were invaded and shared among the three adjacent villages.[8] In Gardenia, the bulk of "recuperated terrains" was given to families of *insurgentes* and *milicianos*, some of whom had been killed in the conflict.[9] Each family received two and a half hectares of the fertile farmland. Sergio, an ex-insurgent who became a close friend during my stay in Chiapas, received a plot and so did his father for having lost a son in the battle of Ocosingo. The terrains recuperated by the Gardenia Zapatistas were flat and close to the road. The new tenants prepared their fields using a tractor made available by their autonomous municipal council for a rental fee of about 10 percent of the harvest value. At the time of my research this amounted to three hundred to six hundred pesos per hectare.[10] Campesinos who were unable to come up with cash beforehand could pay with the respective share of their harvest. The money was used by the autonomous council to fund projects, such as the construction of community schools, that benefited all Zapatista families living in the municipality.

Collective Action and Private Interests

During the first of many long conversations with my indigenous friend Cipriano, I asked about the importance of collective work in La Gardenia, the community where he had grown up. Maybe to yield to an enthusiasm that many foreign visitors displayed about the issue, he made it sound as if collectivism was an integral factor of community life back home. "Everyone in Gardenia works together on *tierra recuperada*. This happens once or twice a week, depending on the season. The fields are up the road on the grounds of the old finca. This is good land, better than the terrains above the village. We use it to grow maize there for the orphans of the village (*huérfanos*), solitary elders too feeble to support themselves (*viejitos sin familia*), and of course for our insurgentes up the mountain."

After visiting La Gardenia myself, I realized that Cipriano had described a practice employed in the 1990s, a somewhat utopian state of affairs that did not correspond to the situation in the village at the time of my visit. Since the early 1980s, the rebel communities of Las Cañadas have seen different levels of collective action. A process of collectivization had paralleled the initial growth of the EZLN's base. This culminated in 1994 when the rebels held sway over a large territory with a strong presence of active-duty guerrillas in the villages. With the invasion by the Mexican Federal Army and the ensuing repression, the loyalty of EZLN supporters was put to the test. The physical distance between the guerrillas who withdrew to the mountains and the civilian population returning to their looted homes encouraged discontent in the villages. The EZLN's failure to protect its supporters from the federal army had met with incomprehension and anger by many long-time Zapatistas. Resistencia policies introduced by the guerrilla movement's command a year later were perceived as austerity measures. All this resulted in a slump in collective projects as locals turned toward private enterprise under the motto "each for his or her own." When waves of dissenters eventually left the EZLN (1998 in San Emiliano and 2001 in La Gardenia), however, new strength arose from smaller numbers and closed ranks. Collective projects, such as the communal support of teachers or the reintroduction of production collectives, became possible once again (see also chapter 4).

Collective action has played an important part in the everyday life of the Zapatista communities and was prerequisite for the clandestine buildup of the EZLN in the 1980s and early 1990s. By employing well-conceived, long-term strategies carried by associations of Zapatista villages (officially organized in the ARIC Unión de Uniones of the 1980s), capital was generated to finance the procurement of arms and equipment (see also Barmeyer 2003). In the context of a government program for the promotion of cattle farming in Chiapas in the 1980s, entire villages engaged in a concerted effort to take out loans from the national Bank of Rural Development (BANRURAL). In San Emiliano, the clandestinely organized Zapatistas, hitherto inexperienced in cattle raising, used the money to buy two hundred calves. After six years, the first credit was paid back through the sale of the bulls. With the sale of the remaining hundred cows, the base communities financed arms, ammunition, and equipment for EZLN recruits. A second BANRURAL credit bought another two hundred calves, which were kept for a few years and then paid for the preparation of the 1994 uprising; that money was never paid back as the rebellion revealed the real objectives behind the cattle raising activities, thereby ruling out the chance of further credits. In addition, individual families systematically invested their maize surpluses to build up the guerrilla movement by rearing pigs. Their sale on the Ocosingo market was one of the rare opportunities to earn cash. That money was either spent in town on necessities not produced in the village itself, such as clothes or soap, or if it was not saved up for a wedding, it went straight toward equipping a family member as a *guerrillero*.

Although the post-1995 period in Zapatista villages of Las Cañadas was marked by the menacing presence of the federal army, there was still a high degree of political unanimity, and community economics was characterized by a hybrid of private and collective work. In San Emiliano the men worked their milpa cultivating maize for subsistence during the week, but on Saturdays all villagers joined forces to accomplish a particular workload that benefited everyone. This included cleaning and repairing works of public facilities such as the road, the church, or the assembly space. Participation was obligatory for men and women alike and was regulated by a rotation system. If

Figure 6: The distribution of beef. At festive occasions, every family in the village contributed to buying a bull for the feast. The small library in the background, furnished by solidarity contributions, is adorned with murals and the Zapatista slogan: "To live for the homeland or to die for freedom," December 2001. Photo by author.

someone evaded these chores or could not participate due to other pursuits, the village assembly decided on a fitting compensation.[11]

Peasant communalism and individualism are not mutually exclusive (see also Wolf 1969, 58). In spite of their collective practices, many Zapatista campesinos did not lose sight of their options regarding individual land ownership. Thus, I couldn't help noticing an undisguised and socially accepted interest, even among some of La Gardenia's hard-core Zapatistas, to retain spaces for the buildup of personal profits. La Gardenia's aforementioned communal social security plan supporting orphans, feeble elders, and insurgentes carried on until early 2000 when decisive changes were made to the taxation system in favor of greater individual control over profits. Thus, the principle of everybody partaking with an equal number of days in the field was abandoned in favor of material contributions of agricultural yields.[12] Notably, this share was not relative to individual harvests but consisted of a fixed amount of three hundred *mazorcas* (cobs of corn), around 15 to 20 percent of the average annual local yield. The new setup privatized the risk of crop failure but also increased the potential for individual profits. After the situation of political division and factional realignment stabilized, collective community projects became more common again. Thus, the social security setup and a collective cattle pasture were reintroduced in La Gardenia in 2002. Work on these projects took place according to seasonal needs and while the maize fed the orphans and elderly, the proceeds from the sale of cows went toward the financing of broadcasting equipment for the community's new radio station.

At the height of communal conflict in La Gardenia in November 2001, Sergio was full of enthusiasm about the new terrains that he and his brothers had received from the EZLN: ten hectares for the families of each of the seven local martyrs who had died in January 1994. The land had been part of a former finca that was occupied during the uprising. Most of it was flat enough to install a cattle pasture, but some of the terrains had lain fallow for eight years and plenty of shrubs and trees had grown back. The families of the war heroes had finally been given the order to take possession of their shares and apparently were allowed to do whatever they wanted with the plots, to plant them, plough them, raise cattle on them, or even to rent them out. Sergio and his brothers wanted to plant maize on their land, but for the five hectares of flat terrain, they planned a cattle pasture. Because they did not own any cows themselves, they wanted to make their land available to someone who did. The going rate was Mex$30 of monthly rent per head of cattle. A herd of a hundred, Sergio calculated, would make them Mex$3,000 a month. He and his brothers made entrepreneurial plans; the money for the rent would enable them to plough the terrains with a tractor to further increase their maize yield.

When scores of Gardenians withdrew from collective ventures in 2001 due to communal strife, the local Zapatista hard core employed a shrewd strategy to make up for their reduced budget. In the face of the desolate state of the dirt track connecting their village with the rest of the country, Sergio and his compas decided to take action and fix the potholes and washouts themselves. After weeks of hard work they set up a roadblock and began a toll collection, extracting a substantial one-time fee of Mex\$2,500 from all passing trucks and buses. It should be noted that this was achieved without the use of arms, solely by employing large numbers of people and strong language. Sergio recounted with pride how they had even managed to stop an army convoy, which after much persuasion eventually paid the amount they had asked for. In 2003 Zapatista factions in politically divided villages had found their feet again and similar actions were undertaken in a concerted effort to negotiate paid road work for community members. In accordance with policies linked to the Plan Puebla Panamá, road construction had begun on the route leading from Ocosingo into Las Cañadas. The dirt track was paved to cut down on travel times and to facilitate access for heavy trucks serving a number of army camps and the large San Quintin garrison at the edge of the resource-rich Montes Azules Biosphere Reserve. In summer 2003, communities making up the Zapatista municipality of Francisco Gómez situated at the upper end of that route came to a consensus to put pressure on the construction company to take their interests into account. This was eventually achieved by continued roadblocks that selectively targeted construction vehicles.[13]

Private profits were not encouraged everywhere in the same way. In a different valley of Las Cañadas, the Zapatista community council of La Utopía decided in November 2000 not to let any of their men work with the Mexican oil company PEMEX, which was recruiting seasonal workers for its operations in Tabasco. This decision was in contrast to the practice in neighboring Tierra Nueva, a new and unanimously Zapatista settlement, where many migrated to the oil fields of Tabasco on a regular basis. The decision of La Utopía's council was probably linked to the severe political division there and aimed at preventing economic inequalities and future conflict within the minority Zapatista faction.

La Organización

In its base communities, the EZLN is often simply referred to as *la organización*. Just how deeply the guerrilla movement was rooted in the lives of the people in the pueblos de base becomes apparent in the many rituals that emphasize the connection between the struggle for land and liberation and everyday tasks such as working in the fields or raising children. The anniversary of Emiliano Zapata's and Che Guevara's death, the annual celebration of the January 1994 uprising, and the commemoration of the Ocosingo martyrs serve as junctures for such celebrations. On these occasions, Zapatista community leaders evoke the prospect of a better future in public speeches and appeal to their constituency to keep up united resistance. Church services are held to ensure divine support for the Zapatista revolution; entire communities repeat a pledge of allegiance in the central plaza or at the graves of those killed in the battle of Ocosingo. For individual Zapatistas, integration into the EZLN can take on three distinct forms depending on their age, their gender, and the strength of their affiliation with the guerrilla organization. These forms are locally known by the terms insurgentes (insurgents), milicianos (militias), and base de apoyo (support base).

During my stay in San Emiliano in 1996/1997, most community members constituted the support base of the guerrilla and were not part of a fighting unit. The activities of the support base are principally civilian and take on many forms; they range from political demonstrations to logistical work and material support for the militias and insurgents (such as providing food and equipment). Milicianos and insurgentes, however, are trained in the use of firearms. Insurgentes are full-time guerrillas living in camps located on inaccessible terrain away from the villages. They do not have a family of their own and often do not visit their home community for years. Milicianos, on the other hand, live in their villages and are mobilized only in cases of crisis, when they retrieve their guns from a secret cache and put on their uniforms to join the nearest unit of insurgents. Similar to the cargos (see chapter 3), the role of a miliciano is temporary and mostly taken on by young men for a number of years during which they attain social prestige. In addition, milicianos participate in communal assemblies and other collective activities. They work their plot of land and contribute to the community's economy.

The contribution of the insurgentes is less tangible for it consists

Figure 7: Ejido land in Las Cañadas usually consisted of steep and inaccessible mountain slopes. A miliciano has burned his milpa in preparation for sowing maize with a wooden stick, May 1996. Photo by author.

mostly in their role as active constituents of the guerrilla movement, which struggles for the long-term improvement of the social and economic situation in the villages. However, they are missing as helpers on the fields, as caretakers of their parents, and (in the case of the men) as potential husbands for the slight surplus of women in their villages. Thus, although everyday material support from the villages to the insurgent camps may be relatively small, their actual net cost to the communities is immense. Their maintenance can therefore be regarded as an investment that the Zapatista base makes into its future.

As I have shown in a study based on fieldwork undertaken in San Emiliano in 1996/1997 (see Barmeyer 1999, 2003), the rebel villages of Las Cañadas adjusted their ways to effectively support a guerrilla movement in the decade following the EZLN's founding on November 16, 1983. On the one hand, villages like La Gardenia and San Emiliano provided the fighters and ensured the movement's readiness for war. On the other hand, the communities financed weapons and equipment for the recruits and at least partly provided food for the guerrillas who, because of their deployment in the mountains, were unable to work on the fields.[14] The financing was either done by donations from the whole community (*cooperación*) or achieved by individual families who, by the sale of agrarian surplus, provided their insurgente and miliciano sons (and in some communities also their daughters) with the equipment necessary for the guerrilla war. In return for this they received prestige from the community. In early 1997, of the one hundred adult men in San Emiliano, approximately twenty of the younger ones formed part of the militia. Additionally, ten of the male villagers were insurgents and stationed in the nearby mountains as part of a guerrilla unit, which received food supplies from the village.

Stephen (2002, 157) points out that the Zapatistas have used collectivization not only as their economic policy but also as a strategy for war to keep people together in one place and to provide safety in numbers. However, collective work as a Zapatista war strategy goes much further than that. An example for this is the *comités de emergencia* characteristic for Zapatista base communities, which operate only in emergencies when they produce food or generate money for the war effort. In times of crisis, the economy in San Emiliano changed over from a mode of individual family subsistence to one of collective production. In this situation, cash was acutely needed and all able community members took part in the exploitation of wood from the forests around the village. Due to the relative scarcity of the resource, this type of strategy would have been useless in the long term but did produce a fast yield when needed immediately. Through the sale of large trunks of *caoba* and other rare woods, the community was able to procure substantial amounts of cash in a short time.

Tierra Recuperada: The New Settlements

According to Rus (1994, 265), the term "revolution" had two meanings among the indigenous campesino population of Chiapas. The
1910 revolution was remembered as "the time of Carranza" or "the
Carrancista war" (in my own interviews) and carried negative connotations. The real revolution for them was the "time of Cárdenas" or
la revolución de los indios in the late 1930s when agrarian reform, labor
unions, and an end to debt contracting and peonage eventually reached
Chiapas. By the mid-1990s, however, the term had taken on a third
meaning. When the Zapatistas from the villages where I conducted my
research spoke of la revolución they referred to the changes that their
1994 insurrection had brought about with regard to autonomy, self-
respect, and most importantly control over their own land.

The lands invaded during the uprising became a crucial resource
for ensuring the economic independence of the EZLN's base. They also
served as a reward for loyal insurgents and militias. Although some of
the recuperated terrains were incorporated into the stock of adjacent
Zapatista villages like La Gardenia, veterans of the insurrection settled
the fertile lands at altitudes between seven hundred and one thousand
meters, which had formerly been used as cattle pastures. They were
mostly young families without ejidal titles and a base for subsistence
in their villages of origin. For them, their new settlements were the
fulfillment of the principal aim of their struggle; the realization of
a utopian vision not unlike the original settling of Las Cañadas and
La Selva by their parents and grandparents. An important feature of
these new settlements was the obligation of continued EZLN support.
Anyone leaving the guerrilla organization faced the sanction of having
to leave their new homestead as well; a consequence that helped ensure
unanimous local support for the guerrilla movement.

Apart from their relatively homogenous social makeup consisting
of young families with strong EZLN ties, the new population centers
also differ from their mother communities with regard to their reproductive base. Whereas older ejidal villages settled in the 1950s have
had to make do with terrains unfit for intensive agriculture, the new
settlements are usually built on accessible and fertile land, fit for the
production of high-yield crops, often complete with cattle pastures and

coffee plantations. At the time of my research, they still lacked basic infrastructure and the resources to invest in cattle, chemical fertilizers, and machinery to make proper use of the land.[15] In the years to come, however, their advantage may well lead to an economic imbalance between winners and losers of the new Zapatista revolution, creating a potential focus for future conflict.

The new Zapatista settlement of Tierra Nueva is situated in a broad river valley high up in Las Cañadas and surrounded by hills covered with pine forests.[16] Before the insurrection and the ensuing land invasions, the valley floor had been grazed on by cattle belonging to one of Chiapas's elite families who owned all this land. In January 1994, the guerrillas seized the land and destroyed the houses of the *patrones* (landowners); all happened so fast that the caretakers had to leave most of their animals behind.

In 2001, cows and horses, albeit in smaller numbers than in the previous decade, were again grazing on both sides of a clear green river. The village of Tierra Nueva built newly on its banks consisted of around one hundred indigenous families from two ethnic groups. The people lived in humble wooden houses clustering around a surprisingly large white church built from concrete. By the time I first visited the place, the Tzeltal and Tojolabal Indígenas who had come here in 1995 had just finished constructing it as a sign for all to see that they were here to stay. In 2004, the Tojolabales moved away to found their own village, ending eight years of pluriethnic conviviality in Tierra Nueva.

Due to the vast size of the former fincas, Tierra Nueva was only one of many new Zapatista settlements in the region. In a concerted effort, the lands that had lain fallow since the uprising were claimed and built on in 1996. The new inhabitants all had strong EZLN ties because they had either been fighters themselves or had lost a close relative in combat. In Tierra Nueva, large-scale support for active insurgents was manifested in a field of three hectares set aside for producing maize exclusively for them. All men in the village took turns in tending that field using a tractor provided by the autonomous municipal council. Existing coffee plantations and beehives were shared between the new communities and, to manage the resources more efficiently, the settlers founded cattle, coffee, and apicultural cooperatives. To generate extra cash income, some of the men in Tierra Nueva left their community for several months a year to seek temporary work on the oil fields of Tabasco.

Arcadia was one of the many new population centers that were part of the same autonomous municipality as Tierra Nueva. Like its neighbor, Arcadia was founded by militias and former insurgents in 1996 at the order of the EZLN. Located at a less accessible spot than Tierra Nueva, Arcadia consisted of thirty families. The village featured coffee plantations instead of cattle pastures, a fact that inextricably linked the earnings of its inhabitants to the world market. Because coffee prices were low at the time of my research, the people of Arcadia were poorer than their neighbors in Tierra Nueva.

The third new Zapatista settlement I researched stands out both with regard to its location and its history. Unlike the other four communities, the small village of 29 de Febrero is situated outside of the EZLN's core areas of Las Cañadas and Selva Lacandona, somewhere in the more populated regions between the central highlands and La Zona Norte. The lands on which the community was built were squatted on in the immediate aftermath of the 1994 uprising by families who were not affiliated with the EZLN and joined the guerrilla organization only ex post facto.

When I first came to the village to work on a water project in autumn 2001, thirteen families lived in humble houses situated between orange trees and banana and coffee plantations. People lived off their milpa, raising some chickens and pigs. Quite a few of the original settlers had both left the EZLN and the village at the time of my arrival. Two families that had severed their ties to the Zapatistas remained living on the land on the condition that they would not join another political organization. When I asked Gualterio, a former local EZLN delegate, how he and his neighbors had come to settle the land 29 de Febrero was built on, I learned that they had worked as campesinos on the outskirts of a nearby town. Most of the squatters had not been politically organized but some had affiliations to the left-leaning Party of Democratic Revolution (PRD). Inspired by the uprising, they formed an alliance to take over the finca land in the hills outside of town. In keeping with the example of the Zapatistas who had taken advantage of the 1994 New

Year's celebrations to cover up their invasion of regional capitals, the campesinos took over their future home in small groups at the height of Carnival only a few months after the uprising. Having expected to be moved off immediately, the squatters soon realized that they were able to stay on their new land only because of the strong Zapatista presence in the rest of the state. Consequently, they decided to join the EZLN and approached the guerrilla movement's regional delegates to become part of the rebel group as early as May 1994.

The settling of former finca land was not limited to the period immediately after the uprising but continued well into the twenty-first century. These more recent settlements by Zapatista bases were not spontaneous but took place according to preconceived plans and in accordance with the guerrilla movement's central command. Thus, a substantial faction of EZLN-affiliated youngsters from San Emiliano moved on to fertile soils up the valley when they received the go-ahead from the *mandos* in 1998, contributing to a subsequent upheaval in their mother village (see chapter 4).[17] In 2001 a new Zapatista settlement was founded in the immediate vicinity of Tierra Nueva on land originally invaded in 1994 and reserved for seven years. The new inhabitants were almost exclusively youngsters who had grown up in a nuevo centro de población themselves and were now old enough to have their own families. More recently still, the Tojolabal inhabitants from Tierra Nueva moved away to new terrains in 2004 that the EZLN had made available to them. At the time of my research, the settling of terrains recuperated in 1994 was far from over. By May 2002, seven Gardenian families whose members had been killed in the 1994 battle of Ocosingo received a substantial two and a half hectares of former finca land each. Sergio, who had lost a brother in the uprising, was among those bestowed. He joined forces with his remaining brothers and rented a tractor, expecting higher yields than those from the inaccessible ejidal terrains of his father. They praised their new plots as paradisiacal and the young families who had benefited from the endowment were making plans to settle there permanently.

CHAPTER THREE

Who Is Running the Show?

The Workings of Zapatista Government

Base democracy and communal governance by usos y costumbres have been key to the demands for indigenous autonomy. But what actually constitutes the traditions that the Zapatistas regularly evoke in their communiqués? Autonomous administrative structures and the ways today's rebel municipalities are run have little to do with Mayan heritage but are actually a hodgepodge of practices ranging from the Catholic cult of village saints imposed by the Spanish Crown to the ejidal administrative structures laid down in Mexico's Agrarian Law and organizational elements introduced by catequistas and Maoist students in the 1970s.

This chapter starts out with a review of the literature on traditional village hierarchies in indigenous Chiapas and focuses on the functions that religious and political offices had for community cohesion and the redistribution of wealth. After an introduction to the ejidal administration characteristic for many Mexican agrarian communities of the twentieth century, I go on to describe the structural elements of communal, municipal, and regional governance found in modern-day Zapatista villages. In this, I place particular emphasis on the parallel existence of two administrative structures; one is civilian and democratically elected in communal assemblies and the other is made up of appointed EZLN military functionaries. Examples from the field illustrate the decision-making processes in small groups and village assemblies, followed by a discussion of the consensus principle that has become a hallmark for Zapatista claims to base democracy. Comparing the situation in the guerrilla camps and in the base communities, the next section focuses on the persistent exclusion of women in many rebel villages. The chapter concludes with an analysis of democratic and more authoritarian elements found in the institutions and practices constituting the various levels of organization in the autonomous administrative entities.

Historical Perspectives on the Administration of Indigenous Villages in Chiapas

In their studies conducted in the 1960s of Tzotzil and Tzeltal communities in the Chiapas Highlands, Favre (1973, 260–64) and Cancian (1965, 1992) describe a hierarchical system of public offices (cargo system). They found this institution to be determinant of a man's social standing as well as crucial for the maintenance of cohesion within the community.[1] Thus, the community expected its (male) members to hold a number of such offices (cargos) in the course of their lives. Each cargo is vested with particular attributes and functions, and Favre (1973) differentiates between religious (e.g., *mayordomo* and *alférez*) and political offices (e.g., *síndico*, *regidor*, or *alcalde*). According to Favre, the religious cargos have their origins in the Catholic cult of saints practiced on the Iberian Peninsula at the time of the *conquista*. Roots of the political offices go back to medieval Spain and stem from the institutions of the administrative units that represented local communities to the Spanish Crown before the ascent of absolutism. After its introduction by the Spaniards, the system of offices was adopted by the indigenous population and merged with an existing local hierarchical system that went by the indigenous name of *jol s'lum* (head of the village). According to Vogt (1961), this system stems from a time before the conquest by the Europeans.

The officeholders (*encargados*) in 1960s highland villages usually spent the day together, each clad in garments denoting their office and rank, while collectively debating community affairs (Favre 1973, 263). These included holding court, the mobilization of villagers for collective work, the levying of taxes, the administration of finances, and relations with the state authorities in San Cristóbal and Tuxtla Guiterrez. In this, the *autoridades* (communal authorities) were usually assisted by young bilingual scribes who took on the correspondence with the centers of administration. This led to a significant increase in the scribes' informal power despite the fact that they themselves were not part of the official hierarchy. Rus (1994) notes that in the deliberations rank was decisive for the weight of individual opinions. The successors for the posts were appointed for one year by the respective officeholders, and the rest of the community could not partake in the decision.

Favre (1973, 267) and Cancian (1965, 24–27) describe the system of political and religious offices in the Chiapas highland communities of the 1960s as an obligatory way of attaining status in the community. Boys embarked on their office career as *mayores*, a kind of village police, when they were sixteen or seventeen. In the following years, the young men took on higher-ranking religious and political offices and, alternating between the two, slowly worked their way up the hierarchy. Especially the religious offices entailed high costs for the encargados as they had to honor saints by financing feasts in which the whole community took part. Thus, in Zinacantán the bearer of the high religious cargo of alférez, had to pay a tenfold of the yearly income of the richest families in that community (Cancian 1965, 126). During their time in office, encargados regularly incurred high debts. Because one had to be free of debt to take on a new office, there were lengthy delays in passing through the higher echelons of the village hierarchy. The cargo system had a strong integrative function, and a marginal position in the community was among the decisive criteria for a prospective office bearer. Thus, the men about whom there was immediate consensus in the authorities' deliberations did not necessarily stand out for their leadership qualities. On the contrary, they might be nonconformist with regard to communal norms and traditions due to their advanced *ladinización* (absorption into the nonindigenous world) or they might even be prone to disrespect, envy, rage, or violence (Favre 1973, 272). Their integration into the office hierarchy aimed at improving their social conduct and to eventually convert them into *bats'il winik* (true people). Another criterion for appointing someone to higher office was wealth, which was perceived as similarly marginalizing. A wealthy person was regarded as dangerous and their advantageous economic position was often attributed to witchcraft (276). The destruction of their wealth to the benefit of everybody in the community, for example, in the financing of communal feasts, allowed these people to increase their prestige and heighten their status, as well as to abide by the norms of their community. Favre disagrees with the view brought forth by Wolf (1955) that the community systematically punished wealth by demanding of its richer members to convert their surplus into social status. Instead, Favre emphasizes the function of the cargo system, which was to prevent social stratification by removing economic resources from the community that could otherwise have been used by individuals to acquire means of production (Favre 1973, 278). However, this has been disputed by Cancian (1965; 1992, 191), who found that the cargo system also reinforced existing economic differentiation by making rich cargo holders socially acceptable.

The past century has seen fundamental changes in the composition of traditional authority structures in Chiapas's indigenous communities, not least with regard to age. As outlined in chapter 1, in the course of reforms by President Cárdenas (1934–1940), literate youngsters took on newly created positions for the management of land and labor issues. In a first phase, these bilinguals were trained to be agents of acculturation and the implantation of state/party institutions. They were appointed as municipal scribes and bilingual teachers and acted as mediators between the community and the institutions of the state, often occupying positions in the local structures of the governing PRI or in subsections of a union. A new indigenous elite emerged, as some of the former teachers and scribes became power brokers by channeling development funds from the National Indigenist Institute (see also Cancian 1992; Gabbert 1999; Olivia Pineda 1995; Rus 1994).

The development of administrative institutions in Chiapas's indigenous communities is obviously a very complex process that has to be viewed in the context of broader developments within the Mexican State and the respective interests that have been behind the creation of institutions such as the ejido, the INI, or certain rural development schemes. On the other hand, local interests have always played an important role in the appropriation and use of institutions introduced from outside. When looking back at Chiapas history before the 1994 rebellion, the emergence of autonomous organization in Las Cañadas appears to be an exception that is closely linked to the relative absence of the state in the outermost fringes of its territory. On the whole, accounts of *cacicazgos*, fraud, and cooptation loom large.[2] The story of indigenous governance in Chiapas is about personal power and about who controls local resources, in particular land, rather than about the ascent of democracy.

Structural Pillars of Rebel Governance

The main pillars in the administrative structure of any Mexican ejidal community are the *comisariado ejidal* (ejidal commissariat), the *consejo de vigilancia* (council for land control), and the institution commonly known as the *agencia* (police agency), which have their origin in Mexican agrarian history. These institutions also featured prominently in the Zapatista base communities I researched. Along with a host of other committees, each associated with a particular function, they constituted the *consejo de autoridades* (council of authorities). Each of the committees generally consisted of several people who were in a formalized hierarchical relationship to each other (*presidente*, president; *secretarios*, secretaries; *tesorero*, treasurer; *suplentes*, stand-in officials). The comisariado was in charge of the day-to-day communal administration, including the coordination of all other councils and the calling of regular assemblies. La agencia, responsible for upholding social law in the village, controlled the community police and served as the first instance of jurisdiction over internal affairs. The agrarian institution of el consejo de vigilancia dealt with all matters concerning land, including forest use and conflicts with neighboring ejidos. Importantly, in La Gardenia and San Emiliano, only ejidatarios with a title to their plot of land were eligible for membership in this key institution. Each of the committees had a certain domain assigned to it and was staffed by the respective local experts; thus the *comité de educación* was made up of local teachers and the *comité de salud* was composed of local health promoters. In fact, any development project that a given community became engaged in prompted the creation of a respective committee. Thus, as a first measure, the villages where I helped with the installation of water systems (see chapter 7) would call a general assembly (asamblea) to elect a committee of delegates in charge of mustering workers, taking care of the tools, and maintaining the system after the NGO team left.

Apart from el comisariado, el consejo, and el agente, as the local population often called the representatives of the three main institutions in the communal authority structure, Zapatista base communities featured a fourth key figure. This was the *responsable de la organización*, the EZLN's direct local representative in the village. Each responsable was in regular contact with his superiors in the guerrilla movement—usually the majors in charge of respective regions—and received his or her orders directly from them.[3] At the time of my research, el responsable was not democratically elected but the guerrilla movement's command rather presented a community member it deemed suitable, who was then endorsed by the assembly (also see Estrada Saavedra 2007, 402). As Zapatista administrative structures have undergone a slow but steady change aimed at slashing the powers of military EZLN institutions in communal affairs, this practice may or may not have changed with the introduction of the Juntas de Buen Gobierno. As was made clear in the EZLN's July 2003 communiqués, the civilian municipal institutions of the EZLN had an interchange with the military ones, but internal regulations proscribed an institutional overlap by making it impossible for individuals to hold civil and military offices at the same time (Marcos 2003, part 2). Be that as it may, the responsables and their commanders constituted a parallel structure of military administration that operated alongside the civilian consejo de autoridades elected by community members.

Each autonomous municipality had its own authority structure staffed by people from the base communities it comprised. At the top of each municipality's civilian structure there were a comisariado, a consejo de vigilancia, and an *agencia municipal* paralleling the institutions at the community level. To match the civilian functionaries, the *regional* was the EZLN's military representative at the municipal level, equivalent to el responsable in the individual base communities. In their official presentation to civil society, Enlace Civil (1998) describes the new Zapatista autonomous municipalities as existing in parallel to the constitutional districts and as being independent of state financing. Representatives for the autonomous municipal councils were elected biannually by member communities and were instantly recallable if they failed to comply with the mandate given to them. All council members had clearly defined duties and worked in close cooperation with "former authorities" or a council of elders. At the time, the municipalities did not manage a budget because each project was directly financed by donations in the respective village (cooperación) or with funds coming from outside (as in the case of a development project). People holding posts in the municipal council did not receive a salary and only their travel expenses were paid for by the community. In some cases, council members were helped with the work on their milpa to compensate for their regular absences. The autonomous municipal council also dealt with minor offences and in cases of "common delinquency" the application of justice was based on customary compensational law. Thus, the council imposed the reparation of damages as a punishment. Instead of prison or fines, this entailed work that either benefited the community or the affected families (Enlace Civil 1998). This account, however, is contradicted by my own findings on the prominent use of fines in Zapatista jurisdiction.

Since August 2003, each of the twenty-nine autonomous Zapatista municipalities has been associated with one of five regions. Their regional governments go by the name of Juntas de Buen Gobierno (Good Government Councils). These councils are staffed by two or three delegates from each autonomous municipality belonging to its administrative sphere of influence. These so-called consejos have an office in the administrational compound of the respective regional center (Caracol) and are elected for a period of three years as representatives of their community of origin. To allow all Zapatista communities of a given region to be represented in the Junta de Buen Gobierno and to avoid the emergence of clientelistic networks, each group of representatives remains in the Caracol's offices only for a period of fifteen days. They are then replaced by another group from a different Zapatista community (Muñoz Ramírez 2003; Castro 2003; Estrada Saavedra 2007, 539–41).

This has raised criticisms about a supposed inefficiency of the regional councils, as each new Junta needs to become acquainted with the current problems facing the administration as well as to adjust to working as a team. However, the consejos are chosen by their communities precisely because they already have substantial experience as holders of communal and municipal offices behind them, sometimes in addition to a military career in the guerrilla movement. The fact that their absence is limited to fifteen days at a time allows them to continue working on their fields and to take care of their family. As with all cargos in rebel territory, the consejos do not receive money but are compensated by their community who helps them on their milpa. Admittedly, the name "Good Government Council" has a slightly Orwellian ring to it. To understand how it came about, however, one has to consider the fact that local terminology identifies official authorities as the *mal gobierno* (bad government) with respect to which the new name seeks to establish a difference.

Another level of government in Zapatista territory consists of the Indigenous Clandestine Revolutionary Committees (Comités Clandestinos Revolucionarios Indígenas, or CCRIs). They draw their members from all communities where the EZLN has a presence. A comité or *cecri*, as these people were commonly referred to, is a civilian representative elected by the general assemblies of each individual base community. While in office, they do not have other important civilian or military functions neither on the communal nor on the municipal level, even though they often have a history of such posts behind them. In their position to decide over crucial matters such as the date of the uprising or the negotiations of the San Andrés peace accords (EZLN 1996), the delegates of these committees have been responsible for steering the guerrilla movement. The local CCRIs sent representatives to the Indigenous Clandestine Revolutionary Committee's General Command (Comité Clandestino Revolucionario Indígena-Comandancia General, or CCRI-CG), which consisted of around seventy to eighty members, and was based near La Realidad (Aufheben 2000). The clandestine committees added another administrative component to the parallel power structures that, at least in theory, kept the military top-down hierarchy in check by a democratically elected body (see also Petrich and Henríquez 1994).

Assemblies and the Consensus Principle

Being a community with strong ties to the diocese, the village of San Emiliano had its own *comité iglesial* made up of the tuhunel (deacon) and a team of catequistas who cooperated with the consejo de autoridades in choosing Bible passages befitting the topics to be discussed in the next communal assembly. These meetings took place on a weekly basis sandwiched between two sessions of church service.[4] During these discussions, which often went on for hours, the congregation split into ten groups, the so-called *asambleas chicas*. According to Harvey (1994, 30), Maoist student brigades from the cities (locally remembered as the asesores) had encouraged the reintroduction of "traditional elements of indigenous democracy" to counteract the centralization of decision making. The asambleas chicas, however, seem to be less of a reintroduction than an importation, as they correspond to the cells at the base of many Maoist revolutionary movements. In Zapatista base communities, such groups were fixed entities made up of adult men or women of the same age group or marital status, which were paralleled by the cells found in the camps of the insurgents. These *secciones* were made up of about six insurgents who lived in the same compound while those in the base communities comprised three or four times as many people.[5]

When decisions had to be made, the functionality of the secciones was eminent: the small groups allowed for the active participation of each community member during debates and allowed everyone to converse in the familiar context of their own age group. This greatly facilitates reaching consensus, a crucial element of the base democracy that has become a hallmark of the Zapatistas. The discussions of each sección were taken down in writing and later read to the whole assembly. Usually, the members of the small groups arrived at consensual decisions, which reduced lengthy debates between individuals during the large plenary sessions of the asamblea. A communal referendum could thus be decided by the spokespersons (*portavoces*) of the secciones. That this practice is not necessarily democratic is exemplified by the case in San Emiliano, where six men's groups faced only four larger ones made up of women. In case of disagreement along the gender divide, the men clearly had a structural upper hand in the decision-making process.

Many discussions during the Sunday assemblies were motivated by selected Bible citations. These often referred to very secular themes, such as the installation of a vegetable plantation by the community's women, the distribution of paid work with a road construction company among the men, a land conflict with a nearby army camp, or a contract on marriage exchanges with neighboring base communities (see also Barmeyer 1999). Less frequently, there were consultations (*consultas*) by which the command of the EZLN gauged the mood among its supporters. Issues included deciding if the organization should transform into a political party, begin or discontinue negotiations with the government, or embark on a nationwide campaign to press for the recognition of indigenous rights to autonomy. The extent to which the support base controlled the ventures of the guerrilla manifested itself in the crucial decision for the rebellion on January 1, 1994. Although the guerrilla command would have preferred to wait for a more opportune moment, it yielded to the insistence of its base, which hoped for a swift improvement of living conditions (Petrich and Henríquez 1994).

On special occasions such as a sudden military emergency, general assemblies were also held during the week. More often, only those community members who were directly concerned by a particular issue held a meeting. Thus, the men would discuss the timing for a concerted burning of their milpas at the end of the dry season while the women met to be briefed by the promoter of health (*promotora de salud*) as she returned from a workshop in the Aguascalientes. The consejo de autoridades met at regular intervals for their deliberations or to hold court. At the weekly asamblea or during ceremonies on revolutionary holidays, attendance and participation were obligatory for all Zapatista community members. There were strict sanctions for noncompliance with duties and for lack of discipline. At assemblies in the new population center of Arcadia latecomers or nonattendees not only had to pay a fine of fifteen pesos, they also had to run several laps around the football pitch after the meeting. With everybody watching, this practice of public shaming was rather effective.[6]

From Espártaco, a former insurgente whom I had the privilege to get to know in the course of my research, I learned that some of the social techniques employed in the communal assemblies of Zapatista communities paralleled those used by the guerrillas in the mountains. In a daily *célula* meeting, for example, everybody from the camp, recruits and high-ranking mandos (commanders) alike, gathered to listen to presentations that the insurgents took turns in preparing, to discuss them, or just to sing together. Whereas Mondays were used to devise the célula schedule for the coming week, Sundays were the time for the weekly *autocrítica*. The autocrítica also was an essential element of evaluating collective actions in the communities. Everyone took turns to speak about the mistakes they made during the past week. In this, the secciones usually referred to *their* mistakes even if an individual was personally responsible. The motivation to own up to "errors" during the first round was great because this was followed by the *crítica* during which participants were expected to criticize each other. Any mistakes not mentioned in the autocrítica usually came up in this session; in this, it seemed to be common practice for lower-ranking insurgents to also criticize their mandos.

In the guerrilla camps, punishments for mistakes usually consisted in communal labor, such as working in the kitchen for a week, cleaning out the latrines, digging trenches, or holding guard. According to Espártaco, there were no physical punishments, imprisonments, or fines in order not to break community morale. Fines, a measure frequently employed for misdemeanors in the base communities, would not have worked, Espártaco argued, for in the camps nobody owned any cash. Imprisonments on the other hand would just "give people a place to kick back and rest." More effective punishments consisted in having to do vigils for consecutive days and nights, for this posed the danger of making more mistakes by falling asleep on the job.

While working in 29 de Febrero in November and December 2001, I witnessed several municipal assemblies, reunions of about thirty to forty representatives of the twenty communities (about three hundred families) that constituted the autonomous municipality. The first people showed up around ten. Each village was represented by a civilian and a military delegate, the consejo (president of the consejo de vigilancia) and the respective responsable. Likewise, the meeting was chaired by a civilian (el consejo municipal) and a military municipal authority (el regional). The civilian spoke most of the time. He was a friendly looking man in his thirties who may have been a teacher. As he was standing at the blackboard of the community school for hours writing names and numbers, that impression was sustained. Only six of the participating delegates were women. The meeting resembled other Zapatista congregations that I had witnessed before. The only difference to an asamblea at the community level consisted in the fact that these people were all representatives from individual villages. Apart from the division into speaker and audience, the meeting appeared like a conference of equals without any visible structuring along rank or individual importance. There was the obligatory prayer session at the beginning followed by long speeches delivered by the two municipal authorities. After communiqués by the Clandestine General Command were read aloud, there was a phase during which everyone formulated their positions on a set of issues in writing. One was about deciding on the sort of produce that individual communities would contribute to the newly devised project for production and commercialization.

The meeting was held in Tzeltal and lasted until the evening. During a break, I got to talk to some of the representatives, one of whom offered to share his food with me. I learned that the meeting was about the "second phase" of the Zapatista revolution, in which the individual municipalities were to achieve economic self-sufficiency by growing and selling agricultural produce. Another topic was the Zapatistas' Arco Iris store in Cuxulhá on the road between Ocosingo and San Cristóbal. It was situated at the site of a former army base, which had been dismantled as a concession to the Zapatistas by President Fox several months after his election in 2000. The compas now used the location as a roadside restaurant and as a store for selling fruit, vegetables, coffee, and dry goods produced in the seven adjacent rebel municipalities. Several weeks prior to the assembly, the shop had been raided by members of the campesino organization ORCAO in a dispute over land it had occupied alongside the EZLN in 1994 when they were still allies. The meeting in 29 de Febrero decided to send a new detachment of people to Cuxulhá to relieve their comrades who had been guarding the place for three days. Individual positions on the issue were then presented to the group and a discussion followed, which proceeded rather calmly. A drawn-out monologue by the charismatic "teacher" concluded the meeting and toward the evening the delegates made their way back to their villages.

The Persistent Exclusion of Women

Women have the right to work and be paid a fair salary.

Women have the right to decide the number of children they want to have and look after.

Women have the right to participate in community affairs and hold posts if freely and democratically elected.

Women and their children have the right to primary health care and food.

Women have the right to education.

Women have the right to choose their partner and not be forced into an arranged marriage.

No woman shall be beaten or physically abused by her family or strangers. Offences of attempted rape or rape will be severely punished.

Women can hold political and military leadership positions.

Women have all rights and obligations bestowed by the revolutionary laws and obligations.

Women, whatever their race, creed or political affiliation, have the right to participate in the revolutionary struggle in accordance with their own will and ability.

(*The EZLN's Revolutionary Women's Law*, quoted in Rovira 2000, 73)

About one-third of all the EZLN's *insurgentes* is estimated to be female. Although this percentage is matched by revolutionary movements such as Nicaragua's Sandinistas and the FMLN in El Salvador, Kampwirth (2002, 84–85) points out that this proportion is remarkably high when one considers that women in the ethnic groups making up the EZLN normally lead extremely restricted lives. This view is supported by my own observations. In any indigenous village of Chiapas, women can be seen working from well before dawn until after sunset. This often involves heavy labor such as carrying large bundles of wood, scrubbing laundry, separating corn from the cob, or milling pozól. In contrast, the men usually take the afternoon off after returning from their milpa. After their siesta they can be seen standing around in groups, talking and smoking along the road. Theirs is traditionally the public sphere; they converse with people who pass through the village or they go to town to sell or buy merchandise or to engage with the state bureaucracy. Traditionally, the women are expected to stay around the house to take care of the children and animals. They spend fewer years at school, are usually less acquainted with Spanish, and their literacy rates are lower. Girls in indigenous communities are often sixteen or younger when they are chosen by a man. "Customs" such as arranged marriages or *robo*, the abduction—and sometimes rape—of a woman by a man wanting to marry her, stand out as particularly abusive.

This situation has been addressed by devising the Revolutionary Women's Law, which was included into the canon of Zapatista revolutionary laws on March 8, 1993, at the initiative of Zapatista women, less than a year before the uprising (Rovira 2000, 73–76). Still, patriarchal practice in Zapatista base communities persists and the influence of progressive attitudes among active-duty guerrillas is hampered by long-standing local traditions. Olivera, Gómez, and Damián Palencia (2004, 37–38) present the biographic sketch of insurgente Margarita, which illustrates the limits to women's empowerment in the guerrilla movement. After marrying in a military ceremony in one of the EZLN's training camps, Margarita and her partner lived and worked together among the other insurgentes. All went well until she got pregnant and her superiors told her to return to her village to have the baby. She was allowed to resume being an insurgente if she found someone to look after her child. Upon arriving visibly pregnant, her parents and her home community rejected her for not having married according to local customs. Margarita eventually had to have her baby at her grandmother's house in another village. Upon learning that her partner had begun a relationship with another insurgente and not wanting to subject herself to the oppressive traditions, she left Las Cañadas to begin a new life as a waitress in San Cristóbal.

Since the founding of the EZLN, the relative number of female *insurgentes* appears to have increased steadily. This is due to a growing number of female recruits and because many men have left the guerrilla to find work in the cities or in the United States. "Men are just better off," Espártaco explained this tendency to me, "whether they stay in their communities or leave to find work up north. In the village, they are free to go where they want and to do what they want. A woman cannot do this. She has to stay in the house, else people start talking badly of her. It is even worse for a woman when she is a migrant because of the constant threat of rape and violence. In the guerrilla organization her position is much stronger. Here she is treated as an equal."

While Las Cañadas was under EZLN control in the year after the uprising many insurgents were stationed in Zapatista villages. That their presence had a direct influence on the position of women is illustrated by the experiences of two women's collectives in La Gardenia. Until February 1995, the local support base successfully ran a bakery and a store. During the raid federal soldiers destroyed the oven, but after returning to their village the women were prepared to rebuild it and continue working. In the absence of the insurgents, however, La Gardenia's male authorities were against the resumption of the bakery project "to protect the women from assaults" by federal soldiers who frequently passed through the village. The collectively run women's store did continue to operate until the male-dominated assembly found a reason to send the women back to their kitchens. Possibly due to local sharing practices (e.g., women working in the store handing out food and merchandise to their compañeras even if they didn't have the money to buy these things), the store seems to have made net losses (five thousand pesos) and the *autoridades* argued that men were better suited for the job. The *asamblea* eventually decided that men should take over the store management, albeit with future profits set aside for the benefit of the female population.[7]

In an early text on the issue of women in the EZLN, Olivera (1995, 168) reports on the disappointment of Mexican feminists during the first National Democratic Convention that the Zapatistas had convoked in the Lacandon jungle in August 1994. They particularly deplored the fact that the rebels had failed to set up women's panels at the meeting.

Among their strongest criticisms, however, was the allegation that Zapatista demands did not include the abolishment of patriarchal practice and that the vertical structures of the EZLN along with authoritarian sanctions for deviance mirrored the patriarchal mainstream society. Even the Revolutionary Women's Law was deemed to be a far cry from feminist demands (169–71).

The Zapatistas clearly reacted to such criticisms and henceforth made sure to prioritize gender equality in their public presentations. However, even fifteen years after the uprising, there is a great gap between the impression that the rebels have managed to create among a worldwide sympathetic audience and the realities on the ground. Thus, in spite of the progressive rhetoric, in most base communities I visited, important posts such as comisariado, consejo, or agente were exclusively held by men. This is contrasted by the fact that, officially, women in Mexico have long had equal rights, particularly regarding the inheritance of land titles, which has also allowed them to take on posts in the administrative hierarchy of the ejido. The respective law was passed as early as 1940 under the presidency of Cardenás (Schüren 1997, 55). The percentage of women possessing land titles throughout the Mexican Republic in the early 1990s is estimated to be around 15 to 30 percent (Stephen 1996, 27). These numbers, however, were not at all reflected by what I found in Las Cañadas, where ejidatarios were almost exclusively men.

The strength of patriarchal tendencies has differed from region to region. Although the Revolutionary Women's Law applies in all Zapatista communities, there are significant regional variations to the degree women have been integrated into communal administration and public life in the villages. In November 2000, I interviewed a young health promoter from the autonomous municipality of 16 de Noviembre. When I asked her about women in the administrative structure of her community, she told me of a female agente, one of the key positions in the communal hierarchy of offices. The local police force, too, was staffed in equal parts by young men and women. After the inauguration of the Juntas de Buen Gobierno, the region that 16 de Noviembre belonged to took great care that of the twenty-eight consejos representing the seven autonomous municipalities at any one time,

Figure 8: At the 1996 women's day march in San Cristóbal an international activist mingled with the indigenous marchers, March 8, 1996. Photo courtesy of an anonymous solidarity activist.

at least seven were women, one for each municipality. This was by far the highest proportion of women in the civilian structures throughout Zapatista territory (Muñoz Ramírez 2004).

In 16 de Noviembre, women generally exuded self-confidence and had a strong presence during public events, participating in activities that elsewhere seemed to be reserved for men only. Thus, of the forty-eight basketball teams participating in a tournament that commemorated the founding of the guerrilla movement in Morelia in 2000, twenty-three teams were staffed by women. Particularly when compared to many new Zapatista settlements where women held posts such as responsable or even regional, communities like San Emiliano, which systematically excluded women from holding important posts in the village hierarchy, appear outright reactionary.

¿Mandar Obedeciendo? A Word on Democracy

The concept of *mandar obedeciendo* (governing by obeying) has long played an important part in shaping the Zapatistas' media image. Described as a "Mayan tradition" (Lynd 2005) or as "the horizontal exercise of power among the population" (Paulson 2001), mandar obedeciendo has become the brand name of what is widely associated with Zapatista-style base democracy. Marcos (1994) has publicly used the term in an interview as early as February 1994 and it has featured in many communiqués since, most notably in the second declaration of the Selva Lacandona (EZLN 1994e), where it is introduced along with one of the Zapatistas' other famous mottos *Todo para todos, nada para nosotros* (Everything for everybody, nothing for us).

Despite its ubiquitous use by the Zapatistas, exact definitions of the concept are hard to find. Probably one of the most detailed approximations to the term is contained in a communiqué issued at the occasion of the inauguration of the five Caracoles. The document states that the principle of mandar obedeciendo is universally applied in Zapatista communities. Thus, elected delegates are obliged to check that all agreements made in communal assemblies are complied with on the municipal level. To take on responsibility by assuming an administrative position is regarded as benefiting the collective, and posts are rotated among adult community members. The functioning of the principle is supposed to be ensured by the *weight of the collective* and the flow of communication. It would therefore be impossible, the communiqué continues, to disguise illicit embezzlement by officeholders for long; anyone found guilty of such trespassing is punished and made to give back what he has wrongfully taken from the community. In case Zapatista authorities deviate, become corrupted, or are prone to laziness, they are removed from their posts and replaced by elected successors. Although none of the cargo holders are financially remunerated, they are helped out on their fields by the community (Marcos 2003, part 5).

The term therefore also stands for a relationship of reciprocal exchange between the respective encargado and the village population at large. As Lynd (2005) evocatively puts it,

Imagine all of us here as a village. We feel the need for . . . a teacher and a storekeeper. But these two persons can be freed for those communal tasks only if we, as a community, undertake to cultivate their milpas, their corn fields. In the most literal sense their ability to take leadership roles depends on our willingness to provide their livelihoods.

(Teresa Ortiz, quoted in Lynd 2005)

Irrespective of its use to promote the Zapatista project, mandar obedeciendo is clearly a local concept comprising viable and long-standing mechanisms of running community affairs. But how democratic are these practices when viewed in a broader context?

Interestingly, in the light of Favre's observations from the 1960s, Marcos (2003) mentions that the collective still uses its power to bestow important cargos, such as those of agente or comisariado ejidal, to reintegrate those individuals who have displayed indifference to common interests. Despite the considerable changes to the practice of communal administration, some of the functions Favre and Cancian have attributed to the cargo system in the 1960s apparently still operate in modern-day Zapatista communities, albeit as elements of a new whole.

In older settler communities such as San Emiliano and La Gardenia the communal authority structure consisted of about thirty-five men who each held a post in the village hierarchy at any one time. Unlike the situation described by Favre (1973) and Cancian (1965), the communal asamblea annually elected these encargados by secret ballot.[8] This democratic element had made popularity rather than age, experience, marginality, or indeed clientelistic ties a prerequisite for election to the top posts in the village hierarchy. Well-connected "elder states-men" types who might have been able to rotate in occupying powerful positions in the past now had to fear being replaced by inexperienced but popular youngsters.[9] Due to high population growth and a young voting age, average voters in the new settler communities were in their teens. In 1997 San Emiliano's *secretario ejidal*, an attractive young man, admired by male and female adolescents alike, was only twenty. Marginal candidates who drank and beat their wives generally stood a bad chance in an election because they had the female voters against them.

A former campamentista who stayed on to live in the new Zapatista settlement of Tierra Nueva for almost two years, told me that one of direct democracy's implications in the village was a high fluctuation among top cargo holders. Having to make compromises on a permanent basis, their decisions were always bound to annoy people, which decreased voter sympathy and led to them being voted out of office by the next round. Abuse of power and embezzlement of funds contributed to the quick burnout of a candidate, eventually leading to a swift if not better replacement. The successor did not need to be popular; not having a history of cheating others was sufficient. Thus, the cargos moved in circles among age groups, shifting to the next generation once all available and consensually tolerable men had been exhausted.

In the older villages of Las Cañadas, about a third of the young men were officially landless, because the distribution of ejido land had ended before they were old enough to apply; titleholding women were an absolute exception.[10] Access to the consejo de vigilancia was restricted to titleholders. This turned the consejo into an obstruction of community-level democracy. This flaw was mitigated by the fact that recuperated lands, shared among the formerly landless Zapatista youngsters, qualified them for taking part in the council of ejidatarios. This was the case in La Gardenia where, in the late 1990s, twenty young men who had either lost family in the battle of Ocosingo or had been insurgents themselves received ten hectares of recuperated terrains by the EZLN and were communally elevated to the status of ejidatarios (also see chapter 4).[11] In the new population centers, where no one held an official title and all families had a plot of land assigned to them, the situation was different and it would appear that in this respect the development of grassroots democracy was more advanced there.

In the older settler villages, remnants of the structures and practices observed by Cancian and Favre still lingered on. Thus, five of the men in San Emiliano's authority structure were *principales*, who were not elected to their mostly ceremonial religious office but appointed by existing officeholders when one of them died. The fact that the community was contemplating to make these offices available for election too

Figure 9: In Zapatista villages, offenders were usually locked up for twenty-four hours in prison sheds for public shaming before the village authorities tried them in court, April 1997. Photo by author.

shows how fluid seemingly fixed traditions become in the aftermath of a revolution.

One of the most striking features of Zapatista administration was the practice of law enforcement and of holding court in the villages. In the base communities where I undertook research, a group of youngsters took weekly turns in staffing the community police, especially on the occasion of a village feast. It was their job to maintain order by detecting drunkenness and preventing fights. Offenders were locked into a prison shed, usually located in the center of the village. A day of public display in the village *cárcel* was usually deemed a sufficient assignment of shame for ordinary offences. On the evening of the day after a delinquent was detained, all cargo holders convened to set a punishment. This was normally a fine (multa) for minor offences such as public drunkenness or domestic violence. The council of autoridades also served as an opportunity for the involved parties to negotiate compensations between perpetrators and victims (see also Speed and Collier 2000). It is worth noting that serial offenders were regularly fined an amount they could not possibly pay themselves. This forced them to rely on relatives for a loan. In such a case, watchful relatives keen on getting their money back ensured the prevention of further transgressions.

When the EZLN proclaimed the creation of thirty-eight rebel municipalities on December 19, 1994, the guerrillas also made it explicit that the legislation in the territory under their control was based on the Mexican Constitution of 1917, the Zapatista revolutionary laws, and any local amendments endorsed by the respective communal assemblies (EZLN 1994a). The local practice of indigenous law (usos y costumbres, *derecho consuetudinario*) has thus been able to survive centuries of oppression (see Cabedo Mallol 2004; González Galván 1997), but the EZLN's declaration of its own legislation publicly challenged the Mexican State. The February 1995 army raid on Zapatista territory has to be seen with reference to the creation of the rebel municipalities that preceded the attack. The destruction of autonomous administrative buildings and the arrest of autonomous authorities by police and federal soldiers in 1998 constituted another attempt at imposing the rule of state law onto an area that had slipped from government control.[12] Failing to consolidate hegemony despite the increased presence of its army, the Mexican State was practically forced to tolerate a de facto judicial pluralism in the indigenous regions under Zapatista control, a situation that has been exacerbated by the establishment of Zapatista regional governments in 2003.

Mattiace, Hernández Castillo, and Rus (2002, 17) point out that indigenous peoples have reinvented the concept of usos y costumbres when rejecting customs they deemed to be oppressive, such as the exclusion of women from village assemblies. However, as has been previously shown, oppressive practices do not necessarily disappear under Zapatista governance but continue to be a challenge under the new setup. Have the EZLN's base communities become a refuge for democracy in a region historically rife with caciquismo, clientelism, and electoral fraud? For an analysis, I regard it as less important to trace the historical origins of the various practices than to focus on the way they are used in a given locality. In this chapter, I have identified the following key structural elements of governance in rebel territory:

- The asamblea and its components function as the core grassroots institution.

- Committees operate on the community level, each consisting of a hierachized set of functionaries elected by the asamblea.

- Committees operate on the level of the respective municipality, in turn consisting of a hierachized set of rotating functionaries from the respective communities.

- The level of regional government consists of five Juntas de Buen Gobierno in charge of administrating five geographically defined regions, each comprising half a dozen rebel municipalities.

- A parallel hierarchy of military functionaries, based in each community (responsables) and municipality (regionales), are appointed by the EZLN command rather than freely chosen by the asambleas.

- The EZLN's civilian steering committee is made up of Comités Clandestinos Revolucionarios Indígenas (comités or cecris), delegates that are elected by the asambleas in their communities of origin.

- In the ejidal communities settled in the mid-twentieth century, only the official holders of an ejido title are privileged to staff the important consejo de vigilancia. In a situation of factional splits, the meetings of ejidatarios could serve as a forum to mediate conflicts (see chapter 4).

Each of these elements gives the issue of Zapatista democracy a certain spin. Whereas village assemblies debating and deciding on burning issues and the transparent election of functionaries theoretically bolster the case for base democracy in rebel territory, administrative centralization and appointed officials, particularly those constituting part of a military apparatus, weaken it. It is an investigation of local practice that has to be key for evaluating the impact of Zapatismo. Any judgment of progress therefore needs to be relative rather than absolute and has to take into account the before and after of a given locality, emphasizing the historical differences between the studied communities.

Likewise, the principle of mandar obedeciendo regulates the relationship between cargo holders and ordinary community members, but it does not guarantee equality and other civil rights. The effects of the principle entirely depend on local usage of the rules it embodies. As I have shown, a regular village assembly making consensual decisions does not automatically stand for true democratic practice if patriarchal, gerontocratic, or clientelistic mechanisms operate through the back door. Neither do recent moves toward reducing the influence of EZLN functionaries (see Marcos 2003) necessarily mean a more progressive practice on the ground if they allow local reactionary elements that have lain dormant to reexert their influence.

CHAPTER FOUR

Resistance, Conflict, and Community Division

At the time of the Zapatista uprising, many of the indigenous settler communities making up the guerrilla movement's base displayed a high degree of cohesion and political unanimity. The years of clandestine organization leading up to the 1994 rebellion, however, saw violent confrontations between those villagers electrified by the vision of a new revolution and those who refused to take part in the armed struggle. In an interview with the French sociologist Yvon Le Bot (1997, 183–87), Subcomandante Marcos explains that the growing Zapatista influence was paralleled by friction in those villages where EZLN cadres neither held key positions in the ARIC nor as local church authorities. Between 1990 and 1993, the challenges to the traditional patriarchal values that also ensured the dominance of village elders caused the greatest contentions and particularly catequistas, tuhuneles, and principales accused Zapatistas of infiltrating women and youngsters with "bad ideas."

In San Emiliano and La Gardenia all dissenters had left their homes and fields behind when the rebellion broke out and the Zapatistas invaded the landholdings that covered the fertile valleys around Altamirano, Las Margaritas, and Ocosingo. The following years were characterized by severe repression from the Mexican army, special police, and paramilitaries. Nevertheless there was a sense of cooperation and mutual solidarity when I first came to the rebel villages of Las Cañadas in 1996. When I returned to Chiapas in 2000, I learned that San Emiliano had undergone factional splits. By the time my research drew to a close, a similar scenario had unfolded in the rebel village of La Gardenia.

This chapter links these divisions in the guerrilla movement's core communities to a major change in EZLN policy, locally referred to as la resistencia, which I regard as key for understanding why so many Zapatistas relinquished their ties to the guerrilla movement. The first of three cases assessed here is based on media reports and covers the events in the town of 20 de Noviembre, which accompanied the first publicized mass defection in a former EZLN stronghold. The section on the Tzeltal settler community of San Emiliano presents local perspectives on recent factional splits in the village canvassed during a return visit in May 2001. The unfolding conflict in La Gardenia was reconstructed from conversations carried out in the community itself and in San Cristóbal between October 2000 and April 2003. The final analysis addresses the question of why the EZLN decided to implement resistencia policies despite the foreseeable risks, and concludes that the rebels did not have a choice if they wanted maintain hegemony in their base communities and keep their outward credibility—a prerequisite for the solidarity support that was to become essential for ensuring government independence.

La Resistencia and Its Consequences

Until 1994, Zapatista core communities had kept up relations with the Mexican State while clandestinely organizing their insurrection. After the uprising, many rebel villages continued to rely on money and goods provided by the government. A decisive change in this practice took place only in 1996 when the EZLN urged its support base in the villages to proceed more thoroughly in their resistance, particularly with regard to accepting "government alms." Drafted years later, a letter by the guerrilla movement's spokesperson Subcomandante Marcos outlines the new policies:

> We have not accepted any government alms (for this is what they are). We have not accepted them in the past and neither will we in the future for, as the living conditions of the Indígenas who have accepted them show, problems are not solved and living standards do not improve one bit. Above all, we do not accept them because we have not made our insurrection to

receive schools, credits, or CONASUPO stores. We have risen
up for a better country where, among other things, our rights
as indigenous peoples are recognized, where we are respected,
and where we are treated as citizens and not as beggars.

(Subcomandante Marcos 1999; my translation)

Before the uprising, many local Zapatistas with land titles had
traveled to town once a month to collect their PROCAMPO money.[1]
Teachers in the village schools were paid and often provided by the
government and, since the introduction of PRONASOL in the late
1980s, many a settlement in the guerrilla movement's core support area
maintained a CONASUPO store that sold subsidized goods. Numerous
rebel communities were engaged in procedures for the solicitation of
additional land or participated in large-scale credit schemes funded
by state agencies such as the national Bank of Rural Development
(BANRURAL) to clandestinely procure money for arms (see chapter 2).
In 1994, state officials put an end to any material and monetary provisions for those communities whose affiliation with the EZLN had
become apparent in the course of the uprising. However, this policy
soon changed and government development programs were increasingly employed to create division in the rebel villages. In response, the
Zapatistas moved toward a general rejection of anything coming from
the government, be it a teacher's salary, subsidized goods, or a health
project. Locals referred to the new policies as la resistencia, a term
emphasizing their defiance toward the state. As the examples from
three Zapatista base communities featured in this chapter show, on
the ground, the realization of la resistencia policies often exacerbated
communal conflict and brought about factional splits.

The Zapatistas' decision of taking a tough line on the acceptance of
"government alms" came about in 1996. An indication for this policy
change (albeit tucked away in a packet of issues) can be found in a
communiqué by the CCRI-CG dating from August 29, 1996. In it, the
guerrilla command mentions agreements, made in consultas by "tens
of thousands of indigenous men and women" in the base communities,
on how to proceed after the failure to find a tenable compromise in the

negotiations of the second *mesa* (panel) of the San Andrés dialogues on Democracy and Justice. According to the communiqué, the Zapatista base affirmed their willingness to "fight to the ultimate consequences for democracy freedom and justice" and asked their commanders to suspend the dialogue rather than to "sell out" (EZLN 1996). Although this was the official Zapatista line, it is likely that positions by individuals in the base communities were more diverse. Thus, the Mexican daily *La Jornada* (September 25, 1996) quotes a government document stating that "the order by the Zapatista command to reject governmental aid is not well received in the indigenous communities of Las Cañadas" (Guerrero Chiprés 1996). Whether the EZLN's resistencia policies came about by democratic consensus is hard to establish. In the light of the political divisions that followed, however, it seems more likely that a majority decided to go along with a request by the movement's command on grounds of faith rather than resolve.

The growing dissatisfaction among the Zapatista base can be traced back to the 1995 army raid, when the guerrilla command ordered the evacuation of rebel communities. Prepared to defend themselves gun in hand, the people who had organized the 1994 insurrection had to watch from the covers as their homes were ransacked by federal soldiers. That humiliation contributed to a growing sense of being forsaken by the EZLN. Some of my informants mentioned that feeling of abandonment in the same breath with economic hardships when I asked for the reasons why they or their relatives had left the guerrilla movement. As people in the base communities began questioning the benefit of their uprising in the face of stagnant poverty and increased repression, the EZLN saw a growing need to assert its claim to be an alternative to the Mexican State. Intended as an affirmation of independence and credibility, however, resistencia policies also exacerbated fatigue among many of those who had helped to build up the organization for more than a decade. In this respect, the guerrilla movement's command, which I assume to be behind the decision to introduce the stricter guidelines, totally misjudged their disastrous effects. This is in line with Bourdieu's argument (1991) that, in their preoccupation with strategies geared to mobilize ever more supporters and resources, political organizations tend to lose sight of the economic plight of their constituencies. I believe that in the present case, this phenomenon led EZLN's policy makers to devise a program that disregarded the will of its base.

The implementation of resistencia policies definitely marked a turning point. Designed to uphold a dignified self-image, the rejection of state resources increased the hardships of life in resistance and exacerbated existing tensions that eventually led to communal divisions. On top of having to support the guerrilla with a share of their work and harvest, the Zapatista base now also had to make do without outside help.[2] Consequences included the suspension of schooling for children from Zapatista families and a subsequent increase in illiteracy, higher costs for basic goods, and no more monthly cash for all ejidatarios who had claimed PROCAMPO grants. At the same time, the government showered neighboring villages that had not taken part in the rebellion with development aid, providing new infrastructure, clinics, and schools. Many people in the original Zapatista strongholds were not prepared to face this bundle of hardships and gave up their resistance in exchange for financial aid and a government teacher for their children. The results of this development were considerable. Whereas a united Zapatista community had been a common sight in Las Cañadas in the mid-1990s, at the turn of the millennium there was hardly a larger settlement without factional splits.[3] The fact that almost none of this found its way into the EZLN's communiqués—of which there was a steady output at the time—hints at the severity of the problem. As many of its supporters were quickly losing faith, the EZLN command may have feared to perpetuate that snowball effect outside of its core area by reporting on it. Indeed, the defections in Zapatista heartland are in marked contrast to what occurred in other areas such as Los Altos, where the EZLN received backing only after the uprising, as the local landless population squatted on terrains from their own initiative. As support for the guerrilla movement grew, however, the region became plagued by paramilitary groups that were part of a state-sponsored counterinsurgency campaign (see also Centro de Derechos Humanos 1998).

Developments in 20 de Noviembre, a town at the edge of Las Cañadas in the vicinity of Altamirano, illustrate how the PRI government was able to capitalize on increasing dissatisfaction in the guerrilla movement's core areas. Hoping to achieve a domino effect, party officials began to stage a series of EZLN desertions in 1999. Postings by news agencies such as CNN (Zapatista Rebels 1999) circulated reports that Chiapas's governor Albores had presided over a ceremony during which sixteen rebels marched out of the jungle and handed their guns over to him. That the EZLN regarded such events as potentially damaging becomes apparent in a communiqué that was issued several days later. In it, the guerrilla movement denounces the desertions as a hoax involving paramilitaries who had lent themselves to the government's propaganda stunt in exchange for cattle (EZLN 1999). Although *La Jornada* seconds the EZLN's allegations, the paper also acknowledges that some former Zapatista families had left the guerrilla movement to take out government loans (Bellinghausen 1999).

In April 1999, another staged desertion took place in 20 de Noviembre. It was followed by local media reports that 442 families, practically the entire local population, had decided to return to "institutional life" and to integrate themselves into the state development programs (Cuarto Poder 1999; Excelsior 1999). A month later, Enlace Civil circulated a posting denouncing that the supposed deserters had received money. The announcement also unwittingly admits that a mass exit *had* taken place by reporting that the four families who remained Zapatista were barred from entering the town (1999). By the time I visited the area in 2000, 20 de Noviembre was a PRIista stronghold.

This example illustrates how susceptible Zapatista communities had become to material inducements by the state after having been denied their ability to play multiple options. Before, the indigenous campesinos had combined their shrewdness with a dignified self-image, clandestinely preparing for revolution while pirating state resources to alleviate their everyday hardships. As such practices were increasingly subject to public scrutiny, they had to be scrapped for being incompatible with EZLN policies. For the sake of their public image, indigenous Zapatistas had to abandon being pirates. They were now faced with the choice between remaining compas living in dignified poverty or of turning into *rajones* who begged for government alms.[4] These new restrictions did not go down well and the following pages show how they contributed to destabilization and division in the settler villages of Las Cañadas.

San Emiliano Revisited

I returned to San Emiliano in May 2001. As the peace camp had been shut down in the late 1990s and the village was not among the lucky few to host an NGO any time soon, I opted for a spontaneous visit. Cipriano had told me all he knew about the division in the village and I expected some of my acquaintances to have left the EZLN. Feeling a bit apprehensive, I took my old friend Barney along for reinforcement. We arrived in the early afternoon as the men were just returning from their milpas. As Barney and I got off the truck with our backpacks, we were instantly greeted by a group of youngsters wearing army boots and pallacates, whom I assumed to be compas. They directed us to a nearby house from which a man in his late thirties emerged. This was Tadeo, a local EZLN representative and son of one of San Emiliano's founding families, whose members had held key positions in the village hierarchy during my stay in 1996/97. In 2001, two of his older brothers were still Zapatistas while his sister and her husband had left the EZLN and joined the ARIC independiente.

Tadeo invited us into his home to eat while his wife warmed up a stack of tortillas and a pot of thin, sweet coffee. He sat down with us at the table to fill me in on four years of absence. Struggling for words, he broke the news to me: "A disaster has happened here, compa! Things are not like they used to be when you stayed with us. San Emiliano is not united anymore. In fact, we are divided due to the greed of a few rajones!" Tadeo did not conceal his anger and resignation as he told me that the majority of villagers had deserted the EZLN not long after I had last seen him in 1997. He knew that I had accompanied the delegation of EZLN commanders on their way to Mexico City a few months earlier and told me how San Emiliano's remaining Zapatistas had received them with a hero's welcome on their way back. "All of us compas were standing by the road. Men, women, the old people, and the children, every single one a Zapatista! Not one of the rajones was to be seen. They were all hiding in their houses in shame when the comandantes came through."

The following paragraphs summarize the narrative of political division in San Emiliano as related to me by Tadeo, who saw the cause for it in the greed and unscrupulousness that drove the deserters to apply for a government-issued permit to exploit rare woods on communal lands. It seems that, initially, the plan to sell the wood had widespread appeal in the community. When the majority decided to seek a deal with the government at a village assembly in April 1998, the EZLN command intervened by declaring the decision incompatible with the organization's principles. However, a group of villagers defied the order and started a mutiny. After the renegades had been officially expelled from the guerrilla organization, they sought contacts with the governing PRI, negotiated the building of a school, and applied for government aid. When it became clear that they had succeeded and came back from town with goods bought with PROCAMPO money, more families decided to join them. A year later, two-thirds of San Emiliano's inhabitants had left the EZLN and were involved in various income-generating schemes funded by the government. Among those, a cattle-rearing project was cause for particular contention because of the increased pressure it bore on the limited village pastures hitherto used by the collective. The majority faction also gained control of the main store, which resumed selling products subsidized by the Secretariat for Social Development (SEDESOL). As the village militia shrank in numbers, the store they had maintained to fund their equipment was dismantled. The remaining Zapatistas stood up to the challenges, got a new store together, and organized their own community school. Three teenagers were chosen as future teachers and remunerated with the yields of a collective maize field. A team of international solidarity activists took on their training. By the time of my visit to San Emiliano, a whole generation of new teachers from all over the region attended workshops on didactic skills held at regular intervals in the nearby Aguascalientes (see chapter 6).

Our visit coincided with the *día del niño* (children's day), one of the many occasions celebrated by Zapatistas along with women's day, the birthday of Che Guevara, and the anniversary of the uprising. Unlike religious holidays that were also celebrated, such dates were used to address the revolutionary struggle in speeches and public performances that the community prepared together. I noticed that the rest of the village celebrated día del niño on the basketball court when I made my way to the new schoolhouse, where the compas had assembled. Inside, about forty people were sitting in a large circle on the same benches their children used during the day. I paced along rows of steadfast Zapatistas, shaking everyone's hands and, as my eyes became accustomed to the half-light, I realized that most of them were women. I knew that several men had died in the battle of Ocosingo and that the mostly male insurgents were almost constantly absent from the village. However, this stark imbalance still puzzled me. With the ban on alcohol and guaranteed equal rights enshrined in the revolutionary laws, EZLN membership may just have a special appeal for women.

Before a protracted show of riddles, poems, and short plays presented by the community teachers and their pupils, the two EZLN representatives embarked on a discourse about the importance of mothers and children for the Zapatista struggle. The speeches concluded with an appeal for unity and perseverance that is requisite of such occasions. In front of everyone, Tadeo then addressed me as someone who had known the community united: "This is what's left of us, thirteen families in the village remain with la organización." With some bitterness, he then proclaimed that, while the others had given up, their humble bunch was continuing the resistance with even greater effort. Tadeo referred to the school whose pupils' performance we were about to watch. He then presented the teenaged community teachers and spoke with pride about how they were supported by all compa families who prepared their milpas and supplied them with tortillas.

On the way back to the hut where Barney and I had strung our hammocks, we passed the basketball court and noticed a couple of inebriated villagers. Four years earlier, this would have been unthinkable due to the ban on alcohol in Zapatista communities. During my stay in 1996/97, anyone caught drinking on communal lands had ended up in the village jail, only to be released upon paying a fine a day later. When I asked a compa whether those drinking would be punished, he told me, "No, only if they are causing trouble." With the division in San Emiliano, EZLN jurisdiction had obviously lost its universality and become restricted to the remaining Zapatistas.

During our brief stay in the village, I also looked up members of the majority faction, whom local Zapatistas referred to as rajones for having deserted their ranks. After I had made my introduction with the compas, it seemed permissible to speak to some people from the other camp, whom I had been close to when staying in the village as a campamentista. Among the ones I visited in their homes was the family of seventeen-year-old Raimundo, one of the kids I had taught to read back in 1996/97. He had never had any other teacher since in spite of the fact that there was now schooling available. Raimundo was too old for this now and already worked as a full-time campesino on his milpa. His younger brother Paco did not go to the new government school either. He had been entrusted to his *padrino* (godfather), a merchant from Ocosingo who used the family's house to sell vegetables when in San Emiliano. Paco now lived in town where he went to secondary school to become a car mechanic with a cash income. Raimundo's justification for his family's change of allegiance focused on the material improvements that had come about since. "Instead of our leaking zacate roofs we now have rainproof corrugated iron over our heads. Things are looking up! Soon we'll be able to buy cars and tractors." With this statement he referred to the future proceeds from the sale of caoba trees growing on village lands still covered by old growth forest. One large plank of wood being worth three hundred pesos meant that a tree could be sold for many thousand pesos. With excitement, Raimundo calculated the riches to be tapped in the very near future. When I asked him how his people felt about the PRI losing the elections, he told me that they were not *meros* (actual) *PRIistas* but *independientes*, ready to negotiate deals with whomever happened to be in government.

Raimundo's mother, Lorena, had been the women's representative in the community when I last stayed in San Emiliano. She takes credit for the memorable line, "Casi ya no somos Zapatistas" (we are *almost* not Zapatistas anymore). Do these words say something about her feeling ashamed for being a rajona or do they reveal local attitudes toward organizational affiliation? Does she imply that her new status may be only temporary? Lorena did not mention anything about the wood issue but instead embarked on a discourse about the poverty that everyone had suffered and the fact that there had never been a school or a clinic in the village, both of which they now had. She also made it sound as if the Zapatista hard core (and here she mentioned her brothers' names) had expelled her and the other ex-compas from the organization for wanting to obtain these essentials. Although Lorena made it clear that she very much approved of what Marcos had done and continued to do, she also said that, in her view, the EZLN had never really delivered anything of what was needed in the community and that the government was different in that respect. "They might give only a little bit," she explained, "but at least they give something."

Hardships of a Heterogeneous Base

The 1995 army raid that turned many Zapatistas from Las Cañadas into refugees caused lasting suspicions toward anything coming from the state. As a result, the inhabitants of San Emiliano took recourse to state aid very carefully. To limit possibilities for government surveillance and manipulation, there was a consensus against PROCAMPO money and government salaries for local teachers. However, some state resources such as the CONASUPO store were indeed tapped. The store was run by Zapatista elders who sold subsidized basic foods such as maize, rice, or beans, but also garments, rubber boots, machetes, and tools of everyday use that were not produced locally. In addition, building materials such as corrugated iron for roofing or even financial aid was sometimes obtained by collective applications to the government.

Such petitions were often shrouded in a way that preserved the dignity of the locals and veiled the underlying objective to outsiders, including the upper echelons of the EZLN. Thus, in spring 1996, I witnessed an assembly of all male adults in San Emiliano, who debated an application to the Secretariat for Social Development, in which they sued the government for the damages incurred by federal soldiers. The congregation sent a letter to the municipal seat stating pecuniary claims amounting to two thousand pesos per family. A year earlier, the same men had already unsuccessfully requested compensation for a harvest lost during the 1995 army raid. That claims such as these, made by communities not allied with the governing PRI, have occasionally met with success has been shown by Collier (1997, 20–21) for the case of Zinacantán.

Figure 10: A CONASUPO truck bringing a fresh delivery of subsidized goods to a Zapatista village. On the shop wall there is a banner pointing out the local peace camp, March 1997. Photo by author.

All efforts to procure money and material testify to the villagers' dire need. Like so many indigenous settler communities at the fringes of the developed world, the people of San Emiliano were extremely poor, as their situation was characterized by a lack of clean water, nonexistent health care, a high birth rate, insufficient nourishment, and the most basic shelters for housing. Due to the high population growth and its location in a steep valley, the village was also overcrowded with regard to arable land. In line with the EZLN's practice of settling lands invaded and "recuperated" during the uprising, a substantial part of San Emiliano's mostly younger population moved to a former finca in 1997. Several hours away from their village of origin, these fifteen families with particularly strong affiliations to the EZLN founded the hamlet of El Arbolito. Their leaving coincided with the implementation of resistencia policies.

With the ban on state assistance, the support of the guerrilla movement became an even greater drain on resources and many Zapatistas

Figure 11: Old-growth trees of the Lacandon jungle were regularly felled to make room for new milpas. They often became a source of conflict, as they were also a lucrative resource that could be sold for cash, April 1997. Photo by author.

began to perceive their guerrilla membership as a sacrifice. When the EZLN command ordered the closing of CONASUPO stores, people in San Emiliano started to voice their discontent and complained about their kids never having been to school. Some saw the solution for their poverty in the exploitation of the remaining rain forest on village lands. To get the trees down from the mountains and into town, they needed to cooperate with regional government officials who had, up to that point, been considered the enemy. Although the plan to sell the wood probably had widespread appeal among all villagers, a warning from regional EZLN functionaries would have put off those whose ties to the guerrilla movement ran deeper than economic considerations. For others, the wood issue might have been a welcome opportunity for a clean break. As my interviews with former compas suggest, opting to improve their economic condition by going for the wood and getting "involuntarily" expelled from the EZLN was consistent with their dignity. As a result of their action, they were freed from the commitments guerrilla membership entailed and could take advantage of government aid.

By November 2000, a clinic and a school had been built in San Emiliano and many former Zapatistas used government credits to invest in cattle rearing. In a region where a large percentage of the population was making sacrifices for the sake of the revolution, the new wealth did not remain unnoticed in surrounding villages and increased existing tensions there.[5] That San Emiliano's dropouts received substantial government funds so quickly indicates that the government regarded financial incentives as effective counterinsurgency measures.[6] In situations marked by scarcity of arable terrains, land-intensive cattle grazing bears enormous potential for further conflict. Particularly new settlements such as El Arbolito that were built on land occupied in the course of the 1994 rebellion became the site of violent clashes. As a PAN/PRD alliance won the Chiapas state elections in 2000, many former EZLN allies, such as ORCAO, saw some of their members take posts in the new government. These contacts provided these organizations with substantial credits, which they used for the purchase of cattle. Thus, by 2003 a vicious circle of increasing pressure on the limited terrains suitable for cattle grazing had pitted the former allies against each other similar to the effect of the PRI's counterinsurgency measures of the 1990s.

It makes sense to look at the conflicts in San Emiliano, La Gardenia, and many other EZLN core communities, proceeding on Bailey's (1969) assumption of moral and contract teams (see introduction). Because the internal links between people in contract teams are solely based on material benefits, they are likely to fall apart when the balance is wrong. Moral teams on the other hand share an ideology and are prepared to stay together through periods of economic hardship. When analyzing the division in formerly united rebel villages, I believe it is important to get away from viewing the Zapatista base as a homogenous bunch. The motivations that compelled individuals, families, and entire communities to join the guerrilla movement have been diverse from the beginning. In the two decades of varying integration into the guerrilla organization—as insurgents, militia, or bases de apoyo—motivations for membership have, if anything, differentiated even further. The degree of integration into the EZLN has varied among individuals and families. Thus, there were people who belonged to the guerrilla movement's hard core because they had a family member killed in battle or had themselves taken part in it, gun in hand. Others were less committed. Only as former insurgents and their families received EZLN orders to settle recuperated lands, a degree of spatial homogeneity was—artificially—created, as the new villages consisted almost exclusively of moral teams. The older villages that had given birth to the EZLN continued to be made up of both moral and contract teams alike. The resettlement, however, tipped that balance.

That San Emiliano divided soon after fifteen families had moved to El Arbolito, suggests that these events were related. The departure of most EZLN loyalists disturbed the equilibrium of interests and powers within the community and fomented the factional split. Interestingly, communal division was accompanied by a boost in autonomous organization. Collective projects such as the community school, which before had been grounded by the lack of cooperation by an unwilling few, once again became possible with fewer participants. During the political unanimity in the mid-1990s there was no schooling as San Emiliano's families had not been able to come to a consensus about remunerating their children's teachers. It took the political division for remaining compas to find the resolve to support their teachers on their fields.[7] Local Zapatista women had raised the substantial sum of Mex$2,500 to buy the building where lessons took place and, when I visited the community in May 2001, the autonomous school had been going for almost a year.

Falling Apart: Political Division in La Gardenia

It took a little longer until factional strife reached La Gardenia. At least outwardly, San Emiliano's neighbor managed to maintain political unanimity until the year 2001. Before that, the last violent clashes had taken place back in 1993 when Zapatistas and government loyalists had bashed each other with clubs after a meeting in the *casa ejidal* (assembly hall). The Zapatistas had won and about ten families who did not want to join the armed rebellion were made to leave. They moved to Ocosingo and, after the rebellion, the government recompensed them for the two hundred hectares of ejido land they had left behind. According to Gardenia compas, they "sold the land to the government" for eighty thousand pesos (eight thousand U.S. dollars) per family. Back in La Gardenia, the most fertile terrains were turned into communal fields, the yields of which supported insurgents, orphans, and the elderly. Some of the land was made available to the growing number of youngsters without an ejido title, who were given use rights to a hectare per year by the community council. In 2002, the bulk of that land was eventually distributed by the Zapatista municipal authorities among deserved guerrillas who also received the status of ejidatarios.

More than seven years after the rebellion, about a fifth of Gardenia's total population, some forty families, asked to be relieved of all obligations pertaining to the Zapatista support base. They consisted mainly of older ejidatarios, many of whom had organized the clandestine buildup of the EZLN before 1994. Cipriano's family described them as "people who have grown tired of the struggle and taken to drink." To avoid conflict with the rest of the community, they promised to neither join another political organization nor to receive government aid. They were, however, allowed a state teacher. The compas I spoke to at the time were all confident that, after taking a break, these people would eventually rejoin the guerrilla movement—an evaluation that proved to be correct in the light of later events.

In October 2001, things came to a head as another group of villagers instigated a mass exit from Zapatista ranks. This threw the whole community into disarray over issues of ownership. Recuperated terrains, collective stores, the tractor, and communal buildings all turned into bones of contention. The situation quickly turned explosive as the dropouts wanted their share of land and collectively owned property, but the remaining Zapatistas held on to what they saw as the legitimate fruits of their struggle. Like most of the inhabitants of their barrio, Cipriano's and Sergio's extended families remained Zapatista. The defectors, who numbered about fifty families, were quick to join the ARIC independiente. In many indigenous villages of eastern Chiapas, this organization, which shares some of the EZLN's roots (see chapter 1) and some of its demands, has occupied a middle position between the EZLN and the PRI, allowing its members to negotiate with both. For Gardenia's dropouts, the ARIC independiente was a choice of flexibility at a time of great political changes.[8] Eighty-three families stayed loyal to the EZLN while the group that had left earlier kept its position of neutrality. Some of those who joined the ARIC had received former finca land for their services as EZLN militants. After their desertion, it seemed a matter of course for the remaining Zapatistas such as Sergio that they would give it back: "Why should they keep the rewards of a struggle they have abandoned?"

While the cargos that some of the defectors had held in the guerrilla organization were subsequently taken over by compas, Gardenia's civilian community council was split along factional lines. To deal with the escalating conflict in the community, the remaining Zapatistas decided to elect a new set of authorities in charge of all issues regarding their faction. Sergio, who had held a post in the previous authority structure, was reelected. While the group of neutrals kept their head down, the ARICistas, too, elected their respective council.[9] Apart from the two new councils, the ejidal assembly kept up regular meetings. As it comprised members from all three factions, this assembly served as an important forum for the dispute over the contested terrains during the following months of indecision and intracommunal strife. After the split, the ARIC council was busy organizing the paperwork necessary to claim PROGRESA and PROCAMPO benefits. Because almost everyone's birth certificates had been destroyed during the 1995 army raid, this proved rather difficult and required the council delegates to make frequent trips to the municipal seat, which the dropouts had to pay for. The Zapatistas regarded this demonstration of how economically futile the decision to quit had turned out for their neighbors with a certain triumph. This changed as the paperwork was done and the situation of the ARICistas improved visibly. The government built a small clinic with a store of medicine and a Red Cross nurse came by at regular intervals. They also provided a new school complete with teachers, which starkly contrasted with the Zapatistas' own underequipped and ramshackle community schools. This came as a particularly hard blow to the remaining compas. The issue of schooling was a sore spot for it touched on the prospects of their children to make a living and called into question notions of a better future associated with the Zapatista revolution.

For a bimonthly allowance of up to four hundred pesos, the PROGRESA program integrated rural women into income-generating or medical projects such as raising chicken or maintaining the clinic. The scheme was thereby in direct competition with the Zapatistas' own health and production collectives that were characterized by a high degree of female participation. Probably the most controversial element of PROGRESA was the requirement for all participants to join a birth control program. Most notably to everyone in La Gardenia, ARIC families received a one-time payment of one thousand pesos for each woman who joined the program. According to local Zapatistas, all of that money was spent on drink and, although this may be a vast exaggeration, alcohol-related squabbles, fights, subsequent arrests, and court rulings increased considerably over that time. In spite of their original aim to honor the local patron saint, the biweekly Sunday fiestas had become a stage for violent drunken encounters. A joint reunion was called and both factions agreed that they would let each other go their ways (*cada quien con su camino*) to avoid conflict. But as the land issue was not resolved, the situation remained volatile.

An Ultimatum and Its Effects

To clear the air and to keep people from remaining undecided, the EZLN command issued an ultimatum for the village that terminated with the Guadalupe festivities on December 12, 2001. On that day, everyone in La Gardenia had to have made up their minds as to which group they wanted to be part of; the ones set to permanently stay away from the EZLN were to face the consequences. First and foremost, this meant losing their right to work on the recuperated finca lands that had been shared among Gardenia's landless in the aftermath of the 1994 uprising. The approaching deadline aggravated the situation and Sergio's mother, Griselda, told me how the growing tensions gave way to outright violence during the November 2001 All Saints (*todos santos*) festivities. Apparently, the ARICistas had used their first batch of PROCAMPO money to buy alcohol for the fiesta. Once in the village,

Figure 12: At times of communal conflict and factional splits, the murals of the Zapatista revolution can turn into symbolic targets. The slogan next to the destroyed Marcos portrait reads, "Everything for everyone, nothing for ourselves," March 2002. Photo by author.

the sugarcane brandy was resold and also ended up with members of the Zapatista faction. As the male village population got progressively drunk during the fiesta, squabbles between individuals turned into physical violence and members of the opposing factions had a go at each other with clubs and knives.

Griselda's son Blas, a dedicated and well-respected *compa* community teacher, was caught dancing around drunk and disorderly at the festivities. In an effort to uphold the prohibitionist policy, the Zapatista village police arrested him and locked him up in the prison shed. Unfortunately for Blas, the cell was already occupied by a drunk ARICista who took the opportunity to vent his aggressions and physically assaulted him. The matter was brought before the Zapatista community court the following day and a fine (*multa*) of a thousand pesos was set for both brawlers. As I was able to observe on similar occasions, the chosen sum was much too high for any one individual to pay, necessitating a joint effort by friends and relatives. Already shaken by the affair, Blas was shocked to hear the next day that the ARICista refused to pay the fine, claiming to be unaffected by Zapatista jurisdiction. Outraged over such blatant injustice, Blas publicly collapsed with a stinging pain in his heart upon drinking the two traditional cups of sugarcane liquor during a communal ceremony at the graveyard. A solidarity activist from Mexico City, who stayed in La Gardenia at the time, diagnosed "liver problems" but Griselda blamed Zapatista authorities for her son's condition. Instead of punishment, she insisted, he deserved compensation for the humiliation of the prison beating.

In another episode, an ARICista refused to participate in the new obligations linked to the applications for government aid and returned to the Zapatista camp, revealing everything about his faction's secret plans to hold on to the recuperated terrains. In the course of the All Saints booze-up, a vengeful ARICista stabbed him in the shoulder. In turn, the enraged mother of the victim attacked the perpetrator and his group with a club, subsequently fleeing the village. Yet another incident involved a government truck trying to deliver one of the first loads of subsidized goods to the newly opened CONASUPO store of the ARIC faction. This outraged local Zapatistas, one of whom chased the driver out of the village by wielding a knife. Shortly before the ultimatum ran out, aversions in the community became so severe that activities such as the church service, which both factions were still engaged in together, were in danger of being suspended. The ARICistas even made plans to build their own church but eventually dropped the idea when the local tuhunel, who had remained undecided until that point, sided with the Zapatistas.

The balance of powers in the community shifted decisively when the neutrals rejoined the Zapatista faction at the end of the year. As their group consisted mainly of older ejidatarios, the threat of being denied the use of terrains appropriated in the course of the uprising affected them only indirectly. However, long-term considerations of having to share their own plots with their sons compelled them to return to the EZLN before the ultimatum ran out. Not so most members of the newly formed ARIC faction, who attempted to hold on to their share of recuperated lands as well as to collectively owned items such as the stores, the tractor, and the guns. To be physically able to do this, however, they would have needed to get the majority of villagers behind them. Until this point a substantial part of the village population had remained undecided about how to proceed. Thus, Cipriano told me about one of his cousins who had kept his head down during the conflict and did not even attend village assemblies. As the situation cleared up with the ultimatum, he resumed going to the meetings "supporting the organization more than before." It looks like quite a few people behaved similarly during that insecure period. After getting a clear idea of their options—and the respective benefits and drawbacks—people made pragmatic decisions as to which side they would join.

From December 2001 onward, events in La Gardenia developed rapidly. Not a month after the ultimatum ran out, the new Zapatista authorities in the village pushed for a high-level municipal meeting to deal with the pressing land issue. Soon after, the leaders (dirigentes) of ARIC independiente and the Zapatista municipal council met to discuss the land situation in La Gardenia. During that meeting, the compa delegates stunned the ARIC dirigentes by bringing up another topic that eclipsed La Gardenia's land situation in importance: the escalating violence in a nearby new settlement where the majority of inhabitants had recently converted to the ARIC independiente. This had triggered persecution, abuse, and even the death of a Zapatista man. The situation had become so severe that the EZLN was ready to dispatch a large contingent of unarmed supporters in a show of strength to stop the harassments. At the meeting, Zapatista authorities disclosed the threat of such imminent action. Wanting to diffuse the situation, the ARIC dirigentes blamed an absent colleague for inciting the violence and offered concessions. They declared that the contested land belonged to Gardenia's Zapatistas and made assurances that their organization had no interest in the compas' land anyway and would concentrate on "petitioning PROCAMPO money from the government." Having publicly rid themselves of any responsibility in local matters, they were reported to have departed in "big cars," leaving their newly won followers in La Gardenia out in the cold. Sergio reckoned that the Gardenia breakaways had not even been aware of the friendly ties that the campesino organization of their choice had with the EZLN. He mused, they would probably have been better off switching to the PRI or some organization that was not in opposition to the government. After the high-level meeting, things in La Gardenia calmed down and, by May 2002, members of the different factions spoke to each other on the streets again.

Upon having established a majority in the village, the Zapatista communal assembly decided in March 2002 that the terrains of the ten families who had left in 1993 would be permanently allotted to twenty formerly landless individuals who had either fought as insurgents or who had a close relative among the Ocosingo martyrs. Each received ten hectares and the status of an ejidatario, thus giving them a voice in the all-important asamblea ejidal, made up of Zapatistas and ARICistas. Incidentally, the number of ejidatarios who were ARICistas had exceeded those of the Zapatistas before the Zapatista land allocation. That structural "shortcoming" had now been remedied by the cunning creation of another twenty Zapatista ejidatarios. That they were able to assume this position without going through official procedures, which would have required the involvement of the state, suggests that the new ejidatarios either relied solely on the leverage of the EZLN's authority or underwent their status change within a framework of locally accepted rules. The latter would point to a strong identification by all community members, with a concept of autonomy stemming from the shared experience contained in decades of political organization.

In retrospect, I share the assessment by Sergio and his brothers that the group who instigated division in La Gardenia had set out to achieve a majority in the village large enough to gain control over the two hundred hectares formerly owned by the 1993 refugees, as well as over the finca lands recuperated in the course of the uprising. By capitalizing on malcontent regarding obligatory contributions to collective projects and the implications of la resistencia, they hoped to recruit those exhausted by more than a decade of guerrilla membership. The defectors might even have hoped to vastly outnumber the Zapatistas and expel the remaining hard core, also taking over their individual plots in the process. As many Gardenians withdrew into passivity from October to December 2001, not attending village assemblies while waiting for some clarity to emerge, this actually might have looked feasible for a while. Eventually, however, the Zapatista hard core made it clear that there were enough of them ready to fight. In a show of institutional backup, the ultimatum by the EZLN command was then strategically issued in close cooperation with local Zapatista authorities. The following escalation saw mutual accusations by members of both factions.[10] However, the land issue remained the focus of conflict throughout. In the end, the strategy of the ARICistas did not work out. They were left with forty-five *solicitantes* in their ranks who ended up *en blanco* (landless). As the terrains formerly assigned to them were shared among the remaining *compas*, the only thing they retained were their *solares*, the twenty-by-forty-meter plots in the village where they lived. All those ARICistas who were not able to share the fields of their landholding relatives faced either having to look for work away from the community or pay a lease of one thousand pesos annually to the Zapatistas to grow maize on spare terrains. When I asked Sergio what would become of these people, he explained that "the door remains open" for them to rejoin the EZLN. Conditions for their return were already set: repentant community members would have to prove their remorse with a forty-eight-hour sojourn in the community jail and also pay two hundred pesos as a fine "for the organization is not a toy to play about with," as Sergio put it.

Struggling for Hegemony

When investigating the reasons for the guerrilla movement's hard line, exemplified by the policies of *la resistencia*, sanctions for deviance, and the ideological stance against the acceptance of "alms," it is important to focus on the new position toward the state that the EZLN has assumed for its base and the wider public since 1994. While operating clandestinely in the decade before the uprising, none of its actions were subjected to public discourse. This allowed its members to be politically involved in a broad variety of ways. Leyva Solano (2003b, 174) has described the common occurrence of "double memberships" by campesinos who had joined both legal organizations such as the Unión de Uniones and clandestine ones such as the EZLN. During that time, involvement of Zapatista communities with the state was justified as a preparation for the uprising. The contradictions implied in taking out a BANRURAL loan or in receiving monthly PROCAMPO crop subsidy payments were resolved by regarding them as merely a provisional compromise, as a means to an end that was more important than a temporary breach of principles.

Since its spectacular coming-out in January 1994, however, the EZLN has challenged the state much more directly and on an everyday basis. It did this by replacing institutions such as justice, law enforcement, and social security, and—as I show in the following chapters—by organizing education, health care, and production. At the same time, the guerrilla movement legitimated its existence also with regard to aspects of the Mexican State that it portrayed as despicable, such as neglect, cooptation, exploitation, and corruption. Although it only briefly challenged the state militarily in 1994, the struggle for hegemony in its base communities has been ongoing. It is manifest in the control of everyday practice and the assertion of loyalty in the villages under its control. This was exacerbated as the Mexican State sought to boost its presence in Las Cañadas and Selva Lacandona by building roads, deploying the army and police, and bringing in development programs that the non-Zapatista population accepted with open arms. Faced with this double strategy, the EZLN countered by enforcing discipline in the villages under its control.

Since its public appearance in 1994, the guerrilla movement has increasingly emphasized indigenous dignity and autonomy. Essentially, both imply staying independent from the government, which the EZLN has persistently portrayed as corrupting and contaminating. Consequently, any display of overt government involvement or ambiguous practices by Zapatistas has the potential to damage the EZLN's image and its credibility both outwardly and within its communities. Having parts of its base engaged with a government it portrays as evil would jeopardize the EZLN's moral integrity in front of the world, making it vulnerable to the prying eyes of the very media that have also ensured its success and the physical survival of its base (see also chapter 9).[11] Moreover, allowing its own members to cut individual deals with government agencies would compromise the guerrilla movement's position of local hegemony. By allocating or withholding development projects, clinics, or schools, the state could easily play Zapatista communities against each other, exposing the EZLN as a powerless bystander and eroding its authority in the process.

To understand why so many Zapatistas in the core regions gave up the struggle and applied for government aid, it is important to consider the linear vision of progress found among settler generations in Las Cañadas. One of the clearest examples thereof I came across in the words of Marcelino, a man in his seventies, whom I interviewed when staying in San Emiliano as a human rights observer in 1997. His narrative about the evolution his village has undergone over the past four decades casts a light on notions of progress prevalent among the settlers of Las Cañadas (see also Barmeyer 2003).

> Look, nothing of what you see now was here when the first of us arrived in this place. There was only *puro monte* [jungle] when we came here some forty years ago. There were ten of us, only men. Some of us had been felling caoba trees in the area before, so we knew there was good water here. We lived in simple shacks and it was hard work to fell the trees. There were wild animals, disease, and the atrocious heat, which we weren't used to; one of us died of snakebite. The women were still in Lumsíc, the village up the valley where we were born. It took two years before we had the first milpas prepared and our wives began to move down here. There was no church here then, nothing, just the ejido.
>
> Things have become much better since then. First, people from the North came here and brought us *la religión*. We walked all the way to Ocosingo to buy our *santo* [patron saint]. This is when we built our humble church. More people moved here and San Emiliano became a *colonia* [settlement]. When the asesores [Maoist advisors] came here twenty-five years ago, they opened the eyes and ears of the people in the village. They

taught us Spanish as well as to read and write so we could petition for land in Tuxtla Guiterrez, which we needed so our grown sons could feed their families.

Now that there is a road here and we have electricity, San Emiliano has finally turned into a *mero pueblo* [proper village]. If people are sick, they can travel to the hospital in Altamirano. Things here have gotten much better. All we need now is for everybody to have their own car.

(Marcelino in San Emiliano, interview, February 1997)

Their rebellion was seen by many Zapatistas as a means to take part in the development that other parts of the country seemed to be experiencing, an inclusion they felt they had hitherto been denied. For most of them, indigenous autonomy, and particularly independence from bad governance, manipulation, and neglect, remained an important goal. However, as continued affiliation with the Zapatista struggle increasingly looked like a dead end on the road to progress, many of the poverty-stricken families of Las Cañadas came to regard it as secondary.

The self-perception of being poor was an integral part of Zapatista discourse justifying the uprising and the austere life one had to endure in a base community in resistance. For people to stick with the guerrilla organization, though, this perception had to be replaced or at least balanced by another self-perception along the lines of "we are enjoying the fruits of our struggle and our hard-earned autonomy." In many places, this balance has tipped, motivating people to leave the EZLN. Accordingly, those who were less integrated into the organizational fabric of the EZLN's support base were eventually drawn by the lure of government development programs. Once they opted for schools, clinics, and financial and material aid, as well as a different self-image as the ones who *were* included in the development that other parts of Mexico experienced, hitherto unanimous Zapatista communities lost their cohesion and divided. When, as in the case of San Emiliano, resources such as the forest were involved, this even led to exploitation of limited goods that might have been regarded as a respected treasure in a situation characterized by political unity.

Over the period in which the conflicts in San Emiliano and La Gardenia unfolded, I also visited the rebel village of 29 de Febrero, helping out in the construction of a drinking water system there. Although the community was situated outside of the Las Cañadas/Selva Lacandona regions, on terrains spontaneously invaded by local landless in the months following the uprising (see chapter 2), it had undergone a similar development. To increase their chances to hold on to the land, the squatters had joined the EZLN in spring 1994 and got together with other Zapatista villages in the region to found their own autonomous municipality. When the policies of la resistencia came into effect, however, the original settler population dramatically dwindled from forty to thirteen families. As most of those who left the guerrilla organization returned to live in town where many still had a small house, lengthy scenarios of intracommunal conflict that are possibly awaiting San Emiliano and La Gardenia were avoided.

Due to the relatively loose ties to the guerrilla movement, the exodus from the EZLN not only occurred earlier and took place quicker here, but infrastructural incentives, a government school or a clinic, were obviously not regarded as worthwhile (and cost-effective) counterinsurgency measures by the state either. One of our local contacts in 29 de Febrero, Gualterio, told me how entire communities had left the EZLN in the hope to get electricity installed in their villages. "But imagine, they didn't get any! The officials in town knew that these people had been Zapatistas. When they applied for a power line, the government told them to get lost." Some subsequently decided to rejoin the guerrilla movement. As a punishment, each repentant returnee was publicly shamed by having to work three days for other Zapatista communities. "After all, this is not a game we're playing here," Gualterio concluded.

CHAPTER FIVE

Global Networks, Local Impacts

The Transformation of NGO Involvement in Chiapas

The following pages focus on post-1994 NGO activities in Chiapas, as well as on the creation of the EZLN's own project coordinating body, Enlace Civil. There is a description of the peace camps, which have become crucial both for the Zapatistas' protection from attack and for introducing a growing number of solidarity activists to rebel communities. After making first contact as campamentistas, many activists have returned to Chiapas to work as volunteers for a number of local NGOs that were founded in the late 1990s. Some of these NGOs have specialized in the provision of basic infrastructure; they will be discussed in detail. Most financing for such projects comes from abroad, raised either by solidarity groups or larger international NGOs (INGOs) that provide funding for grassroots organizations around the globe. The chapter concludes by tracing the changing relationship between the EZLN and NGOs that resulted in only those organizations that adapted to emerging Zapatista policies remaining in rebel territory.

Coordinating Solidarity

In the decade preceding the 1994 uprising, about a dozen nongovernmental organizations had their operational base in Chiapas. They were run by local activists in the urban centers, particularly in San Cristóbal. Their operations spanned a broad spectrum, ranging from the delivery of secondhand clothing, food, and medicine to the training of health and human rights promoters and the establishment of rural production collectives.[1] Immediately after the Zapatista rebellion, these groups founded CONPAZ (Coordination of Nongovernmental Organizations for Peace) to coordinate the multitude of NGOs that converged in Chiapas responding to media images of the war and a call from the EZLN (1994d). Over the following three years, CONPAZ played an important part in monitoring the human rights situation and broadcasting information from Chiapas while continuing to run similar projects as those that had been going on for a decade. Whereas most San Cristóbal–based organizations had moved away from imposed charity and toward community-run projects, many newcomers were less progressive. Particularly some of the INGOs that had been swept into Chiapas on the wake of the 1994 rebellion entertained the idea that the decisions of what project was to be implemented where and how had to be made by outside "experts," some of whom had never even been in rural Chiapas.

From the beginning, the administration of CONPAZ was taken over by a few individuals who lost touch with the organization's base, which had no control over their actions. That way a lot of money ended up within the management structures instead of going directly to projects in the communities. Dissatisfaction among its base and in the villages where projects were run brought the swift demise of CONPAZ. By the end of 1996, internal squabbles within the NGO alliance reached a level that prompted the EZLN to initiate the founding of Enlace Civil. This new Civil Link organization took on the tasks of coordinating many solidarity projects from abroad. Both organizations existed side by side for a couple of months but after a brief period of power struggles, CONPAZ eventually dissolved in early 1997.

Unlike its predecessor, Enlace Civil maintained direct links with the EZLN's command structure. Instead of offering ready-made projects, it took up requests by indigenous communities and coordinated the offers for aid and cooperation by national and international solidarity groups. An important element of the new setup was the establishment of partnerships (*hermanamientos*) between Zapatista communities and labor syndicates, football teams, student groups, or whole municipalities.[2] The partnership was to be reciprocal with each side answering to calls of their partners, be it by raising funds for the purchase of tools or building materials or by publicly denouncing military incursions and exerting pressure on the respective authorities (Enlace Civil 2000).[3]

Figure 13: This former U.S.-American school bus had been donated to the Aguascalientes of Francisco Gomez, which used it to operate its own bus link between Ocosingo and San Quintin, February 1997. Photo by author.

Due to the broad media coverage of the uprising, and its motives and achievements, combined with the generally sympathetic image of the indigenous Maya struggling for dignity, countless activist groups in the "developed world" focused their solidary attention on the Zapatistas. The main support came from the metropoles in the north of the Mexican Republic but also from Europe, principally Catalonia and the Basque country in the Spanish State, as well as Italy, Ireland, Germany, Britain, France, Austria, and Switzerland; from the United States; and from South American states such as Argentina and Chile. Quite a few solidarity groups were brought to life by enthusiastic individuals in the context of the Meetings against Neoliberalism and for Humanity in Europe and Latin America, which the EZLN initiated in 1996. For some, these events marked the beginning of a long career in international activism. The initial range of activities included demonstrations and pickets in front of a Mexican embassy, information events, fund-raising parties, and the organization of preparatory workshops for human rights activists.

Although some solidarity groups dissolved after exhausting themselves in weekly discussions, those that remained active usually managed to establish direct and lasting ties to Chiapas. They got involved in intercultural and material exchanges with indigenous communities by sending volunteers and receiving delegates or by donating educational and technological equipment and buying coffee or crafts produced in the rebel municipalities. These groups often cooperated with local pro-Zapatista NGOs operating from Chiapas and supported them by providing funding as well as volunteers. Over the past fourteen years, there has been an ebb and flow of solidarity activism, with each new wave accompanying the EZLN's political campaigns. Generally, there was a steady decline in activities since the 1998 Intergalactic Meeting in Spain with a reinvigoration of the activist scene in the run-up to the 1999 Consulta, which culminated in the February 2001 march on Mexico City. Frequent media coverage of the Zapatista caravan to the capital rekindled interest, which again dwindled in the two years of self-declared silence that followed the failure to achieve the ratification of the San Andrés Accords. The elaborate inauguration of the Caracoles (the regional administrative centers) served to reinvigorate existing solidarity structures and the initiation of La Otra Campaña and the events that accompanied it (such as the government crackdowns in San Salvador Atenco and Oaxaca) led to the creation of solidarity groups by a new generation of activists. Their work has become crucial for the Zapatista project and in 2004 amounted to Mex$12 million (US$1.2 million) annually for the financial contributions alone (Marcos 2004; Gerber 2005, 158). In the same year, four and a half thousand people from over thirty countries visited the Caracol of Oventic. Many of them were solidarity activists who also lent their workforce to the Zapatista project (Muñoz Ramírez 2004).

Getting in Touch: Hands-on Experience in the Communities

A *campamento de paz* run by the Fray Bartolomé Human Rights Center in San Cristóbal was the setting of my first field research in rebel territory. As I believe that institution to be key for creating and maintaining the Zapatistas' strong ties to civil society that have enabled their independence from the Mexican State, I include a detailed description here. In the aftermath of the devastating 1995 army raid, so-called peace camps were set up in some fifty indigenous communities affected by army incursions and paramilitary violence. The first request for human rights observers was made when mostly Zapatista refugees returned to their villages in March 1995. By mid-April of the same year, nineteen camps had been set up by CONPAZ. In 2001, about forty communities hosted such camps; they were run both by the catholic San Cristóbal diocese and by Enlace Civil (CORSAM 2001).

The idea behind the camps was to provide protection through the presence of foreigners, including nonindigenous Mexicans. Housed in a simple hut and equipped with a camera, campamentistas remained in the respective village for at least ten days. They appeared whenever a military convoy or any other suspicious vehicle passed through, making it clear to soldiers and paramilitaries that any human rights violations would be documented. Especially during the first years, the conditions for becoming a campamentista were minimal to ensure a continuous flow of volunteers. All that a prospective human rights observer needed was a basic knowledge of Spanish and an official looking letter of reference from a civil society organization. By the turn of the millennium, requirements had become more rigorous. In many of the activists' home countries, organizations had sprung up that dedicated themselves to recruiting and preparing potential volunteers by way of informational seminars and workshops. The bulk of Mexican peace observers were students, often affiliated with one of the university sections of the Zapatista Front of National Liberation (FZLN) in the universities of the capital.[4] In the late 1990s, the EZLN introduced a maximum stay of six weeks due to problems caused by foreigners who had become residents in the villages. Some had stayed on for a year or longer and had established personal relationships that benefited individuals rather than the community as a whole.

After a two-day introductory workshop to acquaint the peace activists with the history of the uprising and the rules of conduct in indigenous communities, the volunteers were sent off into the "conflict zone." The respective location depended on the current needs

Figure 14: Campamentistas, such as these at the entrance to the Aguascalientes of Francisco Gómez (La Garrucha), have become a common sight in many Zapatista villages. The sign reads, "Welcome to Zapatista Rebel Territory," December 1996. Photo by author.

of the communities rather than on individual preferences. Once in the village, the campamentistas were accommodated in a hut with cooking facilities and a place to string up a hammock. The villagers took turns in providing their guests with tortillas in return for their human rights work, which consisted mostly of hanging out in front of the campamento while observing passing vehicles and taking note of any incidents. These notes were the base for a report, which every campamentista was required to write concluding their stay; it was filed as a reference to help the Human Rights Center and Enlace Civil keep track of army movements and conflict in the communities. Sometimes, long-term peace campers were invited to help in the fields or to work as a teacher. Thus, a U.S.-American peace camper I spoke to was asked by the local educational promoters of Roberto Barrios to give them English lessons so that they could compete with government teachers.

Before the introduction of the six-week maximum, campamentistas often stayed for several months at a time and were integrated into community life.

In the Aguascalientes or in villages particularly affected by army repression such as Polhó and Amador Hernández, peace camps were staffed by several people at once who were replaced every few weeks. This fluctuation made it harder to get in touch with the locals. When I visited the Aguascalientes La Garrucha in October 2000, campamentistas were confined to the area hosting the school, clinic, and administrative buildings. After five years of peace campers passing through their village, the locals had become used to the sight of internationals, even if they sported exotic and colorful hairdos. People took less notice of me here than they would have in front of a Mexico City hostel. If locals entered the peace camp, it was usually the campamento's caretakers or a group of men wanting to speak casually to a foreign woman. New peace camps were set up in Los Altos due to the increase in paramilitary violence there. Over the years, however, many Zapatista communities in Las Cañadas decided against the camps because the visitors' presence was only sporadic and caused communal conflict as factional splits became the norm in the late 1990s.

At the turn of the millennium, peace camps still were the first port of call for many solidarity activists in pursuit of hands-on experience in Chiapas. However, more and more people embarked on their venture into rebel territory as volunteers for an NGO project. Over the years of running the campamentos, Enlace Civil and the Fray Bartolomé Human Rights Center had devised a set of procedures that were to ensure smooth operation. Thus, peace campers were expected to have a basic knowledge of Spanish, a certain level of training in conflict resolution, and were allowed to stay only for six weeks. Requirements for becoming a project volunteer were still rather informal and contacts to the activist scene tended to be more important than experience. Whereas experience, skill, and particularly contacts to the *comandancia* (central command of the EZLN) were a prerequisite for *running* an NGO in rebel territory, the smooth operation of the projects required volunteers who felt honored to take part in a clandestine enterprise, did not ask too many questions, and got on with their job. The actual work depended on the respective NGO and was geared to either support-ing production collectives, rights promoters, autonomous education, and an independent health system, or providing basic infrastructure. Volunteers became part of a team, left for a remote village at night, and joined the local Zapatistas for weeks of hard work. The teams usually stayed in the respective villages, where they strung their ham-mocks under a tin roof and received tortillas from community mem-bers. In return for their efforts, they got to know a new world and were rewarded with the respect and gratitude of the local population.

Appropriate Technology NGOs

The project volunteers represented a further step on the scale of logisti-cal aides for the Zapatistas' efforts to consolidate their independence from the Mexican State. They were flexible and worked without pay, and their time in the communities was usually too brief to cause a stir. Their organization in teams also meant that their actual workforce was subject to tighter controls and could be used more economically than that of the campamentistas. The two NGOs that I had the pleasure of working for during the time of my research relied heavily on vol-unteers. They both concentrated on the provision of drinking water by way of what has become known as Appropriate Technology (AT). As the majority of technological innovation occurs in industrialized countries and the resulting technologies are neither affordable nor appropriate for people in the developing world, a new approach toward technology was needed to bridge the gap between the capital-intensive and profit-oriented technologies of the "West" and the traditional sub-sistence technologies of developing countries. Appropriate Technology achieves this by using local materials, skills, and labor to enable people with few resources to work their own way out of poverty. By definition, AT is adaptable to a variety of situations and uses, and can be produced in a small workshop and maintained by relatively unskilled commu-nity members; existing skills and knowledge are incorporated into the training, thus fostering self-reliance, local autonomy, and community initiative (SEVA 2002; ITDG 2003).

The San Cristóbal–based NGOs TENAZAS and SHOXEL were specialized in improving health and hygiene in Zapatista villages by employing the basic tenets of AT.[5] Since their founding by international activists in 1996, both groups have focused on building drinking water systems by providing technical advice, logistics, and material for the communities. With regard to basic infrastructure, the situation of indigenous villages that had taken part in the rebellion was generally bleak. In the new Zapatista settlements built on recuperated land there was no infrastructure whatsoever and the need for clean water was particularly pressing. Building water systems in these locations was a prerequisite of rendering them inhabitable in the long term.

The construction process was usually accompanied by training community members to ensure that they knew about water hygiene practices and could repair their cistern themselves. In the context of an integrated approach on preventative health, locals were taught about the causes of waterborne diseases and their treatments, nutrition in general, local medicinal plants, and the basics of allopathic medicine. Due to local necessities, TENAZAS and SHOXEL also began installing dry-compost latrines and low-smoke stoves, and organized community health workshops with a special focus on training indigenous women in reproductive health and herbal medicine. As one of SHOXEL's project coordinators told me, an ulterior motive of this was to provide the women with specialist knowledge to improve their position in patriarchal village hierarchies. In addition to the provision of basic infrastructure, there were occasional donations of money to Zapatistas held in the Chiapas state prison of Cerro Hueco and to various community-run projects. One of the water teams had taken to supplying media such as murals and a mobile cinema.[6] To support the communication of political and social messages to the outside world, the team provided paint and brushes, so the indigenous communities could create their own murals. However, often it was the activist volunteers who ended up painting the icons of the Zapatista revolution at the villagers' request. The idea behind the mobile cinema was to show a variety of social and political documentaries and feature films that people in remote indigenous communities would otherwise not get to see. Examples included reports on the latest Zapatista campaigns, documentaries on 9/11 or the war in Iraq, but also movie classics in which the good guys fight against the system, such as *The*

Matrix, *Robin Hood*, and—due to a growing number of indigenous aficionados—anything starring Bruce Lee.

As many other local NGOs involved with the rebels, the water teams kept a low profile about their affiliation with Zapatista communities. Volunteers and salaried staff lived in the villages while working there in exchange for tortillas and beans. The long-term staff members were in it with their heart and soul. The salary they received from donor organizations was nothing compared to what they could have earned elsewhere and their personal commitment was exemplary. For example, a Mexican coordinator for a San Cristóbal–based water team used the money left over from his salary at the end of the month to buy tools that otherwise would have had to be paid for by the limited project funds. To cut down on overhead costs, some of the long-term workers did without any salary and financed themselves by way of stipends from charity foundations or by working in the United States for half of the year.

Marketing the Zapatista Project

Where does the money come from that funds new water systems, textile workshops, rice husking machines, and coffee roasters? Who pays for the infrastructure that has made the de facto Zapatista autonomy possible, the manifestations of which can be seen throughout eastern Chiapas? Although local efforts to provide material and labor are not to be discounted, at the time of my research a substantial amount of support for the Zapatista autonomy project did come from outside the EZLN's base communities. A good part of support was mustered in nationwide campaigns by the branches of the FZLN and from within national university campuses, but particularly the cash needed for infrastructural, commercial, educational, and health-related development projects was procured abroad, mainly in North America and Europe. Like TENAZAS and SHOXEL, most local activist NGOs did not generate their own funds but relied on money from North American INGOs and European solidarity groups to finance their engagement in Chiapas.

Parallel to the formation of networks among NGOs and solidarity groups in the mid-1990s, a division of labor occurred whereby mostly smaller organizations with strong community ties began cooperating with larger organizations and international solidarity groups. The small NGOs often had local origins, were run by people sympathetic to the Zapatista cause, and worked in the provision of basic infrastructure, the support of production collectives, or the training of health and rights promoters. The funding for these projects frequently came from multiple sources, including international solidarity groups. Often, however, a large proportion of the money was provided by one or more INGOs based in North America. Such organizations provide funding for projects located in the hot spots of war and marginalization all around the globe. To generate the money to finance local NGOs, they use the profiles of the projects they implement. International solidarity groups, on the other hand, raise funds for their own projects and send delegations of volunteers to the communities where they are run. After several weeks of labor, the volunteers return to inform the group back home of the progress and to organize events to keep up the funding.

In his comparative study on strategies of the indigenous people in eastern Chiapas and of those in the Niger Delta, Bob (2005) states that the Zapatistas had to market themselves to survive. Although this was an important objective of the rebels, the author bases some of his assertions on false assumptions. His claim that the Zapatistas have orchestrated their campaigns "all with the aim of maintaining their visibility" is as incorrect as the statement that "before the rebellion, NGOs had neglected the plight of Mexico's poor and indigenous" (175–76). This ignores the significant NGO presence in Chiapas before the uprising, on the experience and contacts of which newcomers were able to build. In his analysis, the author also overlooks the vast number of supporters who are not organized in conventional NGO structures and are involved for reasons that exclude material gain. Nevertheless, Bob convincingly analyzes the Zapatistas' success in framing their movement for international audiences by way of articulating their struggle in global terms, as they did with their initial reference to NAFTA. However, the marketing strategies applied by organizations affiliated with the Zapatistas are a much more complex affair. The ways in which the rebels are portrayed by international NGOs, forming one end of the supply chain that makes the Zapatista autonomy project possible, varies greatly. INGOs funding groups like TENAZAS and SHOXEL do not make any direct references to the EZLN in their online profiles and shroud their revolutionary clients with the inconspicuous veil of "indigenous communities in need." Organizations specialized in selling the Zapatistas' products, on the other hand, have taken to using the rebels as a logo. In between these two extremes there is a range of nuances.

Apart from the relatively low-key and almost clandestine support of rebel communities through projects managed by Enlace Civil and the often equally hushed financing by INGOs, some organizations have used the Zapatista allusion to appeal to broad segments of mainstream society. Organizations such as Global Exchange (GE) or the Human Bean Company share the feature of marketing the Zapatistas as a label for their product, be it an adventure trip or roasted espresso beans. The Human Bean Company and smaller solidarity organizations such as Café Libertad have exported coffee from Zapatista producers at fair-trade conditions, providing them with a much-needed economic base. Global Exchange and Schools for Chiapas (SFC) have channeled volunteer workers and funding to the EZLN's base communities by employing a type of "package zapatourism."

SFC recruits people for caravans to Oventic to support the local Zapatista secondary school—until 2004 the only autonomous secondary school in rebel territory. To finance the school, the NGO had helped to set up the Institute for Mayan Languages, where visiting students from all over the world—but mostly from the United States—study Tzotzil and Spanish as well as the history of the Zapatista struggle (Muñoz Ramírez 2004). International students are put up in "rustic lodgings" and have plenty of opportunity to practice as they "work and play" with the locals. Prices for courses vary according to the student's country of origin and amount to three days of the respective minimum wage (i.e., US$144 in the United States and Mex$250 in Mexico) (Schools for Chiapas 2001). To reach a broad spectrum of clients, sympathies for the rebels are often displayed in a veiled form. On SFC's Web site, communities organized in the EZLN are referred to merely as "the Maya people" and the struggle for autonomy as "returning to the

roots of Maya culture, rescuing lost ceremonies, and studying democratic community practices."[7]

Based in San Francisco, Global Exchange runs campaigns against
unjust trade policies and human rights violations while promoting
humane, environmentally sensitive alternatives. GE's "reality tours"
mean to provide U.S. citizens with an understanding of a country's
internal dynamics through socially responsible travel. The cost of a
one-week tour to Chiapas amounts to US$750 excluding plane fares
but including accommodation, meals, and local transportation. GE's
Web site brochure for Chiapas reads as follows:

> Dialogue with indigenous peasants who have been working for
> the right to own the land upon which they live and work, and
> govern their communities according to indigenous traditions
> and customs. . . .
> - Travel to a highland community to meet and talk with
> members of a successful women's cooperative.
> - Learn about indigenous organizations specialized in bio-
> diversity and medicinal value of local plant life. Make a site
> visit to projects.
> - Meet with internally displaced people living in temporary
> encampments.
> - Participate in a discussion with indigenous representa-
> tives to discuss land issues, their struggles, and their culture.
> - Celebrate the history and the beauty of the people of
> Chiapas with the other trip participants and new friends in
> Mexico.

(Global Exchange 2002)

Reality tours made up half of the financing of GE's San Cristóbal
branch. They also covered the salary for members of human rights
centers or local NGOs such as CIEPAC, Alianza Cívica, or COMPITCH,
which all give talks to the visitors.[8]

International funding organizations raise money by "selling" projects of small NGOs in the developing world to their relatively well-off

urban donors. They recruit professionals such as doctors, educators, and engineers, who often serve as volunteers. The projects and their staff usually stay in a particular region for a limited time and leave behind trained locals to continue the work. Supporters can "adopt" a volunteer whose work they finance. The SEVA Foundation serves as a good example for funding project-providing NGOs in developing countries. According to the Web site of the Berkeley-based organization, SEVA has built partnerships for international health in India, Nepal, Tibet, Guatemala, Mexico, and in native communities in the United States (2001). Its programs are about restoring eyesight, fighting against disease, promoting sustainable agriculture, and helping communities to support themselves economically. In response to the suffering caused by human rights violations in Guatemala and Chiapas, SEVA initiated a program of refugee protection and accompaniment. The INGO began funding or partly funding local NGOs in Mexico in 1997. According to a SEVA worker, the foundation stands out for its low percentage of overhead costs characterized by "even the board of directors only taking very little money for themselves."[9] In the United States, an organization is allowed to label itself nonprofit only if its overhead costs are below 40 percent of the total turnover. The overhead costs of large INGOs such as Greenpeace, Amnesty International, or Americas Watch often approach that margin. SEVA's financial statement for the year 1999/2000 states an annual turnover of just less than US$3.5 million, from which about US$2.3 million was listed as "contributions." A total of US$3 million was classified as "expenditures," of which US$2.5 million went into "program services," presumably flowing directly into the projects benefiting people in indigenous communities. Only US$0.5 million went into "support services," of which US$353,000 was used to pay for "management and general," and about US$118,000 was spent on "fund raising" (SEVA 2002). This left SEVA with relatively low overhead costs of about 16 percent.

At the beginning of the twenty-first century, SEVA was one of several organizations that funded pro-Zapatista NGOs based in San Cristóbal. They trained and coordinated Mexican volunteers, installed basic infrastructure in indigenous Zapatista villages, and gave workshops in herbal medicine aimed at empowering indigenous women.

In the case of a local water team—although not the one detailed in chapter 7—the funding by SEVA amounted to US$10,000 annually. This covered the materials needed to construct two medium-size water systems. A large part of SEVA's money was generated by fund-raising events such as benefit concerts, and from a fund set up by the Buddhist Guru Ram Dass. As a side effect of the division into funding organizations and local project-providing NGOs, the ideological approaches of the organizations, and particularly the individuals involved, could differ substantially. Thus, donor organizations that channeled funds to Chiapas had a broad base among urban liberals or Christian congregations in the United States who adhered to a moderate humanist approach toward development, while the people running local projects in Zapatista base communities sought to support and further revolutionary social change.

Bringing Project Management Home

In the mid-1990s, widely known Zapatista strongholds like La Garrucha or La Realidad were literally inundated with well-meaning project offers designed by outsiders. In time, many of these ventures were abandoned or transformed into projects that the communities in question considered more suitable. The case of La Semillita del Sol (Little Seed of the Sun) is exemplary for this development. The following section illustrates the evolution that this initially Italian solidarity project underwent as it was confronted with the real needs of the local population. Conceived in April 1995 by the Italian solidarity group Tatanka, Semillita was one of the first international projects in rebel territory. The venture took place in the Zona Selva Tojolabal and was laid out for a period of five years. The idea was to further the self-esteem of 275 children in the communities of San José del Rio and Nueva Guadalupe Tepeyac by way of artistic expression, to give back a bit of "true childhood" to those traumatized by the 1995 army raid. The children were also to be taught about their rights, hygiene, nutrition, and the environment. The project aimed at being self-sustainable by recruiting its teachers and their trainers from the respective communities. The first step consisted in setting up workshops for painting, making pottery, and sculpting. Artistic material was to be sent from Italy.

Exhibitions and sales of art produced by the indigenous children were to finance the project. The substantial sum of US$124,437 that Tatanka had raised by October 1996 gives an idea of the sort of money people in Italy were willing to invest in such projects (Tatanka 1998).

A progress report of autonomous education in Chiapas (Enlace Civil 2002b) sketches out the transformation Semillita had undergone in the first seven years of its existence. After their children had taken art classes for six months, the people of San José del Rio expressed the wish for their offspring, whose formal education had been cut short by the rebellion, to learn how to read and write. In response, four educational promoters were provided by Enlace Civil and within a year, another four Zapatista communities requested a school. Due to lacking human resources on the part of Tatanka, the Zapatista villages in the region set up training centers for their own community teachers. By 1997, the first of these centers operated in San José del Rio. A year later, another was built in the Zona Norte and a third in 2002 in the Zona Selva Tzeltal. What had begun as a well-meant bohemian imposition by outsiders was eventually appropriated by the local population. With the support of Enlace Civil they converted the project to address and resolve their needs on the ground.

Such transformations—which took place throughout rebel territory at the time—were accompanied by structural changes in the autonomous administration. From their creation in December 1994 onward, the Zapatista municipalities had gained ever more significance. With councils of elected representatives, a new civilian control structure emerged that began paralleling the EZLN's military hierarchy. This not only introduced more democracy into the ways decisions were made in general but it was also a move toward indigenous project management. By way of village assemblies and the election of delegates, all adult Zapatistas in a given autonomous municipality had a say in choosing if, how, and where a clinic or a water system was to be built. Nevertheless, this process was still slowed down by red tape and the need for approval from the EZLN command for any project to get underway.

In the late 1990s, Zapatista communities also created their own organizations such as the Mut Vitz coffee cooperative and the regional producer association Yaxal Chi (Tzeltal for Green Stag) to manage development projects and coordinate the export of their products.[10] The building of autonomous municipal structures and the creation of communal cooperatives was paralleled by specialization and division of labor within the NGO sector. As small local organizations concentrated on running workshops and building water systems, they left the funding to larger INGOs and international solidarity groups. To complement this development, some specialized in recruiting and preparing volunteers. In a further adaptation to local needs, the organization GANAS was founded in 2000 in San Cristóbal.[11] With its objective to support Zapatista communities in their struggle for autonomy, the group promoted the involvement of Mexican nationals in solidarity projects. It recruited primarily students from Mexico City and provided them with lodging, training, and contacts to rebel communities.[12] The volunteers had to commit themselves for at least three months and were introduced to pro-Zapatista development organizations based in San Cristóbal. They then joined projects engaged in the support and provision of basic necessities, education, media, accompaniment, and human rights defense. The idea was to establish a growing network of volunteers who, upon their return home, would educate and inform others, thus ensuring a continuing flow of Mexican volunteers for local solidarity projects. Solidarity groups such as CAREA in Germany or CORSAM in Switzerland paralleled GANAS as recruitment agencies by training and supplying volunteers. This pool of flexible and unsalaried project workers was a prerequisite for local NGOs and activist solidarity groups to be cost-effective and thus more attractive for international funding organizations.

A decisive factor for continuing cooperation with the Zapatistas was the NGOs' concession to transfer responsibility to local councils and to integrate individual projects into larger schemes associated with the autonomy project. Just as crucial was a good rapport with key figures in the EZLN's command structure. By the new millennium, only those NGOs who agreed to work with the Zapatistas on their terms—and this refers not only to the civilian authority structure but also to the military one—were allowed to continue their work in rebel territory. Without exception, these were people and groups whom

Zapatista key figures considered to be *de confianza* (of confidence), implying that they were predictable with regard to their commitment toward the project as well as to the Zapatista cause. Solidarity activists had an important part in this process. Through contacts they had made during earlier visits to Chiapas, committed graduate students and urban professionals from North America or Europe secured themselves a place in the activist hierarchy: campamentista to volunteer to funded NGO worker to salaried project coordinator. Moving upward from one NGO to the next, these dedicated individuals managed to attain positions within local NGO structures that provided them with a material base for survival in Mexico and allowed them to influence local organizational policies. They created new projects in line with the Zapatista autonomy project and channeled funds from their home countries to Chiapas. The installation of basic infrastructure on recuperated lands by SHOXEL and TENAZAS serves as an example for the success of this "joint venture" between international activists and local Zapatistas. In the course of this development, the contrast between funding organizations and local NGOs has become more salient. INGOs sponsoring these projects do not usually mention the role they have in the Zapatista autonomy project; information on their Web sites is limited to general statements about alleviating poverty and fostering community autonomy. Local NGOs on the other hand recruit their volunteers by explicitly referring to the Zapatista struggle they support with their work. A progressive attitude by project managers toward indigenous autonomy, however, has not kept some of them from using idealized notions of community and images of the indigenous Other as an endangered species when recruiting sponsors and volunteers from an international audience.[13]

In spite of all the advances Zapatista communities have made in past years, "autonomous development" has been achieved at the cost of new dependencies. At the time of my research, this structural weakness was manifest in the fact that none of the local NGOs were able to do without international volunteers. Mexicans with enough time and money to lend a hand for free were simply harder to come by than enthusiastic students and nonconformist professionals from North America and Europe. How much has yet to be done in the way of integration is evident in the sheer number of NGOs in Chiapas that are run by internationals. It is still them and not Mexicans, much less local Indígenas, who have the necessary connections to wealthy individuals and fund-raising agencies to muster the financial support necessary to make any costly infrastructural development project possible.

A main drawback associated with the Zapatista municipal administration at the time of my research was centralism and the structural inequalities this entailed. Thus, the autonomous municipal seat received the bulk of aid and projects at the cost of communities in the periphery. The fact that small roadless villages in remote corners of the mountainous jungle were difficult to access aggravated this imbalance. This situation was by no means particular to the municipal structures introduced by the Zapatistas but was characteristic for the marginalization in the Las Cañadas/Selva Lacandona regions as a whole and one of the root causes for the uprising. But why was it reproduced by the Zapatista administration? This structural imbalance and traces of nepotism (outlined in chapter 8) may well be an indication that the autonomous districts consolidated in the late 1990s had difficulties shedding the menace of clientelism prevalent in the official municipalities. The 2003 attempt to strengthen civilian administration by creating the Juntas de Buen Gobierno (see chapter 3) addressed these problems. Whether it was successful in the long term remains to be seen.

On the whole, autonomous development has proven to be a better alternative to the PRONASOL schemes in the early 1990s. Although smaller in scale, the new projects have not served as inroads for government agents and although they do create dependency on outsiders, they have become increasingly community controlled. At the time of my research, project management was in the process of becoming an indigenous affair. In 2002, most ventures concerning education, production, and health were initiated and controlled by the rebel municipalities themselves; only the funding and some training was provided by outside agencies. The development of relations between NGOs and Zapatista base communities that I have sketched out so far finds its logical continuation in the situation that emerged toward the end of my research. Instead of disjointed projects being implemented in a select few communities, they were now more evenly distributed and displayed a deeper integration of locals. In a combined effort by Zapatistas and solidarity groups, a set of programs was conceived for the rebel municipalities that covered such diverse areas as the production and commercialization of agricultural produce, craft production collectives, and health and autonomous education. In its aim to achieve both economic and educational independence from the state and its institutions, this large-scale integrated approach was part of what local Zapatistas called "the second phase of the revolution."

CHAPTER SIX

The Second Phase of the Zapatista Revolution

Apart from the implementation of policies associated with la resistencia, the "second phase" of the Zapatista revolution involved the construction of self-sufficiency schemes in rebel municipalities, which aimed for an increase of autonomy from the state. This development began in 1998 and was characterized by Zapatistas' efforts to install their own institutions: an independent education system, autonomous public health services, and production collectives for coffee, textiles, and vegetables, as well as a network for the distribution of these products. This process was rather slow in getting started and was often stalled by widespread communal conflicts. When looking at developments in individual communities such as La Gardenia and San Emiliano, it appears that only after the communities had undergone division and the burned-out and dispirited were "purged" from Zapatista ranks, did ambitious community projects became once again possible. These achievements were closely linked to the growing involvement of NGOs in the region, outlined in chapter 5.

In addition to reviewing what I have learned in interviews with people working in the communities where self-sufficiency schemes were implemented, this chapter draws on accounts that were available in the media and on the Internet. These are detailed descriptions of the autonomous hospital school in San José del Rio (Enlace Civil 2001, 2002d), progress reports of agricultural production and trade projects run by the Zapatista base communities of La Garrucha and Roberto Barrios (Libertad Solidarity Group 2000, 2001), and a general overview of developments in all five Zapatista zones (Muñoz Ramírez 2004). After reviewing the areas of production and health, this chapter focuses on autonomous education. My data stems mostly from people involved in the Zapatistas' efforts to establish community schools, such as Cipriano's brother Blas, who has worked as an educational promoter in La Gardenia. The chapter concludes by showing how the EZLN's competition with the Mexican State manifests itself on the local level with regard to the issue of community schools.

Steps Toward Economic Independence

When visiting the Aguascalientes of Morelia for the 2001 New Year's celebrations, I was impressed by the facilities that allowed for the accommodation of hundreds of visitors. All guests stayed in a large fenced-in area with space for half a dozen buildings and a paved basketball court. The largest building was an auditorium with space for a packed audience of five hundred people. There was the peace camp with beds for a dozen foreign visitors, a dormitory, a kitchen, and sanitary facilities for hundreds of people from all over the region, who regularly came here to attend conferences and workshops on health and hygiene, gardening, or teacher training that took place on a daily basis. In addition, Morelia served as a hub for Zapatista campesinos from far and wide who borrowed the tractor and processed their coffee with the electric peeler and a large roasting machine. There were metal and wood workshops complete with tools, a concrete workshop for the production of dry-compost latrines, and finally a shoemaker's workshop. The latter produced all kinds of footwear for peasant farmers, insurgents, and solidarity activists who came to Morelia to buy their shoes. Prices ranged from Mex$120 (US$12) for a pair of sporty sneakers to Mex$150 (US$15) for proper army boots. Similar production facilities had sprung up in all Zapatista regional centers over the turn of the millennium. There were collectively run coffee plantations, countless gardens growing all types of vegetables, and even greenhouses to enable a year-round vitamin supply in high-altitude towns such as the Zapatista stronghold of Polhó. A range of manufacturing collectives run by men and women crafted boots, clothes, and candles for local as well as international customers. The products were sold in San Cristóbal's High Street shops catering for the conscientious tourist, or shipped directly to the United States or Europe to bring hard cash back to the remote communities.

When visiting Morelia more than two years later in 2003 for the fiesta celebrating the anniversary of Emiliano Zapata's death, I caught another glimpse of the efforts to boost local production. The Aguas-calientes was packed with a thousand people from all over the muni-cipality. Apart from villagers who had come for the party or the basketball and football tournaments, there was a conference of the municipality's youngsters that centered on the topic of autonomous production.[1] The meeting featured workshops ranging from concrete mixing to cooking and gave the 250 participants between the ages of fourteen and eighteen an opportunity for social mingling. Excitedly chattering, the young men and women filled the auditorium while the most industrious from their midst stood on a stage in front, speaking about the workshops they had attended and presenting the fruits of the day's efforts. The exhibits included jars of marmalade, loaves of bread, candles, and pieces of roasted chicken. The presentations were interspersed with musical performances and the reading of homemade poems on autonomy and the Zapatista struggle. At the conclusion of the evening, one of the organizers, a man in his late thirties who might well have been the autonomous municipality's representative, initiated the autocrítica (see chapter 3) by first outlining the importance of produc-tion for Zapatista autonomy and then embarking on a discourse about discipline. Due to the multiethnic makeup of the district, he addressed the crowd in Spanish so everyone could understand him. It soon became clear that he was scolding some of the youngsters who had not properly participated in the day's workshops. About ten people were singled out to come forward and explain their idleness. One of them was so ashamed that he could not even speak, but the others critically addressed their shortcomings in front of everyone and were rewarded with applause. Then all of the production teams came forward and publicly evaluated the day's work, at times also criticizing each other.

Following a directive from the EZLN's clandestine indigenous councils from the beginning of the millennium, a particular effort was made by all rebel municipalities to boost collective production. La Gardenia was no exception. After the fronts had become clear following years of intracommunal strife and insecurity, the Zapatista village assembly decided to process sugarcane into *panela* (dehydrated sugarcane juice). This particular project had been chosen because the region was rich in sugarcane and a lot of cash in the community was spent on buying sugar (at the rather high price of eight pesos a kilo). The aim was to become self-sufficient by selling the surplus at the town market and to their neighbors. The Program for Production and Commercialization implemented at the time of my research was meant to boost indigenous culture and rural development by strengthening the productive base of the indigenous communities in resistance. Thus, the program furthered microprojects through indigenous agricultural promoters in the Zona Norte while a schooling farm in the Zona Selva Tojolabal focused on sustainable management, the vaccination of cattle, and basic agrarian training. The cultivation of organic hibiscus in the Zona Norte combined ecological standards with agricultural techniques rooted in indigenous culture. The products were sold to local, national, and international customers while the financial management remained in the hands of community members. The sale of agricultural produce, wood, and crafts was to draw financial capital into the communities, enabling them to acquire much-needed goods and services. The development of a fair internal market was to generate further income for the local population, which could then be invested in projects concerned with education, health, human rights, and communication. The idea was to bring about an improvement of living conditions by boosting cooperation, democracy, and communal organization (Enlace Civil 2002c).

In the Zona Selva Tzeltal an association of Zapatista producers going by the name of Yaxal Chi (The Green Stag) coordinated their agricultural output, coffee exports, and support for autonomous education. One of the association's international donors, the Austrian solidarity group Libertad, meticulously kept track of Yaxal Chi's efforts to consolidate internal trading among the villages in the autonomous district of Francisco Gomez (Libertad Solidarity Group 2000). The original plan was to retain homegrown produce in the Zapatista communities by setting up a center for collection, dispersion, storage, and sale of basic goods. The community-run warehouse was to prevent coyotes (intermediary merchants) from buying products in one community and selling them in a neighboring one at extortionate prices. At the warehouse, Yaxal Chi's members could exchange their produce for goods from town, directly trade with others, or sell to the center at a fixed price. Any profits were to be used for the construction of community schools. The warehouse, however, was not built. Instead, the association acquired a truck to sell the maize, beans, or coffee produced in Yaxal Chi's member communities at the Ocosingo market. On its return journey, the truck brought essential goods such as sugar, soap, clothes, and tools back to the villages at wholesale prices. Although this outcome may indicate local aversions against stockpiling foods away from people's homes, it also shows that local management ensured the flexibility needed to arrive at a solution that suited everyone involved.

At the same time, private enterprise gained pace in Zapatista territory as individual entrepreneurs started to think about how to make most of the lands they had received as a reward for their efforts in the guerrilla. When visiting La Gardenia in January 2002, I spent time helping Sergio in his garden and he showed me his bananas, coffee, papayas, chayotes, beans, and sugarcane. Although he took part in the local Zapatista commercialization program aimed at collectively producing and marketing goods, he had his own plans about privately growing papaya and selling them to passing vehicles for personal profit.

Constructing an Independent Health System

The beginnings of autonomous health care in Chiapas go back to the early 1980s, when organized indigenous communities decided to stop using government health services. As an alternative, they collectively pooled their money to buy medicine and equipment and to pay for trips to a trustworthy Altamirano hospital that was run by nuns (Klein and Castro 2001). After the rebellion, some of the more accessible Zapatista villages started to receive medicine from urban solidarity groups, which also offered courses on acupuncture, medicinal plants, childbirth, and family planning. In the mid-1990s, there were only four doctors for each hundred thousand inhabitants in the indigenous zones of Chiapas. In the face of devastating sanitary conditions and a high occurrence of curable diseases, Zapatista efforts to build a health infrastructure focused on preventative medicine, community participation, and the training of local staff. In 1995, the construction of an autonomous health care system commenced with the election of health promoters in all participating villages. These promoters then attended workshops and shared their knowledge with community members, who helped them on their milpas in exchange for their services (Enlace Civil 2002d).

Yasmin, an educational promoter from Tierra Nueva whom I interviewed in November 2000, took part in a training program for the proliferation of medical knowledge. She told me that her parents had become involved in the Zapatistas' family planning scheme to keep the number of their children at five. Yasmin contrasted this to the situation of other families who had to feed ten and more children, a fact she pointed out as a cause for poverty. In rural Chiapas, where young women often get married at the age of fifteen, she regarded birth control and particularly the sterilization of both men and women as a viable solution for this problem. When I asked her about other methods of contraception, she told me that Zapatista communities associated the Pill and pills in general with the government and regarded them as dangerous and as a source of weakness; condoms were still seen as a curiosity rather than a contraceptive.

For lack of use, the condoms that international solidarity groups included in every aid shipment clogged up the shelves of the autonomous clinics. The account of Jocelyn, an NGO worker from Catalonia, hints at the difficulties of introducing condoms to indigenous communities, regardless of the progressive stance prevalent in the EZLN's public discourse on gender equality. In an effort to raise the issue of contraception, Jocelyn had tried to initiate an "extracurricular" workshop with her women's gardening group without informing the (male) village authorities. To make the exercise more effective, she asked the women to bring their husbands along, but the men refused, arguing that they preferred to discuss contraceptive methods with their spouses in private. When the workshop eventually took place, Jocelyn brought along a banana to illustrate the usage of condoms. As she took out the fruit and began applying the latex, the local women started screaming and insisted that the exercise should come to an immediate stop.

They contended that this was no matter to address in front of children of whom there were plenty in the room. It was eventually agreed that Jocelyn would show them how to use the condoms individually, but in the end only two women invited her home.

In the Zona Selva Tojolabal, the Zapatista health program centered on a hospital and a medical school in San José del Rio, a new Zapatista settlement in the La Realidad area where the EZLN's military central command has been stationed since 1994. The compounds were built and furnished by local Zapatistas who spent three years working on the site in rotating teams. Since 1999, the hospital has lent its services to 239 communities belonging to four autonomous municipalities (Enlace Civil 2002d). I learned from people working in San José del Rio that Indígenas, regardless of their political affiliation, came to seek medical advice and treatment in the clinic and were attended to there. An important aim of the medical school was to train health promoters in herbal treatments using endemic plants. Spreading the knowledge of "traditional" herbal medicine to their communities was to prevent outbreaks of disease and reduce the dependency on allopathic conventional drugs.

By 2001, the hospital in San José was operational. It comprised three patient rooms with three beds each and a separate room for quarantined patients. There was also a delivery room where births were attended to. Two consultancies for general health, a dental consultancy, and a lab for clinical analysis were run by local Indígenas who had been trained over a period of six months. An ambulance, too, was fully equipped and all three paramedics had obtained their driver's licenses. However, there were problems due to a lack of qualified personnel; two incubators and the surgery stood idle until August 2004. The hospital had a total staff of thirty-five full-time employees ranging from doctors to laboratory analysts, paramedics, and assistants to cleaning personnel. A council made up of representatives from all the communities taking part in the project oversaw the hospital's administration (2001). Unlike Zapatista teachers or the holders of positions in the autonomous administration who were not remunerated for their work, the full-time health workers in San José del Río did receive a salary of eight hundred pesos (eighty U.S. dollars) a month. Between 2001 and 2004, one hundred thousand pesos (ten thousand U.S. dollars) of solidarity contributions were used in this way (Muñoz Ramírez 2004).

The hospital in San José was one of two such institutions in Zapatista territory, the other one being La Guadalupana in Oventic. However, smaller clinics such as the one in La Garrucha—which took care of thirty patients per day—were equipped with laboratories that mainly carried out tests for malaria and tuberculosis. Each region counted on between seventy and three hundred health promoters, who took care of the Zapatista base population in their villages. It is noteworthy that in spite of there being relatively few female health promoters, women's participation in the Zapatista health sector was strong in traditional specialist professions. In the Zona Selva Tojolabal alone, three hundred female herb doctors, midwives, and bonesetters had been trained (2004).

Among indigenous Zapatistas, there was often a deep-seated suspicion toward government health services. The extent of this is illustrated by a report from Gem, an activist who accompanied a delegation from a San Cristóbal–based NGO to a politically divided community deep inside the Selva Lacandona. The village they visited in spring 2003 had just received a mass inoculation in the context of an official health program. The Zapatista faction, however, had refused to have their children inoculated for fear that they would be injected venom by the "government doctors." Believing they had an alternative, they waited for the scheduled visit of a solidarity group whom they confronted with the request for their own vaccinating session. However, due to bureaucratic and logistical obstacles faced by the overstretched capacities of Enlace Civil's San Cristóbal office, the venture had to be postponed until the establishment of a regional administration of aid and solidarity by the Juntas de Buen Gobierno (also see chapter 8). By 2004, the Zapatistas had initiated their own autonomous vaccination campaign against tetanus and typhoid. All families in Zapatista territory had received a health pass that allowed them free treatment at their local clinic or at any of the autonomous hospitals in Zapatista territory. The non-Zapatista population was also attended to in these clinics but they had to pay between Mex$10 and 25 (US$1.00–2.50) for their treatment (Muñoz Ramírez 2004).

Educación Autónoma

The concept of autonomous education receives mention on various Web sites concerned with pro-Zapatista solidarity—such as Schools for Chiapas—and particularly on the home page of Enlace Civil (2002a, 2002b). Accordingly, the Zapatistas devised their own educational organization to address the situation in Chiapas's indigenous communities, which were marked by an illiteracy rate of 54 percent above the age of fifteen. Other fundamental criticisms of the official school system range from absenteeism and alcohol abuse by government teachers to their interference in the communities' internal affairs, levying of compulsory fees, disrespect for indigenous language and culture, professional incompetence, corporal punishments, and sexual abuse. In contrast, the educational projects in Zapatista territory sought to integrate schooling with community life (2002b). Their objective was to promote and develop a participatory and inclusive educational system in line with the needs and demands expressed by the communities themselves. The new community schools were to be used as spaces for the generation of knowledge and collectivity to consolidate the process of autonomy and communal self-administration. However, due to the reliance on nonindigenous instructors to train the new community teachers, there was a high degree of dependency on outsiders.

Reports by the Austrian Libertad solidarity group relate the progress of a regional Zapatista education project in concrete terms (Libertad Solidarity Group 2000, 2001). The project was based in the Zapatista administrative region of Francisco Gómez and had started out with an ambitious aim: the creation of autonomous primary education based on indigenous traditions in about seventy villages. All decisions were to be made in cooperation with the communities' authorities based on the principle of consensus. For a period of two years, the project was to provide professional instructors who would train new teachers from within the communities. While still in training, these educational promoters (promotores de educación) were to hold lessons in ways that reflected their personal level of knowledge. It was planned for all families whose children went to the new community schools to support the teachers by taking turns working on their fields. The training

Figure 15: The Zapatista education project relied on solidarity activists who worked as community teachers and teacher trainers. During her social-service semester, this FZLN activist student from Mexico City employed the tenants of Paulo Freire's Popular Education when teaching children from Zapatista families how to read, May 1996. Photo by author.

of teachers from all over the region was to be continued by way of intensive workshops held at regular intervals (2000).

The observer's report a year into the project emphasizes the great enthusiasm on the part of the communities, but also states that the training team from Mexico City supplied neither the financial nor the human resources necessary to do justice to the demand for teachers and teaching materials (2001). At the time of the report, there were bimonthly courses for all community teachers from three rebel municipalities (Francisco Gómez, Francisco Villa, and San Manuel). The promoters and their trainers had just published a new edition of textbooks for mathematics and Spanish. In the observer's analysis, most of the difficulties to provide a well-balanced course program had their cause in the different educational backgrounds of the community teachers; although some had gone through secondary school, others were illiterate. As a reaction, the Zapatista educational commission made literacy training for the promoters a priority. Although it had originally been envisaged to finance all costs pertaining to autonomous education by the sale of coffee grown on communal plots, in 2001 the generated money was barely sufficient for the provision of teaching materials and transportation for the trainers from Mexico City. There were no funds left for further school construction or even for teachers' salaries.

At the time of my research, the curricular content and teaching practices associated with educación autónoma varied due to the broad range of experience by the teachers and teachers' trainers involved. Unless otherwise indicated, the information presented here relies on my own interviews, which I conducted with various actors involved in the autonomous education project between October 2000 and May 2002. During a visit to the Aguascalientes of Francisco Gómez in January 2001, I had the privilege to meet two FZLN activists from Mexico City who conducted a teacher-training course for the region's indigenous educational promoters. One of them was a young student adhering to the subculture of punk, the other a Montessori teacher in her fifties. In the interview, I learned that the teacher-training courses in the municipality of Francisco Gómez had commenced in mid-1999.[2] By January 2001, twenty-four such courses had been held. My interviewees confirmed that, at the time, there was no standardized curriculum in any of the autonomous districts and neither was there a universal ideology behind the concept of educación autónoma. They stated, however, that the trainers themselves were often influenced by various schools and educational concepts such as those of Maria Montessori or Paulo Freire. When asked in what way the content of educación autónoma differed from the material taught in government schools, I was told that the EZLN did not reject conventional teaching methods and content outright, but that anything considered to be either propaganda or not appropriate for indigenous campesinos was scrapped. Thus, official history books were rejected due to the alleged lies and omissions they contained. Official maths books, however, were used by the community teachers, even though some of the examples referring to city life were changed to a context understandable to the inhabitants of rural Chiapas. Teaching materials from Cuba or Sandinista Nicaragua were apparently not used.

In the autonomous primary schools in the municipality of Francisco Gómez, all subjects were taught by one teacher to a particular age group and only in the autonomous secondary school in Oventic did the teachers specialize on teaching individual subjects. La Garrucha's secondary school was still under construction at the time and stood empty for more than four years until it was finally inaugurated. By that time, secondary schools had also been built in seven autonomous municipalities belonging to the Zona Altamirano, overseen by the Junta de Buen Gobierno in Morelia (Bellinghausen 2004a; Muñoz Ramírez 2004). In 2004, autonomous education in this region was most advanced and the schools were best equipped with 280 *delegados* (community teachers) teaching a total of 2,500 pupils. Whereas most of the other four regions had one central teacher-training center situated in the respective Caracol, in the Morelia region there was one in each of the seven autonomous municipal seats. Educational committees of the respective autonomous regions devised the curriculum. In the Morelia region this consisted of the subjects of production, political education, arts, culture, reading and writing, health, sports, mathematics, history, and languages (both Spanish and the mother tongue) (Muñoz Ramírez 2004).

Catalan activists who worked as teachers in communities in the Zona Norte and the Zona Selva Tojolabal between 2000 and 2001 had told me about the existence of a similar range of subjects: languages, taught in Spanish and the respective indigenous language, mathematics, natural sciences with an emphasis on agroecology, history, and *integración*. Along the lines of Paulo Freire's principles of popular education, the subject of integración aimed at the political education of students in the context of the Zapatista struggle. The curriculum included the guerrilla movement's roots as well as its political aims and achievements. Each week there was a special focus on one of the EZLN's basic demands, as well as on contemporary issues such as the Plan Puebla Panamá. In a drive to boost local self-esteem, the base communities of the Zona Norte had compiled a history book focusing on their own origins. Whereas government schools in rural areas prepared students to leave their villages and continue going to school in town, educación autónoma placed particular emphasis on applied knowledge, such as the building and cultivation of gardens for medicinal herbs and vegetables. As communal authorities pointed out to me on several occasions, the idea was to enable the villagers to live and work in their communities in a better and more efficient way. Thus, the subject of agroecology dealt with "traditional" methods of making milpa, and covered practices such as permaculture and other organic farming methods. Apparently, this was already beginning to have an impact in the region around Roberto Barrios. Some Zapatista campesinos refrained from the traditional annual burning of their fields, and instead planted a vine after each harvest, which in spreading suffocated every other weed on the fallow milpa, enriching the ground with nutrients and nitrogen at the same time. As they also used it as a substitute for coffee, locals had breached international copyright laws and christened the plant *nescafé*.

The project of autonomous education required the teachers to be from the communities where they taught. Because most adults in the EZLN's base villages engaged in subsistence farming to feed their families, the only people available for the job were usually still in their teens. At the time of my research, educational promoters in Zapatista schools had an average of six months of NGO-assisted training behind them. Due to the high number of trainees, the workshops took place at all five Aguascalientes on a permanent basis and were conducted by solidarity activists who had a background in teaching themselves. In a May 2002 interview with a U.S.-American teacher trainer for natural sciences at the secondary school in the Zapatista stronghold of Oventic, where two hundred children from all over the region studied, I learned that most community teachers had completed only a year of secondary education themselves. Apparently, as many as 50 percent broke off their training within the first year, often because they started having a family of their own.

Yasmin, an educational promoter from Tierra Nueva, was only fifteen but already had worked in San Cristóbal as a medical assistant and translator for indigenous languages before taking on the cargo of teacher in her home community. There, she was in charge of about twenty children at the level of third- and fourth-grade primary school. The lessons she taught were indigenous history, the history of the EZLN, and the struggle for land and freedom, as well as the laws and workings of the new autonomous administration. Yasmin worked alongside four colleagues, two men and two women, who were in charge of an age level each. Lessons took place only three days a week to give the children a chance to participate in working in the fields and at home. Having gone through two years of secondary school, a lot by local standards, Yasmin had been elected to be a teacher trainer on top of her other chores. Apart from teaching didactic skills, Yasmin also taught future educational promoters about the uses of endemic medicinal plants. The workshops for new community teachers from all over the region were held at the autonomous municipal seat at regular intervals.

When I visited 29 de Febrero as an NGO volunteer in November 2001, fifteen boys and girls aged between six and twelve years attended the autonomous primary school in the center of the small village. Underneath a tin roof and inside of a fence, there were benches and a blackboard. Books and teaching materials were stored next to the basketball court in a small shack painted with the icons of the Zapatista revolution and emblazoned with the word *biblioteca* (library). It contained a dozen volumes of reference books ranging in topics from the animal world to human anatomy, a few dictionaries, and the Zapatista teaching materials. For each child there were two photocopied booklets compiled in the Aguascalientes of Morelia and Oventic. One consisted of songs, stories, and political discourse in Spanish; the other one was in Tzeltal and was made up of little stories and riddles. Both were about the history of the 1994 uprising and the Zapatista struggle, with the main points packed into little poems and songs, which the children learned to know by heart. They ranged from historical and legendary descriptions of the guerrilla movement's origins to the concrete demands and political slogans of recent times. Whenever we passed through the village on our way to have lunch, we could hear the children sing together at school and observe them march around on the basketball court. In the afternoon, the teacher played football and basketball with the older boys. He was a man of twenty-three from a village in the hills, several hours of walking distance away. There, he had a wife and a son but got to go home only during the weekends; he spent weeknights on the benches under the tin roof. The fact that he did not stay with local families might have had something to do with him being new on the job. His predecessor had left six weeks before our arrival in the community.

In the mid-1990s, the first Zapatista schools had relied heavily on activist teachers from outside of the communities. This was also true for La Gardenia. During my first visit in 2001, I noticed the remains of a large schoolhouse built by the government in the early 1990s and destroyed in a raid by its own army a few years later. Until the turn of the millennium, activists from Europe and Mexico City had taught the children here in return for food and lodging. The ones I spoke to had stayed for up to a year and complained about a lack of support by the villagers who allegedly failed to provide them with tortillas. Eventually, the foreigners were asked to leave after the communal assembly decided that they were inefficient and therefore not needed anymore.

Cipriano's brother Blas, who lived in La Gardenia and worked there as a community teacher, was a regular visitor to our San Cristóbal quarters. He told me that, in the years of repression by army and police in the late 1990s, education in the predominantly Zapatista settlement was reorganized with the creation of small decentralized schools. The school where Blas taught in exchange for community help on his milpa was one of five in La Gardenia and consisted of a little shack by the road with a blackboard and a few desks and benches on an earthen floor, not enough for the twenty-seven children who attended. The children were between five and fourteen years old, and Blas kept the younger ones occupied drawing pictures. The older children were making progress reading and doing math. Most Zapatista schools were in desperate

Figure 16: In the late 1990s, Zapatista community schools often had to make do with the bare minimum of furnishings and teaching materials. Sometimes there weren't even enough desks for all the pupils. The girls usually brought their younger siblings to the lessons with them, April 1996. Photo by author.

need of basic teaching materials such as notebooks, colored pens, and schoolbooks. Here, the blackboard was worn out by use and Blas received chalk only when attending an occasional teacher-training course. What he considered to be the biggest problem, however, was that there were no teachers willing to commit themselves for longer than a couple of months at a time.

After having been a community teacher for six months, Blas himself terminated his job for what he considered a lack of communal support for his efforts. This was in mid-2001, when the growing rift between interest groups in the once-united rebel community led to a suspension of collective projects in the village (see chapter 4). When the people of La Gardenia eventually made up their minds and split into two opposing factions in 2002, there were renewed efforts by the remaining Zapatistas to get the autonomous school project going.

In this, the competition with the rivaling faction, whose teachers were provided by the government, might have been an additional motivation and every Saturday the compas took turns working on two hectares of recuperated terrain to grow food for their children's teacher. By May 2002, Blas was again attending to thirty compa children three days a week. The number of children attending school varied according to what kind of agricultural work had to be done in the community and to the degree the children were involved in it. In the framework of this part-time setup, he was able to take care of his bean harvest and vegetable garden. Another young community member who assisted Blas in the lessons was trained by a solidarity worker from Mexico City.

Competing with the State

In many communities with a Zapatista presence, the existence of government schools aggravated the competition between the two systems. The prospect of a better education and therefore a subjective betterment of their life chances became an important motive for individual families to quit EZLN membership and switch allegiance to the Mexican government. Thus, in February 2002, a Basque campamentista reported from Roberto Barrios that within a week a dozen families had left the guerrilla movement to be able to send their children to "real school." The everyday tangible presence of a seemingly better alternative constituted a problem in many places where different political factions lived together. Thus, an activist from the north of the country who had settled in one of the rebel communities, where he married a local woman with whom he had a child, recounted how he was subjected to the most humiliating situations. In the small village where he worked as a surrogate teacher, the autonomous school was right next door to the official one. Twice a week the government teachers handed out free lunch packets to the children while his own pupils watched with hungry eyes.[3] After six months, the man was deeply demoralized as Zapatista parents had complained about their municipal authorities not having sent them a "real" teacher.

This problem is exemplary for the situation in many older villages marked by political division. But even in unanimous Zapatista communities such as Tierra Nueva, people considered all their possible options, even if they were in breach of Zapatista rules. Although the autonomous primary school in Tierra Nueva dates back almost to the community's founding days in 1995, there had been difficulties from the start. Most crucially, many locals were not prepared to pay a salary to their community teachers or to support them by growing their food. Thus, the teachers eventually discontinued their work. Not wanting to put up without education for their children, inhabitants of Tierra Nueva decided to request teachers that were paid by the government. This was in spite of resistencia policies, which were already widely adhered to in rebel territory at the time (1998). The state provided two deeply frustrated pedagogues who were transferred to the remote backwoods for disciplinary reasons. They were put up in the same house as the peace campers and are reported to have dreamed about teaching in San Cristóbal. After less than a term, they returned to their hometown. Whether the reasons for this had something to do with their incompetence, their frustration, or with the fact that their employment breached the rules of resistance remains to be explored, but the community of Tierra Nueva has not requested any government teachers since. Instead, they reinstated their autonomous primary school, which has been in operation since February 2000.

Even though by 2002 there were autonomous community schools in most Zapatista communities, the project of educación autónoma seems relatively ineffective when comparing it to the educational successes of other Latin American guerrilla movements as in El Salvador or Nicaragua. One of the most obvious causes has to be seen in the high fluctuation and relative inexperience of the community teachers and the limited resources to sustain them. Another is the omnipresent lure of government schools linked to the failure of the EZLN to consolidate exclusive administrative control over its territory. Yet another weakness stems from the widespread involvement of foreigners and urban Mexicans in the project of "autonomous" education. This does not only create dependencies but also makes it more difficult for the local population to identify with the project, rendering it susceptible to internal criticism. Paradoxically, the effectivity of educación autónoma is reined in by the openness to outside solidarity and the very lack of dogma and authoritarianism that have won the Zapatistas their widespread appeal.

The urgent and fundamental necessity for the Zapatista base to press ahead with the campaign for community schools dawned on me as I became aware of the full extent of illiteracy in rebel territory. During a visit to the Aguascalientes of Morelia in April 2003, on the occasion of the anniversary of Emiliano Zapata's death, I witnessed a meeting of about 250 local youngsters who had congregated in the main auditorium of the compound. After a speech about recent successes in the construction of new community schools, a top EZLN representative asked everyone in the hall who could not read to come forward. Slowly, some of the youngsters in front started to get up from their seats; first, only the boys and then throngs of young women and girls came to the front of the auditorium. After a while, the benches had emptied significantly and around 100 people crowded the space around the microphone. Almost in the manner of a talk-show host, the representative then walked around to ask individuals whether they were ready to learn how to read and write in the new autonomous schools. Eventually, everybody up front replied with a resounding "¡Sí!" in a chorus as the audience cheered them on. As they returned to their seats, all of them received new school bags from a dozen energetic educational promoters, who matched their future students in both age and appearance.

CHAPTER SEVEN

Projects and Their Impacts

Observations by a Volunteer Water Worker

The first part of this chapter illustrates the construction of water systems in Zapatista villages in which I have participated as a volunteer worker. Apart from the technical side and my observations regarding our reception by community members, I include details about the impact on the social fabric in the villages. These are discussed with regard to three key issues: (a) the creation or perpetuation of communal division due to partisan involvement by the NGO, (b) contradictions between NGOs and local communities, and (c) the introduction of capitalist marketing models to rural communities, with an eye to the activities of those NGOs focusing on production collectives.

Clean Water for the Revolution

At the beginning of the twenty-first century, the scale of deficiencies regarding basic infrastructure in rural Chiapas was massive. Many villages did not have access to electricity; hardly any had sewage systems. Most people lived in wooden shacks with earthen floors that were moist in the rainy season. Few had proper beds, and several family members usually shared wooden bunks. Cooking was done over open fires, with the smoke causing health problems, especially for women. Clean drinking water often had to be carried from distant springs if it was available at all. Toilets were usually nonexistent and, due to contamination by human and animal feces, water was a constant source of intestinal diseases such as amoeba, typhoid, or even cholera. Due to their recent establishment on cow pastures occupied in the course of the uprising, the lack of infrastructure was particularly grave in the new Zapatista settlements. Addressing the needs of the EZLN base, the NGOs remaining in Zapatista territory from the late 1990s onward focused on remedying these problems. As so many villages required clean water, the systems had to be built at minimum cost and by enlisting community members as a workforce. Most of these systems were based on gravity flow, by piping water downhill from a spring to a reservoir tank and then into the village. Each family compound had a tap installed that was connected to the main supply line. Making use of gravity avoids employing pumps, which are expensive to fix and often unreliable. A fresh water supply takes an average of three months to build and can last for thirty years, if maintained well. The systems we installed consisted of one or two reservoir tanks and provided water to communities comprising ten to sixty families. A population growth of about 3.5 percent annually was taken into account, leaving the growing community the option to expand their system.

The first stage in building a water supply consists in prospecting for a water source. Once a spring has been found, a geological survey is done to ensure the water can reach its destination by gravitational pull alone. Chemical and bacteriological tests are sometimes used to establish the water quality. The actual building starts with the construction of the spring tank, an open basin of several square meters that rims the source and funnels the water into the main 1.5-inch supply pipe, which feeds into a reservoir tank at the edge of the village. In hilly terrain, the supply line has to be fitted with valves to avoid blockages by air bubbles. If there is a great difference in altitude between the spring and the village, small intermediary tanks have to be installed at every fifty meters of altitude drop to break the pressure that would otherwise destroy the pipe work. Because most components are made of plastic to limit the cost of a system, susceptibility to leakage is considerable, particularly under conditions of high pressure over prolonged periods. Fixing the resulting breaks and blockages in a supply line can be particularly time-consuming if, as is often the case in rural Chiapas, the line is buried over a distance of several kilometers and there is no way of telling exactly where the problem is located. Furthermore, the spring tank needs to be cleaned out at regular intervals, so the filters at the upper end of the main line do not clog. To protect the tube from the heat of forest fires, which frequently occur at the end of the dry season when the campesinos burn their milpas, the main line needs to be at least sixty centimeters deep in the ground. A typical reservoir tank holds about fourteen thousand liters and is built of concrete supported by a wrought iron basket. The location of the tank needs to be high above the compounds it serves to ensure a sufficient pressure in the individual taps. From the main tank, a 1.5-inch plastic pipe leads down into the village, and from that line an extendable number of 0.5-inch pipes branch off to taps installed in front of individual houses.

About Losing One's Head: La Utopía

My first visit to a rebel community as a water volunteer started with an adventurous trip along dark country lanes. To avoid army and police roadblocks, the water teams generally travel at night. There were three of us and, as a newcomer, I had to contend myself with riding in the back of the pickup truck among concrete bags, pickaxes, and plastic tubing. Up front were my indigenous friend and housemate, Cipriano, and Charlie, the project coordinator. Charlie was an international activist from a well-to-do background who had recently found his vocation with appropriate technology in Chiapas after finishing a university degree in an unrelated discipline. We were heading for the Zapatista stronghold of La Utopía to conclude a study of the terrain in preparation for the renewal of the water system there. Despite the late hour some of the army posts were staffed, but the soldiers waved us through; it was long past midnight when we arrived in the village. All was quiet when the 4WD truck pulled up in front of the peace camp, the usual place for foreigners to spend the night. The door was locked and, not wanting to wake anyone up, we crept into the nearby dormitory used by people from all over the municipality who regularly came to La Utopía to attend workshops. Even though there already were about thirty men and women sleeping, we found a space on the wooden bunks.

It must have been about four in the morning when someone turned on a radio full blast with the worst of ranchero tunes (folklore music) and people were getting up, chatting away in an apparent effort to drive us out into the dawning day with them. Doggedly, the team managed to stay wrapped up for another two hours before we found our way into the kitchen, where the local water committee was already expecting us. Charlie spontaneously cancelled breakfast to not make them wait. Appalled at such rigidity, Cipriano and I shouldered the equipment needed for measuring altitude changes and followed a group of local men into the wooded hills. After walking for twenty minutes, we arrived at the spring that was to feed a cistern, which in turn would provide water for the clinic in the village. If this worked well, a larger storage tank was to be constructed to provide water throughout the village. Another team had already done a study to establish the altitude difference (head) between the spring and the projected storage tank. After working two days in difficult terrain, they had calculated the head to be a mere five meters, just enough to create the pressure necessary to ensure a steady flow. In the meantime, villagers had discovered a shorter, more cost-effective passage between the village and the water source. This necessitated another survey, which we were about to undertake.

While three local men hacked a breach into the underbrush and Cipriano and I set up the transit, Charlie explained how to use it. After all, one of the principles was to train the villagers in all the skills needed to build and maintain a water system themselves. While Cipriano was measuring the angles from the apparatus to the poles held by two stoic locals at a distance that was determined by the visibility of the terrain, it was my job to calculate the altitude change from the angle and the distance, using trigonometry and a pocket calculator. The idea was to keep a sufficient amount of head throughout the entire passage. If the distance between any point of the pipe system and the spring was to fall below ten meters in the hilly terrain, air could get trapped in the pipes and an expensive automatic valve would have to be installed to prevent eventual blockage. At one point we got down to three and a half meters of head, necessitating a valve. Then there was a drop in terrain down to the river below La Utopía and it looked steep enough to increase the pressure to ensure a reliable water supply at the clinic. The final ascent, however, was longer than expected and we lost all of our accumulated head, ending up with half a meter of altitude difference between the spring and the cistern. One of the two studies was obviously faulty, but the spring was definitely situated too low in relation to where the water was needed, meaning that a system relying on gravitational pull alone could not be built. Possible alternatives involved pumps fueled by an erratic electric grid or expensive gasoline, or complicated hydroelectric contraptions that would have been difficult and costly to fix once they broke. The work was exhausting, and after a hard day of futile labor there was a general sense of disappointment both among the team and the locals. Charlie bought a round of Pepsi for all workers before we retired to the peace camp.

The camp was staffed by a motley crew of Europeans, sitting about reading or playing cards. The peace campers' only job in La Utopía was to record military movements along the road, which was visible from the shack. No Humvees or army trucks had passed for a week but there were daily overflights by light planes and an occasional helicopter. The bulk of vehicles driving up and down the road were logging trucks, heaping with the trunks of old-growth pines, which one of the communities down the road was selling to improve their financial standing. The campamento featured eight bunk beds, a table, and a light bulb. The walls were adorned with photographs, drawings, and political slogans left by generations of activists from the Basque country and Italy. Among the potpourri of Che Guevaras, indigenous faces, red stars, and the odd trinket left behind as a token memory, there was a sheet of paper pinned to the wallboard. It bristled with regulations prohibiting everything from leaving the camp without asking to displaying revolutionary décor or radical statements on buttons or garments, making gifts to locals, and public kissing or nudity. Only those campamentistas who had committed themselves to hold out in such dire conditions for many months were able to get to know local families, who took them out to work on their fields or to help with the coffee harvest. Most people here, however, were short-termers, eager to volunteer with the water team to fend off the boredom that their monotonous days entailed. After an alternative spring was found weeks later, a group of these campamentistas worked along with the villagers to build the water supply for the local clinic.

Building a Tank: 29 de Febrero

About a year later, after the work in La Utopía had been completed, Charlie's team began working in the new Zapatista settlement of 29 de Febrero, which held an important position in the autonomous municipality despite its few inhabitants. The spring was located seven kilometers away from the community and the amount of tubing needed to cover that distance was pushing the limits of what the NGO considered cost-effective. Digging the trench for the main tube was hard work and time-consuming. After clearing a hillock above the village for the tank, we left for other engagements, to return only after locals had finished the trench. All male adult members of the families that were to receive a tap took part in the digging but, as the village consisted only of fourteen families, this wasn't enough to complete the seven kilometers within a reasonable time frame. Help was needed and the autonomous municipal authorities wisely chose who was to lend a hand. Only people from neighboring villages that had very recently joined the EZLN were picked. Apart from providing a much-needed workforce, their participation in the collective project also allowed for conversations, interpersonal exchanges, and invitations. This integrated the newcomers further into the network of local Zapatistas, improving intercommunal cohesion in a region otherwise characterized by factional strife.

Holding fourteen thousand liters, the tank was far too generously laid out for a community of only fourteen families, but since the land was able to sustain many more people, the autonomous authorities had wanted it to be big enough to serve a larger population in the future. The chosen hilltop location measured about twenty square meters and needed to be scraped even and freed from rocks and roots. All materials had to be carried, with fifty-kilo cement bags guaranteeing a truly backbreaking toil. Under the supervision of Charlie, the wrought-iron basket for the concrete tank slowly went up until it resembled a giant birdcage. Layer by layer we applied concrete to the base and later to the walls and roof. Working inside the now closed structure was atrocious. With outside temperatures approaching forty degrees Celsius, the tank turned into a simmering cauldron of abrasive vapors stinging the eyes and itching the skin; Cypriano, Charlie, and

I had to take turns to come up for air. There was only space for half a dozen men to work with spatulas while the others carried cement bags as well as buckets of sand and gravel. For want of a cement mixer, a group took turns preparing the concrete by patiently turning the ingredients over with a shovel, slowly stirring in water until the desired result was produced.

Community members displayed a very welcoming attitude toward the team. We were put up in the school building and ate with a family that was financially better off than the other villagers, for the father worked as a driver in a nearby town. There was an almost intimate contact with people in the village who, apart from working with the team on a daily basis, came to talk and play ball games with us in the evenings. The inauguration of the water system was a big event. A bull was slaughtered and two hundred people from all over the municipality showed up for the fiesta. In a ceremonial procession, everyone made their way up to the tank, which had been decorated with banana trees and a white ribbon. On arrival the principales, the catequista, and the *magrina* (female holder of a ceremonial church office) blessed the tank with water, incense, and prayers. The congregated assembly, divided into gendered groups, followed suit. Three old men started playing two guitars and a fiddle, producing something slow and rhythmical that sent the congregation swaying from side to side while moving their feet back and forth. The water team took part in this dance, a recurring feature at religious ceremonies, which Charlie affectionately referred to as the "bus-stop shuffle." Back in the village, the consejo read out a letter drafted by autonomous municipal authorities thanking the team for their efforts and praising international solidarity. Then it was our turn to speak. We encouraged the villagers to remain steadfast in their struggle while Cipriano addressed the congregation in Tzeltal. In the end, many people came up to thank us individually. There were handshakes by men and women, young and old. Some of the women spoke to us in Tzeltal, insisting on a hug. By the time it was over, all of us were very touched and filled with a rare and precious warmth that stayed with us for a long time.

Figure 17: The inauguration of a drinking water system was a festive occasion for Zapatistas from all over the region. The tank was made with a capacity of fourteen thousand liters that can serve up to fifty families, December 2001. Photo by author.

Sources of Conflict

With their offer to provide basic infrastructure, NGOs in Chiapas unintentionally became competitors to the Mexican State, which delivered the same services. In 1996, a European solidarity group decided to remedy the devastating parasite infections by building a water system in the new Zapatista settlement of Tierra Nueva. A North American INGO took on the financing and the European activists running the peace camp were integrated as a building team. The people involved did not have a great deal of experience and, as the first two hundred meters of pipe leading down the mountain from the spring tank were tested, not a drop of water came through. The trench had to be dug up again to check where the problem was. The local Zapatista authorities quickly lost faith and began to consider other options without informing the NGO workers. Together with a neighboring village, they eventually entered into negotiations with government agencies, which offered to build a water system as well.[1] The activists knew nothing of this, until the villagers did not show up for work one morning. Only after a lengthy inquiry did they learn about a consensus that the community members had come to at a meeting the night before; they had unanimously decided to have their system built by the government, which was to either bring in workers or pay for the ones supplied by the community. The activist in charge of running the project is said to have been so outraged upon hearing this that he threw all building materials into the back of the truck and drove off at once without saying good-bye. The government's water system was never built. A year later, it became clear to the locals that the offer had been a scam designed to divide their community. The official explanation for canceling the plans was that that the government did not want any Zapatistas to benefit from the project. Over the following years, Tierra Nueva's authorities repeatedly approached members of a San Cristóbal–based solidarity group with the request to resume work in the community, but it took until 2002 when the money and the will were there to make another attempt.

La Utopía is a large indigenous village of about 1,500 inhabitants with origins that predate those of La Gardenia or San Emiliano. Although it had been a Zapatista stronghold in the years after the uprising, the place was severely affected by factional splits in the late 1990s. By the time of my first visit in October 2000, the people had divided into three political factions of equal strength (Zapatistas, PRD-militants, and PRI-militants). Many of the pastures beyond the village used to be finca land occupied by the EZLN in 1994 and settled by young families affiliated with the guerrilla movement several years later. When I arrived in La Utopía, SHOXEL had just started work on a water supply for the local autonomous clinic. If the spring proved to be copious, SHOXEL planned to build a larger system that would provide water throughout the village. The local *perredistas* (PRD-members) had teamed up with the Zapatista faction and both groups would benefit from the project. The remaining third of the population—government loyalists—however, would be left in the dry. SHOXEL collaborated with this deal on the assumption that the local PRIistas could apply for their own system with government authorities. The vast potential of this sort of partisan NGO involvement becoming a cause for communal conflict was obvious to everyone involved but I doubt that such details made it into official reports to SHOXEL's donor organization.

As Middleton and O'Keefe (2001, 129) point out, ethical codes applicable to development work not only should insist on consultations with the communities where a project is to be implemented but also achieve a participation of all the people who live there. First and foremost, these ethical codes stress the importance of taking into account the political context of any intervention. With regard to comportment in the politically divided communities of the Las Cañadas/Selva Lacandona regions, I have found that local NGO coordinators repeatedly breached ethical codes by taking their partisanship with the Zapatistas too far. Obviously, data for such assumptions need to be procured from relatively close up and are generally hard to attain due to the pressures on NGOs to portray their ventures uncritically to secure further funding (see also Bob 2005, 181–95; Earle and Simonelli 2005, 141). In the case of La Utopía, SHOXEL's estimation that local PRIistas were privileged in obtaining governmental aid not only ran contrary to the experience of the NGO's long-term staff, it also ignored the changed power balance after the 2000 presidential and state elections, which the PRI had lost. As a consequence, local PRIistas had a much harder time obtaining state assistance.[2] Moreover, SHOXEL's project managers knew the region well and were aware of the frequent shifts of political affiliations in local communities. Nevertheless, they agreed to the terms set by Utopía's Zapatistas and surveying got underway.

The water project in 29 de Febrero exhibits similar ethical problems. After several days of work in the community, it became evident that all but two families in the hamlet were sending their daily detachments of workers for the building of the tanks and trenches. These two families had left the EZLN, and the Zapatista majority in the village did not expect them to get a tap installed in their compounds. I could not establish if this was simply due to the lack of communication or whether this exclusion was a logical consequence of their political affiliation. What surprised me was that SHOXEL simply executed the will of their Zapatista clients, rather than attempting to mediate between factions with the aim of providing infrastructure to everyone who needed it.

When the pipe between the spring and storage tank in 29 de Febrero was connected for the first time, it became apparent that a family from a neighboring village had been using the source as their own water supply. They had nothing to do with the Zapatistas but when they saw their spring basin drained by seven kilometers of pipe, they voiced their fear of being left without water. The Zapatista water committee assured them that there was no need to worry, as they would make sure that there was enough water left for them. As spring output varies according to the season and to the amount of rainfall, a lack of water can quickly become a cause for conflict in times of scarcity. Another factor that could aggravate this situation is the probable population growth in the Zapatista settlement, which would inevitably lead to a greater demand for water.

Efforts to build a water system in 29 de Febrero attracted hostilities by neighboring communities almost from the beginning. As the source that supplied the village with water was relatively far away in the hills, the feeder pipe to the reservoir tank had to cross "enemy territory" before getting to the village, thus rendering it vulnerable to attacks by anyone wanting to harm Zapatistas. Already during the construction of the water system, the exposed supply line had been damaged by unidentified assailants. We repaired the pipe, covered it with earth, and eventually it was hidden by vegetation. By its sheer existence in the periphery of the village, however, costly and complex infrastructure such as a water system represents a perpetual Achilles' heel in times of intercommunal conflict. Thus, 29 de Febrero's spring tank was destroyed by members of political factions loyal to the government and in opposition to the Zapatista autonomous municipality in May 2003, one and a half years after its construction. Even though the locals can repair their spring tank without outside intervention, it is questionable whether they will go through the effort as long as the threat of repeated destruction remains.

Contradictions between NGOs and Local Communities

The people of rural Chiapas have adopted the term "white elephant" for those prestigious government projects that are inaugurated with much publicity but do not live up to expectations in the end. The epitome of such a project was the huge hospital built in Guadalupe Tepeyac in the Lacandon Jungle as a showcase for President Salinas's National Solidarity Program (PRONASOL) in the early 1990s (see chapter 1). Even the president himself was flown in with a helicopter for its inauguration, which was broadcast far and wide by Mexican television. Only weeks later, all the expensive equipment that had been displayed to the media crews was packed up again and driven to another state where it was needed for the next inauguration. The concrete shell in Guadalupe Tepeyac stood empty until federal soldiers used it as a brothel from February 1995 onward. During my time in Chiapas, the term "white elephant" was widely employed by those in the NGO scene, who also used it to refer to the following projects, some of which they themselves had taken part in.

The hydroelectric generator in the Aguascalientes of La Realidad was probably the most expensive single machine ever built in rebel territory. The spectacular turbine project was conceived during the 1996 Intergalactic Meeting when Italian activists—one of them the vice mayor of Venice—and EZLN commanders had the idea to equip La Realidad with its own hydroelectricity plant (see Avilés 2000). There were several attempts to deliver the generator to its jungle destination after it had been designed by engineering students from Rome's Sapienza University. The turbine got stuck in a Mexico City customs office for years until it was finally shipped to Chiapas in a joint effort by the Ya Basta Movement, Enlace Civil, and the Union of Mexico City's Electricity Workers (SME).[3] By the end of 2001, the river passing by the village of La Realidad was diverted to feed the turbine and two kilometers of cable were installed to provide the houses with electricity (Bellinghausen 2001). That the story has been promoted as a great success is evident by a host of media announcements informing of the project's impending or final completion.[4]

Sponsors such as the city councils of Venice, Rome, Palermo, Reggio Emilia Romana, and Trieste; the Italian Greens and Communist parties;

and Catholic congregations were mobilized by Ya Basta to generate the funds necessary for the venture. This money paid for the construction, its shipment to Mexico, and its eventual installation in La Realidad. Great care was taken to design the generator in accordance with ecological standards: unlike ordinary turbines, this one did not heat up the water that drove it. Depending on the source, the total cost of the project amounted to at least US$150,000 (Avilés 2000) and, according to the Ya Basta delegate Donatella, who was sent to La Realidad two months after the completion, some of the debt had still not been paid back.[5] Donatella's mission was to check on the project and send pictures of La Realidad as it was illuminated by electricity from the turbine. The sponsors back in Italy wanted to see how their project was doing. Unfortunately, there was no power in the village when Donatella arrived. After running for only three weeks, the turbine had given up the ghost and no one had been able to fix it. What puzzled Donatella most was that Ya Basta hadn't been informed about the breakdown.

In an effort to save the project, she spent the following months traveling back and forth to La Realidad trying to organize the transport of the faulty turbine part to the state capital of Tuxtla. Even though La Realidad's Zapatistas owned a truck, other factions in the village and neighboring communities who did not benefit from the project prevented them from leaving. The plan to train a team of ten compas to fix and maintain the turbine, which had a projected life span of fifty years, also met unexpected obstacles. Even though enough people had volunteered for the training course, their own community refused to take care of their fields while they were away for the workshop. Eventually, two technicians from Italy who had taken part in building the turbine were flown in from Rome to repair it. After several weeks, the turbine was finally up and running and 2001 New Year's Eve in La Realidad was celebrated in electric splendor. Even for the team of volunteers a solution was found. Their community finally agreed to tend their milpas and the Don Bosco Center for Continuing Education in San Cristóbal offered to train them as mechanics.

Although it does not fully explain local reluctance to help getting the turbine working again, this narrative provides a glance at the complexities linked to the acceptance of a particular project. For the people of La Realidad, the benefits of having their own electricity might have been outweighed by the potential conflict created by the Zapatista faction having exclusive access to it. As most communities in the region pirate the electric grid anyway, La Realidad's compas might not have perceived the possession of their own turbine as an expression of autonomy but, in the face of not being able to fix it themselves, rather as one of dependence. The sum of US$150,000 would have been sufficient to finance the construction of a dozen water systems, which given the human resources to build them, could have provided for up to five hundred families. But, after all, the Aguascalientes at the heart of the Selva Lacandona was a symbol not only for Zapatista autonomy but also for the link between indigenous rebels and (inter)national civil society. For the decision to build the turbine, this fact might have outweighed the real needs of the population who lived there.

Particularly in the first phase of post-1994 NGO involvement in Chiapas, rural communities often agreed to projects in which they did not see any sense, fearing that they would not receive any aid at all if they refused. All the while, they were hoping that the next project would be more along the lines of what they needed. The changing attitude toward such aid shipments comes across in the story by a Danish journalist with a long history in the Central American activist scene. The group responsible for implementing the project in question was a small alliance from Barcelona with a success story in Sandinista Nicaragua, where it had distributed eyeglasses among the urban poor. After having established sufficient connections to progressive opticians in Barcelona who were willing to contribute glasses, they wanted to repeat their venture in Chiapas a decade later. The Catalans made their way out to a Zapatista community they had selected beforehand and then waited two weeks for a village assembly to deal with their proposal. After they had presented their project, the local Zapatistas politely thanked them but showed no further interest. No more meetings to organize the distribution of the glasses were called and the Catalans eventually returned to San Cristóbal without having achieved anything. Similar narratives of failure abound among NGO activists in Chiapas and among development workers the world over. They show how even small-scale development aid organized by experienced activists can be a complete flop when the initiative doesn't come from the people in the communities themselves. In this particular case, a project that had met with success in a culture of readers turned out a failure among rural people who were possibly unaware of the benefits of glasses and who lived in a context where spectacles might even carry a stigma as attributes of unloved state officials.

But how do NGOs deal with such obvious resistance and the ensuing lack of cooperation to their projects, on the success of which they themselves depend in many ways? Failed projects not only risk getting them into disrepute with the Zapatista command but also jeopardize future funding by donor organizations and thereby their livelihood in San Cristóbal, as well as their career. Earle and Simonelli (2005, 140–44) report on the Chiapas-based NGO Desarrollo Mujeres (DESMU) that veiled negative results of their projects to ensure continued funding. Sometimes this type of strategy can take on very subtle forms. Against what should have been common practice, in 29 de Febrero, the water quality of the spring was never tested although SHOXEL possessed the necessary equipment. As the team already worked on the system, it was still not clear if the actual source for the system was a spring or an underground stream. When we first filled the tank, the water sprawled with yellow organic matter but even this was not followed by testing. Instead of bringing the issue before the communal assembly, Charlie imparted his conviction of the superior water quality to the local water committee, who passed it on to the whole community, thereby lowering their guard against any health hazards. Prior to our arrival, 29 de Febrero already had a rather limited but working water supply from a small spring, which dried up in the hot season. Eager to bring the project to a close, Charlie disconnected the old supply once the tank was filled although the water from our system still tasted of solvents due to the new plastic tubing.

Far from being caused by ill will, such detrimental practice was caused by lack of experience, the ambition to present flawless results, and an atmosphere of competition that prevented the sharing of disconcerting information with other groups engaged in similar projects. Nevertheless, such negative aspects cast doubt on the concept of "mutual solidarity" as possessing essentially novel and different qualities, as Olesen (2005, 107–11) claims. Along a similar line, Bob (2005, 194) notes that, in spite of the high principles of many NGO workers, their motivations are not fundamentally different from other international actors. They therefore base their decisions not solely on the needs of the population they have come to help but also on the objective to ensure their own survival and organizational maintenance. For similar reasons, NGOs in search for a project location do not necessarily look for the neediest cases. Due to the competition for membership and funding and the resulting pressure to produce positive results, they rather choose those groups who appear the most capable of using aid effectively. This tends to reinforce existing inequalities (186), which is particularly salient in regions where many NGOs become engaged due to a sudden rise in media coverage (also see Terry 2002).

Introducing Capitalism?

The San Cristóbal–based NGO Kinal Anzetic focused on the empowerment of indigenous women in Zapatista highland communities by setting up production cooperatives. In their workshops the group trained local women to design, produce, and market *artesanía* (crafts), principally textiles, to achieve their economic independence. The villages where the NGO worked were organized in the Mut Vitz coffee cooperative. Even though the women participated in the production process, they did not have a say in the coffee councils because the land titles belonged to their husbands. The artesanía workshops had the explicit aim to give local women control over their income at a time of low coffee prices on the world market and the resulting conversion of coffee plots into maize fields. The merchandise was produced on location and then shipped to Mexico City and the United States, where it was sold.

Are such workshops a motor of capitalist transformation? When I presented a European activist who had done volunteer work for Kinal with the question, she told me that rather than being passive receivers of something imposed on them, the women she worked with expected the NGO to provide them with the connections necessary for access to international markets. Often, they were even disappointed when they realized that there was not a bigger demand for their embroidered blouses in the United States. In the case of coffee production the issue is more complex because the cash crop usually replaces subsistence cultivation of maize and beans. Under conditions characterized by a limited amount of largely inaccessible terrains with low yields, campesinos often have to choose between one and the other. As coffee takes five to seven years before the first batch of beans can be harvested, there is no easy reversal to subsistence production, leaving growers at the mercy of fluctuating prices dictated by market forces beyond their control. Another problem arises from the fact that in good years the sale of the harvest provides plot owners with relatively large amounts of cash, increasing the risks of conflict caused by economic inequalities between those villagers who own coffee plots and those who don't. According to Lucio González Ruíz from Mut Vitz, the harvest cooperative members employed landless neighbors or seasonal workers from other regions (Gallardo Caballero 2001). Such practices further increase the potential for tensions. For if these hired workers are compas, how does this fit with Zapatista notions of collectivity? And what happens to community cohesion if they aren't? The cases of former Zapatista villages who left the still clandestine guerrilla organization after starting to export organic coffee to Europe in 1988 (Benjamin 1996, 239) show that the strategy of empowerment by market integration can also backfire; with growing prosperity, would-be revolutionaries may actually abandon their revolutionary ambitions.

On the whole and in view of future market integration on the terms of multinational capital, Zapatista communities are indeed put into a stronger position by projects that allow them to take charge of capitalizing on their available resources. Although garment production taught in artesanía workshops is geared toward export production on the capitalist market, the workers of community-based collectives remain in control of the production process. Furthermore, by training indigenous women in garment production and marketing, NGOs such as Kinal not only brace them against exploitation by multinational corporations, in the case of Mut Vitz they have also given them an edge over the men from their own village. Involvement in those NGO projects that the Zapatistas ran at the time of my research also allowed campesinos to continue having their mainstay in subsistence agriculture. That said, I don't see milpa cultivation, the land for which is usually obtained by clearing rain forests, as a long-term solution in an increasingly crowded ecosanctuary such as the Selva Lacandona, as Earle and Simonelli have suggested (2005, 21). I also don't believe that this is what most Zapatistas want. It seems clear that only projects that are profitable for the people in the affected communities have a chance of functioning by themselves in the long run. Zapatista autonomy is going to last only if the communities also become economically independent. The image of labor associated with a commodity is another important aspect to consider. In choosing a product handcrafted by a Zapatista women's cooperative over one produced in a sweatshop, for example, international customers can contribute to a change in the practices of global trade. Thus, a future scenario is indeed imaginable in which indigenous communities adapt to their fragile ecosystem, optimizing on their space and selling products that are special because of their origins and the way they are produced; this could include maize that is labeled as Zapatista, organically grown, and derived from a genetically diverse strand.

Perspectives for Sustainability

Despite the pitfalls I witnessed, most projects implemented in rebel territory, and particularly those centered on appropriate technology, had a predominantly positive effect on the ground. After all, that basic infrastructure contributes to the survival and well-being of the people who would otherwise not have the means to improve their living standards as drastically, especially not while retaining their independence from the state. By the time my research came to an end, most projects in rebel territory were initiated by the people who lived in the villages and they were sustainable in the sense that they could be maintained by locals without any further outside input. However, there were still problems with imposing outsider's ways of doing things, retaining hierarchies within the NGOs, and depending on paid locals (see chapter 8).

It should be stressed that such problems were less likely to occur if the people involved in running a project were unpaid activists from a solidarity group rather than resident NGO workers. If there were long-term contacts between activists and community members, the resulting relationship of trust was likely to increase the chances of integrating locals into a project and thus making its success more probable. Because of the absence of salaries in volunteer work, hierarchies too were less likely to develop. The example of Tierra Nueva, where a solidarity group had run various projects over several years, however, shows the difficulties that were characteristic for such solidarity projects: every time the staff changed, it took some time both for activists and community members to get used to each other and for the project work to become effective again. Alternative development projects that prove to be both successful and sustainable in the sense that locals can maintain them without further input (such as those introduced in chapter 6) could well become organizational models for a whole society. Of course, an entirely new scenario becomes imaginable for the indigenous communities of Chiapas if they were to gain control over the resources above and below their soil, such as oil, hydroelectricity, minerals, and pharmaceutical resources, and also over the yields of an environmentally and socially responsible tourism.

CHAPTER EIGHT

Mobility and Cultural Change in the Face of Outside Involvement

This chapter focuses on the cases of two indigenous men who found employment with San Cristóbal–based NGOs during the time of my research. The story of Cipriano illustrates how the presence of international activists contributed to him escaping from the confines of his community to see the world. Having found a livelihood elsewhere, he became a role model for others who followed suit, further integrating parts of Las Cañadas into wider patterns of migration. Fausto's case, on the other hand, hints at some of the possible effects of a local community member receiving a regular NGO salary while remaining in the context of his village. The stories of these two men serve as examples for the complexities involved in assessing the impact of outside involvement in Zapatista communities and puts Earle and Simonelli's (2005) thoroughly optimistic assessment into perspective. However, they also show evidence of functioning communal defense mechanisms. Feeling threatened by nonconformism and emerging economic inequalities, the people of La Gardenia and Arcadia reacted by sanctioning the two individuals whom they perceived to threaten their cohesion.

Nuijten (2003) points out that intervention by the Mexican State has often contributed to the generation of divisions by privileging individuals with good connections: "Personal relationships, rather than collective organizing, have been central to obtaining village projects, jobs, access to credit, important information" (198). According to Nuijten, any government program fosters divisions and reproduces clientelism. Why should this apply only to state involvement? What about other types of outside intervention? In spite of all Zapatista claims and efforts to the contrary, I have observed the tender beginnings of a similar trend happening in villages where independent projects are run. Wherever an individual or a group of experts is generated by providing them with privileged access to information, material, and money, there is the danger of breeding a new generation of power brokers who will undermine the democratic elements of the Zapatista project. The last part of the chapter outlines Zapatista efforts to stem the negative aspects that have emerged with regard to outside involvement, epitomized by the 2003 administrative restructuring manifested in the creation of the Juntas de Buen Gobierno.

The Career of an Indigenous NGO Worker

Cipriano is not a new character to this book. He has been introduced as my main informant, housemate, and fellow water worker. Chapter 4 has sketched out the recent conflict in his village of origin, La Gardenia, and he has appeared in action as a member of the water team in La Utopía and 29 de Febrero. This chapter takes a closer look at this young Indígena's biography. The following pages provide an account of what I consider to be key events for Cipriano's gradual estrangement from his home community and for the shaping of his identity not as a member of a close-knit campesino community but as an individual precariously selling his labor in an urban setting. I believe that Cipriano's case is not isolated and, as his northward migration along with three other men from his village shows, people like him are fast becoming role models. Cipriano's story emphasizes the link between what he has become and the involvement of outsiders, albeit in the context of alternative development that Earle and Simonelli (2005) so praise as a solution to "arrest the flow of migration and help promote healthy communities in their current places of rural residence" (21).

Because his mother had come from a mestizo town, Cipriano grew up in the indigenous village of La Gardenia speaking both Spanish and the local indigenous language Tzeltal. His was a big family of eight sisters and brothers, one of whom was killed in the battle of Ocosingo in the course of the uprising. As a teenager, he witnessed the preparations and outbreak of what the locals call the Zapatista revolution. Terrified by the 1995 army raid, Cipriano fled to the mountains with his family, while their belongings were stolen or destroyed by federal soldiers.

When they dared to return to La Gardenia, a CONPAZ peace camp had been set up in the community and Cipriano made his first contact with international activists. A year later, the San Cristóbal diocese that organized the peace camps offered him the chance to attend courses at its Don Bosco Center for Continuing Education. Cipriano obtained permission from Gardenia's communal authorities and moved to San Cristóbal, where he learned how to drive and work on leather and wood. However, he spent more time at the site of the peace dialogues that were taking place in nearby San Andrés. There, he helped out with the security cordon and worked as a cook for the comandantes who conferred with COCOPA. Half a year later, Cipriano returned to La Gardenia to make milpa as a campesino. In time, his family's house became a popular hangout for activist teachers and Cipriano's relations with campamentistas soon grew closer than his community's agreements allowed. At that stage, he had already turned into a renegade, listening to reggae music, smoking grass, and refusing to participate in community church services.

When a water team installed a system in La Gardenia in 1998, Cipriano mingled with the activists. After the team left, he used his new connections to return to San Cristóbal against the explicit wish of the community council. In the city, he was able to stay rent-free at an activist's house, while working on building sites and in road construction to make a living. When he returned to La Gardenia for a brief visit a couple of months later, the communal authorities summoned him. To his shock, Cipriano was told that he was excommunicated and had his right to make his milpa on recuperated land revoked. Upon his return to San Cristóbal, he took up an offer to work with the TENAZAS water team even though his salary there amounted to less than what he had earned in construction. A year into his second stay in the city, Cipriano was in a steady relationship with an international activist and had enrolled at a secundaria (junior high school equivalent) evening school. To concentrate on his studies, he quit his job and moved in with his girl-friend, who could afford to support him financially. After another year, she returned to her home country and Cipriano took up work again. This time, he found a job as an assistant for SHOXEL, which paid him a monthly salary of two thousand pesos. Cipriano was just about able to integrate his studies with his new task and successfully finished the secundaria in early 2001. He was eager to enter the *preparatoria* (high school equivalent), along with his fellow graduates, but his employers made him choose between continuing evening school and carrying on working with them. At the time, Cipriano had no health insurance and still struggled with the malaria he had caught when installing water systems in a remote corner of the Selva Lacandona. The prospect of losing his job was daunting in several ways. Apart from depriving him of his livelihood, it would have challenged his rebel identity, as he had justified life away from his community with working for the advancement of the Zapatista project. Cipriano eventually decided against school to adapt to the schedule of his employers. He plunged himself into the job and devoted all his time to building water systems. Although he enjoyed his work, he felt increasingly uncomfortable about receiving only half the salary of his international colleagues. When SHOXEL's funding organization sent a project evaluator to San Cristóbal, Cipriano resolved to ask for a pay raise. However, when the moment came he could not muster his self-confidence.

As a result of Cipriano's prolonged residence in the city, people back in La Gardenia harbored fantasies about his foreign friends and his new affluence. The following episode exemplifies the advancement of his alienation. While we shared a house in San Cristóbal, he tried to maintain regular contact with his family. His relatives stayed at the house when they needed to work for a bit of extra cash to support a newborn or to contribute to a village fiesta. Cipriano also made a point of visiting his home community on special occasions. One of them was the first *cumpleaños* (birthday) of his brother Sergio's daughter in January 2001, when I accompanied him to La Gardenia. The day after the fiesta, Sergio and Cipriano took me to a beautiful green river, cascading from pool to pool in the jungle. We spent most of the day there, and then made a detour on the way back to the village because Sergio wanted to show me his milpa. When we finally got to La Gardenia, we were completely exhausted. Unfortunately, there was no time to rest. People from the village had spotted us on our way through the woods and Cipriano's family received us with the news that the community police had come looking for us. My friend went off to see the consejo about the issue straight away and when he returned I could tell he was angry. All he revealed was that the authorities wanted to see us both. While we found our way through the mud and the night we discussed my imminent appearance before the council. Cipriano asked me to keep quiet about the close ties I had with his family and advised me to tell them I was an acquaintance from work.

A thin man in his forties received us in front of the church and then asked me to accompany him to the main assembly space under a tin roof. Five men had gathered around a light bulb and were looking at me expectantly. I was told that three of them belonged to the consejo and one was the translator; a doyen seemed to be included because of his age. I shook everyone's hand and was offered a bench. A man with a moustache began to speak in Tzeltal, pausing at regular intervals for the translation: "We are Zapatistas here in La Gardenia. The community has an acuerdo [agreement] that every visitor from outside needs to have an official accreditation from the autonomous municipal authorities. What if you disappear or if a snake bites you and we are later blamed for it? We used to have campamentistas staying in the village and there is a special hut for them. There is therefore no need for you to live at the house of Cipriano's parents. How long are you planning to stay in our village and where is your accreditation?" I replied that I did not have an accreditation for I had come at the invitation to a birthday party. I also told them that I had been a campamentista in a neighboring village four years ago, but that this time I was here just for a private visit and planned to leave the next day. The men did not need a translation to understand what I said and started talking among themselves. After a few minutes, the council faced me again and their speaker declared, "Cipriano doesn't live here anymore, so he can't just invite people. Every outsider coming to the village has to present himself to the authorities first. So do you, next time round. And don't show up again without accreditation." Then they summoned Cipriano and interrogated him for half an hour. He was outraged when he finally joined me again: "I have been denounced by people from my own community! They are envious of my family receiving foreign visitors. They obviously think you shower us with all kinds of presents. I have hardly ever brought anyone here and still they scold me for doing it 'all the time.'" What particularly angered Cipriano was the authorities' reiteration of his no longer being part of the community where he had been born and where most of his family still lived. "This is only because I left without their permission in 1998. They'll do anything to pin me down with a wrongdoing now." In an attempt to dismiss the incident as insignificant, he then said, "The men who spoke to us are not even EZLN officials but just ordinary community delegates who have not consulted the asamblea and are therefore acting without a mandate."[1] With pride, he then repeated the words he had said to the village authorities before leaving for San Cristóbal back in 1998: "I do not need to ask for your permission to be free!"

At the end of 2001, Cipriano was sacked from his SHOXEL job over discrepancies with his superior. Upon hearing about his misfortune, both his father and his uncle asked him to come back to Las Cañadas and share their plot of land. Cipriano seriously considered the option but was obviously attracted by alternatives to campesino life. He seldom visited La Gardenia in those days and when he did, he was taken aback by the repercussions of factional strife. Once he participated in a football game when the two village teams played against each other. Cipriano joined in on the side of the Zapatistas and, to his shock, came under heavy attack by his former friends who had turned ARICista. Fearing for his safety, he eventually broke off the game. When he told me about the incident back in San Cristóbal, he stated that before returning to live there again he would rather lead the life of a free rover.[2]

It seems that the cosmopolitan existence that had come with Cipriano's NGO job contributed to rendering him incompatible with community life. On the other hand, it failed to provide him with long-term material stability. Cipriano alternately entertained visions of becoming a shrimp fisherman on the Pacific coast, teaching Tzeltal in San Cristóbal, or making off to the United States *de mojado* (without documents). He even entertained the idea of starting his own NGO. In 2002, an existing NGO eventually took him on as a prospective coordinator in an attempt to "indigenize" local team structures. This time, Cipriano's salary matched that of his colleagues and he continued to live in San Cristóbal, mingling with the internationals and sharing their world, yet set apart by his origins. At first glance, and for many of the first-timers among the activist crowd, he represented the people and the struggle they had come here to experience and support: the arcane Indígena who had put an end to his oppression. Being the only tangible Zapatista in town you could hang out with in a bar, he soon became the newcomer's object of desire. People who stayed longer were irritated when they realized that he did not correspond to their fantasies. Some were even put off when they noticed that he mimicked the international activists in their ways, having taken on their somewhat decadent leisurely lifestyle.

There was a general ambivalence in Cipriano's attitude toward his home community. When asked about his birthplace, he regularly denied his origins and just answered "Ocosingo," even to people from the solidarity scene. When going out with a group of internationals in the streets of San Cristóbal, he usually hurried ahead to avoid the suspicious looks by the *coletos* that any Indígena was subjected to who associated with scruffy-looking foreigners in public.[3] When staying in San Cristóbal, Cipriano went through strenuous efforts to retrieve his birth certificate, as well as to organize all the documents necessary to apply for a passport. Part of this procedure included the procurement of the *carta liberada*, certifying undertaken military service or the exemption thereof, which is either bought from a corrupt military official or obtained by serving the lowly tasks of recruits at the nearest garrison. The first option was closed to him for a lack of the necessary cash to bribe the relevant officials. Cipriano was not willing to undertake the second, especially because it entailed cleaning the roadsides of the San Cristóbal thoroughfares of garbage in full view of anyone, including people who knew him. Ironically, it was a liberalization in federal legislation introduced by the Fox government that eventually allowed him to apply for a passport without completing his military service.

By the end of 2002, Cipriano had been dismissed from his third NGO job for not living up to the expectations of his employers. He had not turned into the conscientious successor for the out-of-town project coordinator as they had hoped he would. Instead, he had further worked on his version of life as a rover by prioritizing leisure and experiments with his freedom. Upon losing his livelihood in San

Cristóbal, he headed for the northern border in search of work, taking three men from his village with him. As he told me, two of the men, along with many others in Gardenia, had parents who had recently left the EZLN and joined the ARIC in hopes for a better future (see chapter 4). Although their fathers were able to hold on to their ejido titles, the sons faced a dilemma. Staying Zapatista meant falling out with their families, but joining the ARIC entailed losing their rights to grow maize on recuperated lands. For those still not bound by a family of their own, migration was the best way out. Many people in this situation had originally planned to take a company bus to the sugarcane fields of Nayarit, where men from a neighboring village had done seasonal work for years. When the two men found they were not on the passenger list, they joined Cipriano and his comrade Mauro on their way north. They were in their late teens and, as Cipriano explained, represented only a fraction of restless youngsters ready to leave the village. For many others, they were the scouts.

The fact that the group ended up in Tijuana was coincidental. Mauro, the oldest one of them, had an acquaintance there who put them up while they were looking for jobs. After three months of carrot packing, Cipriano proved that his experience among the international crowd of San Cristóbal was a worthwhile investment. Unlike the other three, he was granted the option of (temporarily) escaping the ambivalent spoils of migrant labor. All expenses paid, he got on the plane to Europe at the invitation of a solidarity activist who had fallen in love with him back in Chiapas.

After contemplating a marriage offer that would have allowed him to stay in Europe indefinitely, Cipriano eventually returned to Chiapas to continue his way of life there. As he did not find work in the NGO scene, he went back to La Gardenia as his family had eagerly expected. Instead of choosing life as a campesino, however, he put his acquired skills to good use, taking up work as a driver. At the time of writing, he was conducting a pickup truck (*camioneta*) somewhere along the roads between San Cristóbal and his home community. Although Cipriano's journey to the north and across the Atlantic turned out to be a round-trip affair, the other three remained in Tijuana without an inclination to return to Chiapas any time soon.

Local Reactions to Outside Influences

The continued international presence in indigenous communities has certainly affected the way their inhabitants look at the world and at themselves in it. The first thing that springs to mind is the impression of affluence caused by gadgets, clothing, and well-fed international activists who can afford to pay for airplane tickets at a cost that is enormous by local standards. Stories about highly paid jobs, social security, education, the concept of holidays, recreational drug use, and sexual promiscuity may have an even greater impact. For some, like Cipriano, Mauro, and the two youngsters who headed for the border to improve their prospects, the protracted exposure to such narratives might have brought about the desire to participate in this imaginary world of well-being. Of course, indigenous Mexicans have wanted to leave their home communities as economic migrants before NGO workers came to their lands, but the close involvement of international activists with the inhabitants of remote communities is a relatively new occurrence, at least in Las Cañadas and Selva Lacandona. For many indigenous Zapatistas, migration has fast become an option, influencing their lives' choices. At the time of my research, the story of a former EZLN major who left Chiapas to find work in the United States made its rounds in activist circles. Cipriano and Mauro had come to live in the city to enjoy such things as cash-paying jobs, privacy, mobility, and the option of changing their girlfriends. It appears that they were only the first of many more to come.

Apart from such unintentional value imports by solidarity activists, other new ideas were purposefully brought to rural communities by way of workshops and training courses. In contrast to common clichés about indigenous Zapatistas, the concepts of ecology, natural healing methods, or feminism are novel for most inhabitants of the EZLN's base communities. Some of these ideas are adopted while others are rejected by indigenous Zapatistas, who decide which values appeal to them and which ones they feel they can do without. The following episode from the work of our water team in 29 de Febrero illustrates this point.

The autonomous municipal councils often decided to have water systems built in those villages that served as a meeting point for the area's communities, be it for assemblies, workshops, or fiestas. Due to

Figure 18: The presence of internationals in the indigenous village of Las Cañadas was an absolute novelty in 1996. This kitchen hut, made from hewn poles thatched with zacate reeds, was representative of many houses in Las Cañadas when I first went there, March 1996. Photo by author.

the function that 29 de Febrero had as a meeting place for the entire municipality, a tap and two public showers were to be installed in the center of the village. A wooden shack with two compartments and a door on either side was to shield users from view. After individual family dwellings were connected to the storage tank, efforts focused on the construction of the showers. While Charlie and I undertook a final check for leaks and blockages of the main supply line, Cipriano and three men from the village were building the shower doors. As they presented their work, Charlie looked dissatisfied. Privately, he vented his frustration by saying: "Aw, it hurts me to see a job badly done. Just look at that! Apart from the fact that they have hammered in the hinges with nails, the doors are far too small. On top and at the bottom, there are gaping slots almost half a meter across!" When I asked the group of local workers why they had made the doors so small, one of the boys present at the scene piped up, "So you can see who is in there!" Realizing that the product of their efforts did not agree with the foreign supervisor, one of the older villagers interjected, "People are only going to be in there for a very short time." Feeling challenged by Charlie's perfectionism, Cipriano later removed the doors and built new ones, surrounded by a crowd of locals. After he had finished, there were only gaps at the bottom. The villagers had insisted that "the water had to flow out somewhere," in spite of the obvious fact that there was a gutter in every shower. To keep the doors shut while taking a shower, the locals used a simple string-and-nail contraption and politely declined to have the bolts installed that we had brought from San Cristóbal. Before inaugurating the showers, they insisted on painting a woman on one door and a man on the other.

At first glance, the shower reminded me of the flimsy public restrooms you find in the United States, meant to keep people from taking illicit drugs in privacy. I believe the men who constructed the doors in 29 de Febrero had similar intentions: they wanted to prevent the creation of a truly private space with solid walls and lockable doors. Indigenous communities in Chiapas do not have any such private spaces. In many of the villages where we worked, bathing was done rather publicly in a stream. There was hardly any personal privacy there. The women bathed separately in a group without removing their skirts, and the men bathed around a river bend upstream. I spoke with Cipriano about the practicality of assigning a cubicle fixedly to each gender and he told me he found it hard to imagine that a woman would use one of the cubicles at the same time as a man was taking a shower in the other one. The paintings on the cubicles were an added element of control, making the new facilities gender exclusive. This episode clearly portrays an act of communal resistance against the creation of a private space, where unmarried couples could escape surveillance to engage in proscribed sexual acts. In a masterstroke of appropriation, the local population embraced the introduced technology while successfully ridding itself from the cultural baggage that came with it.

Shifts in gender relations were probably among the biggest changes affected by the presence of internationals, especially by women who

Figure 19: After the public showers were completed in the village of 29 de Febrero, the locals insisted on a strict separation of the cabins by gender. International activists often participated in painting the walls of public buildings in Zapatista villages, December 2001. Photo by author.

came in from outside. Particularly among indigenous men, resistance toward any change in that field was fierce. This is exemplified by the occurrences at a meeting of representatives from seven rebel munici-palities in autumn 2001, where SHOXEL coordinators presented a project that focused on the training of women as health promoters. The male-dominated assembly eventually turned down the proposal on the grounds that it would foster splits in the communities by pitting men and women against each other. Instead, the delegates requested the workshops to be gender mixed. The reaction by women activists from San Cristóbal was one of frustration but, as they wanted to continue working in Zapatista territory, they had to go along with local (male) conceptions of gender and collectivity.

The first wave of post-1994 solidarity activism had also swept a group of feminists into the Zapatista communities of Chiapas who sought to better the situation of indigenous women in patriarchal social structures. Among San Cristóbal activists, a favorite narrative circulated about such a group (Colectivo de Mujeres, or COLEM) who suppos-edly organized a gender-mixed workshop in a Zapatista village in the mid-1990s. They related the mechanisms of patriarchal exploitation to their intrigued audience by putting special emphasis on the situation in the respective community itself. It is reported that for weeks some of the older local men talked of nothing else, debating the accusation that for generations they had oppressed their wives and daughters. COLEM was eventually expelled from Zapatista territory on the accusation of trying to incite a gender war.

Money Doesn't Stink: Implications of Paying a Community Member

A hub for both activist NGOs and Zapatista efforts to boost market-able output, La Utopía was brimming with specialized production facilities. Among machinery for the refining of coffee and vegetables and the manufacture of shoes and the sale of beef, the village featured an appropriate technology workshop for the production of energy-efficient ovens and dry-compost latrines. San Cristóbal–based NGOs and their North American funding organizations endowed the local builders of latrines and ovens with the didactic and monetary means to forge ahead with their venture. The appropriate technology workshop consisted of a wooden building filled with cement bags, workbenches, and a variety of molds. Under the supervision of Fausto, an indigenous expert in his late twenties who was both trained and paid by SHOXEL, six local men were making cement casts for toilets as well as clay components for energy-efficient stoves.

In remote rural areas recently settled by campesinos, such as the Zapatista new population centers in the Las Cañadas/Selva Lacandona regions, there were hardly ever any efficient latrines. Human feces were often eaten by domestic animals and ended up in the drinking water, putting people at risk of diseases such as dysentery, typhoid, and intestinal worms. Dry-compost toilets keep human feces away from animals and prevent germs from entering the soil, thereby protecting people from getting infected. Combined with health- and hygiene-awareness programs, this can significantly reduce such diseases. Compost latrines are built with two chambers that are used alternately. Decomposition continues in the chamber that has filled up while the other one is in use. Each chamber has its own opening for the removal of mature compost. The chambers are built on the ground and over them is a hole for feces, as well as a funnel to receive the urine. The chambers are designed to have an accumulation time of about nine months to allow thorough composting of the contents and the elimination of pathogens. The compost produced is an almost dry, crumbly, black product described by the designers of such latrines as "having a light, pleasant, earthy odor" (Calvert 2003). It is high in nutrients and can be used as fertilizer for vegetable gardens and coffee plantations. Such latrines were very much in demand with the Zapatistas living in and around La Utopía for reasons of convenience and prestige, but especially for their economic use as production facilities of *abono* (compost). This fertilizer they produced was valuable and could either be sold or traded, for it replaced expensive chemicals that would otherwise have to be bought in town.

According to a consensus by the autonomous municipal council, Fausto's home community, the new Zapatista settlement of Arcadia, was chosen to have the first latrines in the region installed. The measure was intended to stem parasite infection—which was rife in the village—by preventing human feces from getting into the food chain and the water supply. Arcadia had been founded on recuperated coffee plantations and cattle pastures a couple of years earlier and had no infrastructure whatsoever. Tucked away in a river valley, the shabby hamlet sheltered thirty families. Although in possession of coffee groves once owned by a finquero, the inhabitants of Arcadia were poor. Coffee prices were way down on the world market and fertilizer was beyond their means. Understandably, the local population enthusiastically welcomed the arrival of compost-producing latrines.

The inventors of these latrines had anticipated this use and facilitated the appropriation by community members. What they had surely not intended was that the local latrine builder would allot them to his cronies along clientelistic ties. Conspicuously, the first latrines all ended up with Fausto's own family members. At closer look, it also turned out that all the men building the contraptions were his cousins, some of whom did not even live in Arcadia. As a result of this, the latrines were not installed evenly throughout the village, thereby foiling the attempt to break the connection between excrement and food.

SHOXEL had hired Fausto as an assistant half a year earlier in connection with its agenda to combat intestinal disease in Zapatista communities. After training him, the NGO put him in charge of the latrine workshop in La Utopía. With the help of local youngsters whom he taught his skills, he cast concrete toilet bowls and urinals at the rate of a latrine a day. To do his new job efficiently, Fausto needed to be away from his milpa most of the time. Since his parents lived in La Utopía, he had a place to stay when working there. In 2000/2001 SHOXEL paid Fausto a monthly salary of two thousand pesos. Within months, he was the richest man in Arcadia. Apart from the fact that he was the first to own all the gadgets the organization provided, he also built himself a new three-roomed house with a concrete foundation and proper wallboards, in a village of humble shacks. He soon was the proud owner of a stereo system, and began saving for a car and paying his compañeros for planting his milpa for him. A little more than a year into Fausto's employment by SHOXEL he had turned his father's house in La Utopía into a *bodega* (store), selling foodstuffs and household wares.

Cipriano was torn between being impressed and outraged: "Fausto is the boss now (*está chingón*). He doesn't even touch a shovel or a pick ax anymore; he's got people working for him. All he ever does now is manage NGO money. He drives to town and buys a ton of gravel or tools. I bet he can even get the prices down with his suppliers and keep the leftover money for himself." Cipriano's statements might say more about his own misgivings rather than Fausto's actual activities, but his account of what happened in Arcadia shows that he was not alone with his sentiments: "Fausto is in trouble already. The compas in Arcadia have threatened to disown him because he hardly comes to the village anymore. He's always in La Utopía training new AT apprentices and looking after his store. If I had that kind of money," Cipriano conclusively opined, "I'd share it with my community." In the course of restructuring community relations with the NGO and the EZLN, SHOXEL eventually discontinued Fausto's salary payments. It should be noted that he kept on building latrines even without getting money for it.

May these be the beginnings of a new indigenous elite in rebel territory? A comparison of recent NGO involvement in Selva Lacandona and Las Cañadas with what Rus (1994) has described for indigenous communities in the Chiapas Highlands of the 1930s would seem farfetched, particularly in the light of the Zapatistas' own measures to counteract clientelism. However, just as the Mexican State has relied on mediators to implement rural development programs in remote villages, so do NGOs. As long as development projects are run or even paid for by (cultural) outsiders, Gilsenan's (1977) proverbial gap (see introduction) will be there for someone to fill it. My point is that it does not take state-orchestrated development for the emergence of cronyism. The issue of remunerating a local assistant with NGO money is always problematic, both with regard to employment equality and its local implications. On the one hand, it is only fair to pay an indigenous colleague at least the same salary as someone who has come with altruistic motives from abroad. On the other, paying cash to someone who then spends it in the context of a communal subsistence economy has immediate and often detrimental repercussions on the ground. To do justice to both the individuals as well as the communities involved, it is therefore crucial to consider the social contexts within which a local NGO employee is embedded. Thus, the case of

Fausto, who did not have to pay rent and subsisted from the yields of his milpa, differs significantly from that of Cipriano, who lived in San Cristóbal where he had to pay for his rent, food, and maintenance from the salary he received.

Lessons Learned

NGO activists who felt privileged to work in rebel territory often displayed a great tolerance toward the EZLN's strategic use of development projects as rewards for loyal base communities and as a measure to keep down the dropout rate in villages rife with malcontent. Although this was a recurring topic for discussions among the activist crowd, no one seems to have been seriously put off. There were stories of communities who had confronted the EZLN with the choice to either provide them with infrastructure or else they would request it from the government. Indeed, some Zapatista villages felt passed over by their municipal authorities. The following episode dating from May 2001 illustrates how ready some were for striking individual deals with outsiders regarding "foreign aid." It also sheds light on the way centralized project administration was perceived in villages beyond the reach of the gravy train.

When I visited San Emiliano after a four-year absence, a local authority approached me with an illicit proposal. After he had made sure there was no one outside his house, he started talking to me in a low voice. "Look, you've seen how few of us are left here," he said, referring to the fact that most people in his village had quit the EZLN. "It is hard for us here, but we are keeping up the resistance," he continued. "We have bought a schoolhouse and organized communal teachers for our children but we still are very poor. In fact, we have nothing." He looked at me imploringly. "All the solidarity projects stay up the road in the Aguascalientes. We don't even get chalk for our school here. We are in need of help and this is why I ask you now if you yourself or people you know could come up with some money to support our resistance." Considering the implications of such a move, I asked what the autonomous municipal council would say to this. With an expression of dismay he then declared, "If you want to support the people of San Emiliano we have to do this quietly. If you go by the prescribed route, any donations will get stuck in the Aguascalientes. It always happens like that." I did not go along with his wishes and when we met again a year later, neither he nor I brought up the issue.

The EZLN had long become aware of such grievances and made policy adjustments to address them. Major administrative changes were announced in 2003 at the inauguration of the Juntas de Buen Gobierno in charge of—among many other things—reviewing, coordinating, and managing solidarity and NGO projects. In his analysis of the relations between the Zapatistas and civil society, Marcos particularly addresses issues of inequalities arising from centralized administration as well as from connections between outsiders and individuals or whole communities. He concedes that the well-known and accessible communities have received more projects and more support and also points out that special relationships between outsiders and a Zapatista family breach the Zapatista principle of "to each according to his needs" (Marcos 2003, part 5).

The restructuring of relations between NGOs and the rebel municipalities already emerged in spring 2002, after the issue had been debated in the Zapatista municipal councils. Gem, my well-connected activist friend, recounted the discourse prevalent among the Zapatista echelons at the time. There were two approaches. One proposed to leave organizational matters as they were, in the hands of the NGOs. The other sought to pass all responsibility, such as the management of funds and the supervision of projects, to local communities. Gem anticipated economic implications for NGO employees to be drastic: salaries would be cut to 10 percent of what they were and control over vehicles would switch from individuals to the autonomous districts. Transport of material and people to and from the Selva would take precedence over personal use by NGO managers in San Cristóbal. Some voices in the councils advocated leaving things as they were. After all, they already had a say as to what kind of project was implemented where. One of the principal fears was that locals in charge of large sums of money were more prone to mismanagement than urban professionals. And why change something that has worked pretty well so far?

A little more than a year later, the advocates for change had prevailed.

New policies were announced at the inauguration of the Juntas de Buen Gobierno in August 2003 (Bellinghausen 2003; Ramírez Cuevas 2003). The new policies amount to nothing less than a regional administration of NGO and other projects by the central Zapatista councils, to ensure a more just distribution of aid by way of stricter controls. They also seek to prevent non-Zapatista communities from marketing their products as "Zapatista," a label that had become similarly attractive to international customers as "fair trade" or "organic." Another regulation prevents donations and help from national and international civil society to be earmarked for any specific community or municipality. Instead, it is up to the Juntas to decide, after evaluating the circumstances of the communities, where the help is needed most. Moreover, the Juntas impose a "community tax," amounting to 10 percent of the total cost of any project. Thus, any community, municipality, or collective that receives economic support for a project has to make 10 percent of that support available to be used by other communities in the region, chosen by the Juntas with the objective to balance out the economic development throughout Zapatista territory. In addition, surpluses or bonuses from the sale of products from cooperatives are to be made available to the Juntas for distribution "to help those compañeros and compañeras who cannot market their products or who do not receive any kind of aid" (Marcos 2003, part 6).[4] After one year in office, the Juntas de Buen Gobierno presented a balance of their activities in front of hundreds of support bases at the Caracol of Oventic in September 2004. The total amount of solidarity contributions that all five regions had received in that first year amounted to Mex$12 million (US$1.2 million), of which Mex$10 million had already been spent on equipping autonomous schools and hospitals, buying collective trucks, and building water systems (for details see Bellinghausen 2004b; Marcos 2004; Gerber 2005, 158).

It has to be seen how these policies are accepted by the people in the cooperatives who have just begun to experience a higher level of living standards as the result of their combined efforts. It might well be that the strict regulations lead to a further wave of defections, particularly among economically successful communities. Especially in the new settlements that often have lucrative coffee plantations or cattle pastures located on former finca lands, people may soon find themselves torn between old loyalties and new hopes for affluence. Another issue that holds potential for future conflict is the question of how non-Zapatistas are integrated into the new administrative structures. Although the EZLN gave its assurances that everyone would be attended to on a basis of strict equality—and even the non-Zapatista population appears to be making use of the new autonomous law courts and clinics (Muñoz Ramírez 2004)—the fact that regional government is likely to make strong decisions about the allocation of resources is potentially problematic. A lot will depend on how well the structures for collective decision making and the support of more disadvantaged groups enshrined in the new setup actually work in practice and whether the Juntas de Buen Gobierno will resolve the problems that produce mal gobierno elsewhere.

CHAPTER NINE

Accommodating Home Base and Civil Society

The EZLN's Many Facets

Many who have spent time in a Zapatista community will testify to the contrast between local perspectives and those conveyed outwardly, be it in the EZLN's communiqués or in the alternative media. Solidarity Web sites, pro-Zapatista publications, and the parables of Subcomandante Marcos emphasize grassroots democracy, gender equality, and ecology while drawing a timelessly grim picture of the low-intensity war and stressing the urgent need for volunteers and financial contributions. Zapatista campesinos, on the other hand, proudly describe the achievements of their revolution, noting that the slavery that their parents knew had been replaced by freedom and self-determination. They talk about the fertile recuperated lands some of them now live on and praise the beginnings of economic self-sufficiency and independence from government institutions. When addressing a solidarity activist, they also point out their poverty and the plight of living under siege and repression.

This apparent discrepancy highlights the different functions that the EZLN has served for two distinct sets of "clients." The guerrilla movement has been built up by the indigenous communities of eastern Chiapas to serve their interests as a counterstate in the sense of Wickham-Crowley (1991) by providing protection and enlisting NGOs as service providers, but its other and more recent roles are less obvious. In return for assistance in the autonomy project, the guerrilla organization has also made itself available as a campaign engine for national and international social movements. For it, and for Mexico's indigenous groups, the EZLN has become an important ally in the promotion of their own various projects. While this cooperation with civil society actors outside of Chiapas has also aimed at transforming social realities, it has kept up all-important publicity for the base communities. Continued outside attention has been vital to them as it has provided safety from total military assault and offered a long-term perspective for economic development.

After the following brief overview of the various mechanisms at play in the EZLN's efforts to mobilize civil society, I argue that the utopian notions linked to the *comunidad indígena* (indigenous community) constitute the common denominator behind the Zapatistas' attraction for solidarity activists. During my fieldwork, I had the chance to observe the 2001 caravan to Mexico City and the National Indigenous Congress in Nurío, Michoacán. The bus tour by twenty-four EZLN comandantes, a growing number of Indígenas from various Mexican states, and hundreds of international activists was the culmination of the Zapatista campaign to achieve a ratification of the San Andrés Accords. It physically brought together large numbers of people that made up the guerrilla movement's broad spectrum of clients. This occasion put the contradictions between them into sharp relief and illustrates the practical aspects of their merit to the EZLN. But what about the indigenous base? An account of a Zapatista military exercise in one of the Aguascalientes is the background for an analysis of loyalty and hegemony in rebel territory. The chapter concludes with an assessment of the broader implications of the type of development described in this book.

Serving Base and Supporters

The Zapatistas' achievements in attaining media coverage have been widely discussed (Burbach 1994; Halleck 1994; Ronfeldt and Arquilla 1998; Leyva Solano 1998; Lins Ribeiro 1998; Yudice 1998) and so have the EZLN's efforts to transcend the narrow bounds of rural Chiapas to forge alliances with students, workers, civil society in the broadest sense, and most notably with the nation's many indigenous peoples (Díaz Polanco 1998a; Harvey 1998; Leyva Solano 1998; Mattiace 2003; Burguete 2003).[1] In an effort to turn their struggle into a *national* project, public relations events such as the National

Democratic Convention, the consultas, the marches to the Mexican capital and initiatives such as the founding of the FZLN have been crucial for the Zapatistas. With the increasing inclusion of indigenous questions, the EZLN has also sought to become the vanguard of Mexico's indigenous peoples.

In the promotion of their movement, the Zapatistas have been enormously successful, not least due to their expedient use of symbols. In the cases of the *pasamontañas* (balaclavas) or the recognizable spokesperson Marcos with his pipe, it is fair to speak of proper innovations that at once protect personal identity and facilitate collective identification. In addition, symbolic iterations such as the use of the Mexican flag and frequent allusions to the 1910 revolution and the agrarian hero Emiliano Zapata can be considered classic examples of successful branding. As Yudice (1998, 366) points out, with an "artful guerrilla media war . . . the Zapatistas have been able to carve a space for themselves and their civil society project by remaining newsworthy—virtually rewriting the manual for marketing—and pushing the normally unidirectional means of communication into a back and forth dialogue" (see also López 1996, 30–31).

By promoting their image in mass events such as the taking of San Cristóbal or the 2001 march on Mexico City, coupled with political initiatives ranging from their first eleven basic demands to the promotion of the COCOPA law, the Zapatistas have managed to establish a triangular dialogue between themselves, civil society, and the Mexican State.[2] EZLN discourse has emphasized the necessity of connecting Mexico's existing popular struggles that had taken place in "isolated nuclei" over the decades preceding the uprising. The Zapatistas have achieved this by creating appropriate spaces for meetings and for the discussion of relevant national matters (Leyva Solano 1998, 47). Drawing on pre-1994 rights and autonomy discourses by popular movements, the Zapatistas have both created an opening for democratic change and contributed to the redefinition of citizenship in Mexico (Harvey 1998, 199–200). With regard to their communities, which came under siege from February 1995 onward, the EZLN exposed the state's lack of commitment to democracy and human rights in front of the world and thereby prevented an all-out assault.

In this, the peace camps staffed by international observers were crucial as they provided the Zapatistas with their first batch of volunteers who served as human shields and of media-skilled foreign correspondents, whom they could hardly have mustered from their own ranks, at least not in comparable numbers.

On the international level, the Zapatistas have managed to keep attention focused on themselves for more than a decade. With the aid of a multitude of sympathizers, the sometimes poetic and often captivating communiqués by Subcomandante Marcos attained widespread distribution. Just as significant was the support by the Mexican left-wing daily *La Jornada*, the compañeros of the FZLN, Enlace Civil, and a host of alternative news outlets that have faithfully disseminated any pronouncements coming from the EZLN's headquarters in the Lacandon jungle. It struck me that, in its portrayal of social organization in the communities under its control, the EZLN readily catered to utopian visions so cherished by their sympathizers around the globe. Accounts from rebel villages were generally rather vague, leaving it up to the readers to fill in the gaps with their own favored images; poetic fiction characteristic for Marcos's communiqués has usually prevailed over concrete and self-critical assessments of the situation on the ground. The way the situation in Chiapas was conveyed in the alternative media has been far from uniform. Some publications have been more differentiated than others (e.g., Midnight Notes Collective 2001; Land und Freiheit 1995–1999; Irish Mexico Group 1998–2003a and 1998–2003b) in focusing on issues such as cultural survival, grassroots democracy, and independence from globalized capitalism, but especially in criticizing patriarchal hierarchies and the subordinate role of women.

Imagining Zapatista Communities

When entering a Zapatista community, the first thing a visitor is likely to notice are the murals adorning the walls of schools, clinics, or collective stores. They usually depict the icons of the Zapatista revolution, such as peasant leader Emiliano Zapata, Che Guevara, or Subcomandante Marcos. Often, these images are complemented by slogans such as "*Vivir por la patria o morir por la libertad*," "*Todo para todos,*

nada para nosotros," or "*Para un mundo donde quepan muchos mundos.*"[3]
Just as often, the murals show scenes from indigenous Zapatista communities. Often, they contain utopian elements that depict an ideal
state rather than actual reality. A famous and detailed example is the
mural of Taniperlas that adorned the autonomous town hall of this
important EZLN stronghold until the hall was destroyed during a
police raid in 1998. The mural portrayed an ideal Zapatista village.
A relative affluence came across in the presence of horses, vegetable
gardens, and fruit orchards and in a connection to the electric grid. In
the center of the village, people had gathered in a circle before leaving
for work on their milpas. In the foreground, an autonomous community school was visible with a promotora expecting the approaching
children. The village was surrounded by wild and untamed nature. A
jaguar prowled the jungle and in the mountains in the background, a
phalanx of masked guerrillas was visible. Two of them, a man and a
woman, were depicted larger than life. Armed with ammunition belts
and guns, they were protecting the community in the foreground.
The picture was framed by a frieze of birds with olive branches
in their beaks.

Similar images are transported in communiqués by the guerrilla
movement. Particularly the letters by Subcomandante Marcos often
work with metaphors, fables, and references to a utopian parallel
reality of the Maya. In the following excerpt of a text from 2004,
Marcos links the guerrilla movement's founding myth about the cultural merger between the urban and the indigenous guerrillas to the
importance of international support networks for the continuation of
the Zapatista project.

> I don't quite remember how it came up in our talk, but Old
> Antonio explained to me that the indigenous always walk
> as if they are hunched over, even if they aren't carrying any-
> thing, because they carry the well-being of the others on
> their shoulders.
>
> Old Antonio told me that the first gods, the ones who gave
> birth to the world, made the men and women of maize in such
> a way that they always walked together. And he told me that

walking together also meant thinking about the other, about the compañero. "That is why the Indígenas walk bent over," Old Antonio said, "because they are carrying their hearts and the hearts of everyone on their shoulders." I thought that two shoulders wouldn't be enough to carry that weight.

Time passed and things happened as they did. We [the urban FLN-members] did not prepare for battle, and our first defeat was to these Indígenas. They and we walked bent over, but we did so because of the weight of pride, and they because they were also carrying us (although we didn't realize it). Then we became them, and they became us. We began to walk together, bent over, but all of us knowing that two shoulders were not enough for that weight. And so we rose up in arms one first day of January in the year of 1994 . . . in order to seek another shoulder which would help us to walk, that is, to exist. . . . As with the origin of the Mexican nation, the contemporary history of the Zapatista indigenous communities also has its founding legend: those who inhabit these lands now have three shoulders.

To the two shoulders that the usual human beings have, the Zapatistas have added a third: that of the national and international "civil societies."

———————————————

(Subcomandante Marcos 2004, my translation)

I have chosen this piece for its unusually straightforward emphasis on the importance of civil society for the Zapatista autonomy project. The language is typical for such texts. They have been eagerly received by sympathizers the world over, translated and dispersed over the Internet and in solidarity publications. Often, this work is not limited to mere reproduction. Regularly, certain elements are amplified, others are omitted, and new ones are added. An example for this is the Mexican artist Beatriz Aurora, famous for posters available in Mexico City bookstores and San Cristóbal souvenir stalls alike. One motif, issued on the occasion of the 2001 Zapatista caravan to the capital, shows an arc in an ocean of flowers before the backdrop of the Mexico

City skyline. The arc is filled with Zapatistas wearing ski masks and pallacates. They are portrayed as an endangered species, the last of their kind. Above their heads, birds, butterflies, and a rainbow fill the sky. Although such idiosyncratic interpretations deviate from the Zapatistas' own discourse—in this case by way of added biblical elements—they do provide a vehicle for their agenda.

North American and European supporters are usually attracted to the rebel army because of other attributes. The excerpts from online brochures by Global Exchange and Schools for Chiapas presented in chapter 5 are examples for providing stylized messages catering to essentialist notions of Mayan culture and utopian pipe dreams of a base democracy untainted by individual power trips. A look into the archives of the Chiapas-1 and the Chiapas-95 mailing lists provides an overview of the discourses among sympathetic international audiences spawned by that type of information.[4] The protagonists of international solidarity have largely ignored these mechanisms of discourse production. A truly heterogeneous multitude, they exhibit a broad spectrum of worldviews and ideologies, as could be expected from Basque nationalists, Italian communists, Swiss anarchists, and all manner of other socially engaged people who eschew any such label. But their ideologies do have a common denominator. In my view, this is the notion of the *comunidad indígena*, which is central to utopian projections of pro-Zapatista solidarity groups far and wide. In this imagined community, harmony reigns among the autochthonous inhabitants. Guided by ancient Mayan wisdom, gender equality, and a deep respect for their natural environment, it is a matter of course that all their decisions are consensual. As most activists tend to lead lives of individualized city dwellers, an idealized Zapatista commune attracts them. Even if they do not attempt to realize it for themselves, they like the idea of contributing to its existence in that faraway place called Chiapas.

However, today's indigenous communities are historical products of colonialism, of the elites that have exploited their workforce, and last but not least of their inhabitants' own agency. Idea and practice of community *do* play a central role not only for the Zapatistas but also for Mexico's indigenous population at large. In Chiapas, community has been an important instrument of indigenous self-organization at the periphery of state control. All matters ranging from agriculture to conflicts between neighbors had to be solved in the absence of state institutions, a prerequisite for the emergence of the EZLN. However, these communities are far from being the primordial entities that many EZLN sympathizers imagine them to be. They are characterized neither by a special harmony among their inhabitants nor by a particularly caring attitude toward the nature that surrounds them. Patriarchal structures are all-pervasive and even "consensual decisions" are often the result of undemocratic processes. Privacy and individual liberties that are taken for granted by most EZLN's solidarity activists from North America and Europe are almost nonexistent. Collective work, however, does indeed play an important role. Conflicts between individuals and interest groups are sometimes carried out violently and, contrary to the assumptions of most solidarity activists, political affiliation usually is not static but guided by pragmatism rather than loyalty. Thus, it is not unheard of for Zapatistas to change over to the progovernment camp and back again within just a few years. In the midst of a tropical rain forest, agriculture always constitutes an interference, with negative effects on existing ecosystems. Although—due to inaccessibility and a lack of funds—simple methods are used for cultivation (sowing stick, machete, fire), slash-and-burn agriculture does not exactly correspond to current notions of ecology. That said, organic farming methods have indeed come into use recently to achieve higher yields with little cash input. However, the use of permaculture, nitrogen-producing vines, and compost instead of chemical fertilizers often constitutes not traditional knowledge but techniques taught to the campesinos by urban specialists in the context of recent development projects (see chapter 6). Absurdly, the very organizations sponsoring such projects refer to imported knowledge such as organic farming methods and the use of certain medicinal plants as indigenous traditions in order to enlist new donors.

For the supporters from a technicalized metropolis, the seeming primitiveness of a Zapatista village possesses romantic attraction. For the inhabitants it is a deficiency that needs to be remedied. When I first stayed in San Emiliano as a campamentista back in 1996, I rejoiced about the starlit night sky, untainted by a single light bulb. I was horrified when engineers showed up to arrange a connection to the electric grid. That evening, a group of encargados gathered around the candle-lit table of my hut and I tried to dissuade them from the idea. "What do you need electricity for?" I asked them in my naivety. "Haven't you been happy the way it is?" I was surprised to learn that they were not and knew exactly what they needed electricity for. They wanted to bring light into their ill-lit huts, conserve their food by refrigeration, cook with electric stoves, and watch television all evening. "Just think about the electricity bills," I tried. "Do you think we'll pay for the power?" they replied. "After all, we're rebels."

Working as human rights observers or project volunteers does give solidarity activists an opportunity to experience indigenous villages from close up and to attain deeper insights into their complexities. Particularly women are struck by the ubiquity of patriarchal structures because in this regard Zapatista rhetoric and everyday reality clash particularly harshly. Inconsistencies between actual and imagined reality can lead to a differentiated perspective on the part of the activists. Often, however, they are ignored or not even registered. Upon returning to their home countries, former Chiapas activists usually become involved in mobilizing others to either donate or become volunteers themselves. Sometimes an in-depth portrayal of the situation in the communities is attempted at first. In order not to obstruct the efficiency of fund-raising rallies and volunteer recruitment, however, critical overtones are often omitted and the proliferation of idealized images is perpetuated.

La Marcha del Color de la Tierra

In February 2001 a caravan of hundreds of indigenous Zapatistas and an equal number of Mexican and international sympathizers set out on a tour that would take them through many towns and cities of southern and central Mexico. They were accompanying twenty-four EZLN comandantes, among them Subcomandante Marcos, on their march on Mexico City, where they were to promote the inclusion of the San Andrés Accords into the constitution before the Mexican Congress (Congreso de la Unión). I joined the Marcha del

Color de la Tierra (March of the Color of the Earth) as a correspon-
dent for the newly created Chiapas branch of the open-source news
agency Indymedia.

On its way to the capital, the caravan stopped off in the small
indigenous village of Nurío, Michoacán, where the comandantes
appeared before the third National Indigenous Congress, which was
convened by countless groups representing Mexico's indigenous communities to synchronize with the Zapatista campaign. The conference
brought together large numbers of people representing the Zapatistas'
three main constituencies: Mexico's indigenous peoples, its foreign
supporters, and the Zapatista base from the villages where the guerrilla movement originated. The participants gathered on the premises
of a secondary school and more than fifty buses jammed the muddy
thoroughfares of the village. With more than three thousand delegates,
many of them in colorful traditional dress, and over seven hundred
special guests, the congress was a big event. They were joined by
about five hundred international observers who had followed the
Zapatista comandantes from Chiapas, several hundred journalists, and
thousands of students and workers who had come from the nearby
metropoles to partake in the spectacle. Throngs of people pushed
past booksellers, food stalls, and peddlers vending jewelry; Zapatista
paraphernalia such as flags, pasamontañas, and T-shirts; and countless
copies of the San Andrés Accords for three pesos apiece. A big stage
was set up on which the Zapatista delegation addressed the audience before, during, and after panel discussions, which took place
in smaller groups dispersed over the three acres around the stage.
Security was clearly an issue among the organizers of the event as there
were several body checks to get onto the premises and near the stage.
Notwithstanding, Marcos made it a habit during the comandantes'
speeches to stand in the most exposed position at the edge of the stage,
making sure that if someone wanted to snipe him, no one else would
get hurt for being in the way.

A group of disciplined Italians from the Ya Basta Movement, the
monos blancos (white coveralls), quickly evolved into the bodyguard of
the comandantes. There were about fifty of them, set apart from the
rest of the caravan by their white coveralls and red neckerchiefs. Every

Figure 20: The main stage of the National Indigenous Congress in Nurío, Michoacán, was the site for speeches by the Zapatista delegation and indigenous representatives from throughout the Mexican Republic. At the congress and throughout the 2001 caravan to Mexico City, the twenty-four EZLN comandantes were accompanied by their white-coveralled Italian bodyguards from the Ya Basta Movement, March 2001. Photo by author.

time the comandantes moved between their bus, their lodgings, or the stage, they formed a human chain around them, thus shielding them from potential assailants or overenthusiastic fans. The indigenous delegates usually appeared in groups adorned with festive garments and displaying attributes of authority such as staffs or headdresses. Most had been sent by their home communities with the mission to represent their concerns. This was not easy, for delegates had to limit their panel contributions to three minutes. The procedure was standardized throughout the congress; five contributions were followed by a summary of the content and a decision whether to hear another five contributions on the same issue. Overall, participants were very disciplined, listening attentively to each other and abstaining from interventions.

This practice contrasted starkly with the unending discussions among the activists in the caravan that focused on differences rather than on finding consensus.

Discourse among indigenous congress participants was generally supportive of the EZLN's endeavor to get the San Andrés Accords ratified, with groups from various parts of Mexico announcing impending declarations of autonomy in their respective communities. While there was widespread agreement about institutionalizing cultural autonomy, many delegates pointed out that their communities considered the issue of land and who owns it to be more important, at times even displaying a more radical position than the Zapatista delegation. Some speakers voiced skepticism toward the EZLN, demanding to take part in the parliamentary hearings to prevent the comandantes from making any deals with the government (for example, by changing the wording of the accords). Another issue of great concern was the ubiquitous extrajudicial killings, torture, and disappearings of indigenous activists throughout Mexico. The Zapatista comandantes attended the panels in small groups without contributing much to the debate at the time, addressing the main points only in the closing ceremony. They reaffirmed the importance of the land issue for the Zapatista struggle, making it clear that there was to be no peace with the government as long as this remained unresolved. All indigenous delegates were then invited to join the comandantes in their appearance before the Mexican Congress. The event ended with a fiesta, complete with music and dance, vividly displaying Mexico's diverse indigenous cultures. Early the following morning, the caravan continued its journey, doubled in size, for most indigenous delegates had decided to join the Zapatistas on their march to the capital.

Many activists had come to Mexico especially for the occasion, only to surrender control over their own lives and be carted across the country as extras for weeks. I witnessed the idealized images many had brought along with them clash with realities on the ground. The bus with the comandantes usually traveled ahead, being the first to pass through a town. Close behind followed the others, adorned with banners expressing support for the guerrillas. About half of the motorized supporters consisted of international activists, NGO workers, and "revolutionary tourists." Whenever the buses entered a town, throngs of people lined the streets, standing in doorways, on balconies, or in front of restaurants and stores. Many of them waved and cheered us on as we passed. There were shouts of *"Viva el EZLN,"* *"Viva Zapata,"* *"Viva Marcos,"* and most of all *"Viva Mexico."* All of them seemed to have great expectations and many appeared to be stunned by the sight of hundreds of scruffy-looking foreigners. The windows of the buses were open, with many of us looking out and waving and cheering back to the people on the street. At regular intervals we also got to hear the shouts that made many of us cringe: "What are you doing in that caravan, damn gringos?" or "Where are the Indígenas?"

Apparent absurdities such as the participation of so many foreigners in the Zapatista Caravan for Peace in Chiapas have to be seen against a background of both security and economic necessity. Although the EZLN's association with foreigners has had the side effect to corroborate doubts about the Zapatistas' indigenous authenticity among the wider Mexican public, the guerrilla movement needed its international supporters there with them. To a lesser extent, we served as a protective shield against potential attacks by police or assassins during the journey. What eventually secured the front-row tickets for internationals, however, was our function in the grand scheme of things. As part of the spectacle, we increased the global significance and hence the media coverage of the event; upon our return, many of us served as emissaries to keep the Zapatista issue burning for a broad international audience of potential donors.

As many Zapatista campaigns, the 2001 march operated on multiple levels. With its focus on the San Andrés Accords and participation in the CNI, the EZLN attempted to consolidate its role as the spearhead of Mexico's indigenous movement. By touring the main squares of the republic, instigating a debate among politicians in the national media, and eventually appearing before Congress, the Zapatistas once again emphasized that their project was not limited to eastern Chiapas but about bringing democratic change to all of Mexico. The inclusion of internationals was to add to the EZLN's profile as a "global player" and, not least, to brighten the prospects for economic independence of its base communities by keeping international aid on the flow. The input of goods, money, and people into the remoter parts of Chiapas has enabled many Zapatista base communities to come closer to their aim of a life in dignity by raising the living standards in their villages. However, independence from the Mexican State has been achieved only at the cost of new dependencies on outsiders with regard to assistance, funding, and volunteers. Of course, the other crucial reason for the Zapatistas not wanting to do without internationals in their communities is the threat of annihilation and repression by the army, paramilitaries, and special police units, which remains to this day.

Considering the internal dynamics of the EZLN, it springs to mind that its indigenous grassroots supporters have kept surprisingly quiet about the obvious failure of the campaign to ratify the San Andrés Accords. To explain this by steadfast loyalty alone would mean overlooking the quintessential flexibility of these people with respect to political affiliations. To me, it is obvious that local Zapatistas were fully aware of the somber prospects of a law that endorsed real autonomy. I think they half expected that their twenty-four comandantes would not come up with the goods but realized that the political theater of the march on Mexico City was also about mustering national and international support in the interest of their own long-term agenda.

Of Loyalty and Local Hegemony

On April 10, 2003, in the Aguascalientes of Morelia, I was able to witness the commemoration of Zapata's death. As had most of the visitors, I arrived in the evening before the festivities and spent the night on the premises of the convention center. At sunrise, I awoke to the sound of running and shouted orders. As I struggled out of my hammock to see what was going on, I found the lawn before the auditorium full of people who all seemed engaged in some sort of military training. A thousand visitors from all over the municipality had gathered in groups separated by gender, age, and military rank and were now busy running or doing gymnastics. Each group was instructed by a superior as to which tasks to perform. The men were running, marching, doing push-ups and various warm-up routines, while most women were engaged in lighter exercises such as running, because many had their babies strapped to their backs. Close to the pole where the Mexican flag was flying, about eighty men and thirty-five women were busy working out. Most of them were in their late teens and their trainers addressed them as milicianos. Their performance was particularly martial as they marched around presenting imaginary guns as well as performing kicks and punches.

The experience emphasized the strong connection between civilian and military elements contained in EZLN membership. Rituals such as marching exercises, flag-lowering ceremonies, and the singing of the Zapatista hymn were part of everyday life in rebel territory. Additionally, dates with relevance to the Zapatista struggle (anniversary of the uprising, commemoration of various martyrs, women's day, etc.) served as junctures for Zapatista residents of a region to take part in political-military ceremonies together. Apart from military ritual, fiestas such as the one I attended on April 10 consisted of political lectures, the inauguration of community schools or clinics, and displays of locally produced goods. Milicianos, insurgentes, parents and siblings of a war hero, and all those who had proven their commitment to the Zapatista cause were publicly praised for their efforts. Such occasions clearly served as affirmations of loyalty and aimed at renewing everyone's commitment to the cause and conduct of the Zapatista revolution as well as strengthening the bond between individual rebel communities.

Whereas the large ejidal organization Unión de Uniones had already been multiethnic in the sense that it comprised campesino communities pertaining to different ethnic groups, Zapatista membership not only encompasses the four main indigenous peoples of eastern Chiapas: Tzeltal, Tzotzil, Tojolabal, and Chol, it also cuts across religious divides. A common jurisdiction, as manifested in the EZLN's revolutionary laws, is enforced throughout rebel territory both in community courts and at the municipal level. The jurisdiction is but one manifestation of everyday practice rooted in a common ideology and a set of values, which provides cohesion at a time of uncertainty and upheaval. All this contributes to a shared sense of solidarity and identity as empowered Indígenas, campesinos, and Zapatistas. Moreover, families whose children decide to become insurgents and militias not only receive prestige but are also privileged with regard to more tangible premiums. As I have pointed out earlier, the EZLN has ensured continued allegiance among its base by using development projects and land as rewards for loyalty as well as an incentive to remain involved in the guerrilla movement.

When taking a look at the sociodemographic changes that have taken place in Zapatista territory since the uprising, two developments are particularly salient: (a) the slow but persistent deterioration of allegiance in the guerrilla movement's historical core areas of the Selva Lacandona, Las Cañadas, and Los Altos, and (b) the founding of new Zapatista settlements on former finca land, which has led to the creation of more homogenous communities with regard to age and EZLN affiliation.

The rebels' loss of support was largely a result of individual and collective choices among indigenous campesinos over which the EZLN lost control. These choices were based on the assessment that continued guerrilla involvement was not worth the effort, whereas a new alliance with the PRI or an independent peasant organization might be more advantageous. The founding of new population centers, on the other hand, was a realization of the paramount purpose of Zapatista mobilization: the settling of fertile plots by the landless who had risked their lives for the revolution. The allocation of recuperated terrains to veteran fighters and their families brought about spaces of unanimous support for the EZLN. Continuity was ensured by the rule that dissenters were punished by having to leave these villages, losing their livelihoods in the process. The new villages were relatively homogenous with respect to the age and ideology of their inhabitants but they also represented a tabula rasa in economic terms because the new settlers all started out with the same amount of land. Whereas the relative poverty of many of the ejidal communities in Las Cañadas can be explained by the poor quality of their plots, the resource-rich new settlements could well lead to a steady increase in living standards for their inhabitants if current programs for production and commercialization (see chapter 6) are pursued successfully. It remains to be seen whether the EZLN will be able to assure a steady and, most of all, uniform growth among its base communities to prevent a split of its constituency along economic lines. It is imaginable that the more affluent new population centers will leave behind the larger, older, and poorer communities riddled by political divisions.

As noted in chapter 1, the EZLN and its predecessor organizations developed in the way they did because the institutions of the state were barely present in the remote settler communities. By taking on judicial, police, and administrative duties, the guerrilla movement came to replace the state with regard to these functions at the local level. After the 1994 uprising, this process was consolidated further in spite of the strong presence of the police and federal military. Particularly during the "second phase of the revolution" (see chapter 6), la organización also took over health and education in parallel to creating structures of autonomous municipal, and later regional, administration. Due to the many police posts and army camps along the roads leading through Las Cañadas and into the Selva Lacandona, the Mexican State undoubtedly had military supremacy in the region. Considering the way people lived in these communities, however, provided they were Zapatistas, the EZLN was "defining the boundaries of the possible" by "enforcing the terms on which things *must* be done on the most everyday of levels" (see Sayer 1994, 375). Not agents of the state but elected EZLN functionaries locked up the drunkards after a fiesta, held court over land conflicts, and decided on issues ranging from matrimonial questions (Barmeyer 1999) to who was allowed to do commerce in the villages. If one was to define the state as an ideological project, a claim that tries "to give unity, coherence, structure and intentionality to what are in practice frequently disunited attempts at domination" (Abrams 1988, summarized in Sayer 1994, 371), one has to diagnose the Mexican state's failure to achieve hegemony in the remote rural communities of Chiapas. However, taking into account the heterogeneity of political affiliation a decade after the uprising, the EZLN too has proven relatively unsuccessful in sustaining local hegemony, particularly in its original core communities. In larger villages characterized by factional splits, such as Morelia, Roberto Barrios, or Taniperlas, not any one party held sway. As in the case of Taniperlas, different factions tried to control the same territory, with the Zapatistas setting up roadblocks and inspecting vehicles going in or out of town while PRIista police officers were simultaneously patrolling other areas (Leyva Solano 1999). Nevertheless, if the creation of the rebel munici-palities was to boost the EZLN's efforts to achieve hegemony in the area of its influence, the further administrative centralization in five regions as proclaimed in August 2003 can be seen as an attempt to consolidate it.

Comparing the EZLN to other guerrilla groups in Latin America that have realized exclusive administrative control over their territory to effectively "become the state," the failure of the Zapatistas to do the same can be sought in their relative absence of authoritarianism. As this happens to be a key feature for winning the movement widespread appeal both in Mexico and abroad, there might be a connection. The need to cater to ethical notions of a "clean guerrilla" to maintain the sympathy of foreigners and urban Mexicans might well have played a role in keeping the EZLN from establishing stricter and possibly more successful control in the area of its influence. Statements by Subcomandante Marcos describing the EZLN as an "undemocratic element" in a relationship of direct community democracy, and its military structure as "contaminating a tradition of democracy and self-governance" (Marcos 2003, part 5), do indeed indicate that that the EZLN's own ideological agenda has become incompatible with a more authoritarian setup.

To understand the contradiction in the Zapatistas' insistence of not wanting to secede from the Mexican State (see Marcos 2003, part 4) while doing their utmost to replace its institutions, it is necessary to return to the notion of the guerrilla movement's distinct clients. To realize their autonomy project, the EZLN needs to cater to the expectations of not only their base in the indigenous villages but also of their supporters from around the globe. As the campesinos in the base communities have sought to establish maximum control over their material, social, and administrative resources, they also require maximum autonomy. In its ultimate consequence, this could be con-gruent with a separate state as, say, the Basque country would be in a federation of autonomous states like the European Union. Although this approach was not in line with EZLN discourse at the time of my research, Burguete (2003, 204) has pointed out that in February 1994

Marcos remarked to a Spanish TV reporter that the Zapatistas were aiming for a relative autonomy with its own institutions similar to the one in Catalonia or the Basque country. Seen in this light, it is no coincidence that the EZLN became mixed up in the politics of the Iberian Peninsula (Marcos 2002); several Basque activists I have spoken to in Chiapas explained to me that they identified with the Zapatista struggle for national liberation because it resonates with their own. Suffice it to say that I, as many others, was originally attracted to the EZLN in spite of the N in their logo rather than because of it. I believe that most internationals who have come to Chiapas were drawn by notions of egalitarianism, communal living, and an independence from globalized capitalism, and the example testifies that the Zapatistas have appealed to the broadest possible spectrum of potential supporters by addressing utopian visions across the board.

Assessing Alternative Development and Guerrilla Membership

NGO involvement in Chiapas has increased the Zapatista population's independence from the Mexican State. However, it has also brought about new contradictions. Apart from the obvious dependence on outside assistance and the problems outlined in chapters 7 and 8, the EZLN's use of NGO projects has in some cases been reminiscent of the way that the Mexican State has employed rural development programs to ensure loyalty from its rural constituencies. When NGOs such as SHOXEL and TENAZAS came onto the scene, the installation of basic infrastructure such as drinking water systems in Mexican rural communities had long been used by the PRI as a means to ensure their loyalty, as well as to get access to resources such as oil located on their territory (Rus 1994, 290). Local caciques organized in the PRI have arranged the distribution of development aid to their clients in exchange for their reelection (see chapter 1). On a global scale, institutions such as the World Bank have used development projects as a means to integrate peripheral communities into the world market. Cooperation with sympathetic NGOs has enabled the indigenous communities organized in the EZLN to bypass both of these options by allowing them integration with the outside world on their own terms. They thus chose to use certain aspects of the imported technology while disregarding or even rejecting others (see the episode of the public shower in chapter 7). As in the case of Arcadia, the introduced technology represented a production unit for valuable fertilizer. Eventually, the dry-compost latrines became so sought after that their principal health-related purpose was torpedoed, as they became a means for establishing a clientelistic network by an indigenous entrepreneur. It is not hard to spot the similarities to practices employed by power brokers in PRI-controlled municipalities. The example shows that ways of doing local politics cannot necessarily be replaced by outsiders in the same way an NGO replaces a state institution as a provider of basic infrastructure.

Assuming that the EZLN has taken on the role of the state in parts of eastern Chiapas—particularly with regard to the administration of development aid—arguments drafted with regard to the relationship between NGOs and states in the developing world can be applied to that between the guerrilla movement and its service providers. Husson (1998) points out that by "doubling" the state in taking on its traditional role as a service provider, NGOs are actually strengthening it. The argument that developmental aid supports state control is a common perspective in the discussion on development. Bierschenk, Elwert, and Kohnert (1993) argue that those segments of the population supportive of a particular state in many developing countries even owe their survival to developmental aid. This does not apply only in the sense that these people live off development money or serve their clients with it. Successful development aid also has the side effect of legitimizing the sovereignty of the state and the classes associated with it in the eyes of the population. In the communities where living standards have improved due to the provision of infrastructure, education, and health services, NGO projects strengthen both the EZLN as an organization and legitimate those community members holding key positions in the guerrilla movement. However, there are empirical studies on the effects of NGO activities and their relation with the respective state administration in West Africa that come to an opposite conclusion. They find the state is weakened rather than strengthened by developmental aid because the population tends to compare the efficacy of developmental projects with that of the local administration. Because the former are generally perceived as superior, if only due to their superior financial and material resources, people turn away from the state administration and approach the NGOs instead (Reijne and van Rouveroy van Nieuwaal 1999). Until the implementation of la resistencia policies in the mid-1990s (see chapter 4), development projects in the base communities, if they existed at all, were delivered by the institutions of the Mexican State. One can assume that later NGO performance contrasted previous experiences with state-directed development. In cases of successful projects, this would indeed have contributed to a continuing delegitimization of the Mexican State. Likewise, unsuccessful NGO projects reflect negatively back onto the EZLN.

Whereas some authors have suspected a vanguardist in-group puppeteering an army of obtuse Indígenas (see chapter 1), I hope to have shown that the guerrilla movement was ultimately controlled by its indigenous support base. Through more or less democratic mechanisms (chapter 3) and by way of exit or the threat of it, the indigenous communities have steered the organization, which for two decades they have also staffed and shaped as their instrument for social change. The wave of dissenters seen in the late 1990s (chapter 4) show that EZLN policies were not always in accordance with the interests of some of its base. Of the many communities that had affiliations with the EZLN in the twenty years of its existence, I estimate that at least half of all the people that once constituted the guerrilla movement's base de apoyo have since terminated their allegiance; some of them resumed it later. The fact that so many people came and went, however, highlights a strong democratic element linked to organizational membership for, had affiliation been maintained by means of repression, there would hardly have been the observed degree of fluctuation.

There were various reasons for people in the base communities to want to quit the EZLN. As outlined in chapter 4, membership entailed duties that were at times perceived as strenuous, and deviance carried social and material sanctions. However, the perception of being poor and differences over how to best deal with communal crises (that usually had strong economic components) have been principal causes for leaving the EZLN. Upward mobility was an aspiration of those communities and individuals who left the organization, but it is questionable if the dropouts actually achieved this. Far from experiencing a visible improvement of their economic situation in the short term, some of the families in La Gardenia or San Emiliano lost their base for subsistence as a result of quitting the guerrilla. However, the case of 20 de Noviembre, where former Zapatistas were able to hold on to lands squatted on in the course of the uprising, shows that concerted action by all community members can be a way of avoiding such sanctions.

On the whole, I have found a puzzling tendency for EZLN affiliation among the poorer segments of population, at least with respect to the settlers of Las Cañadas. That these people, who have constituted the bulk of the organization's base, have also influenced its policy became once more apparent in the changes announced by the EZLN in August 2003 that aimed at a more equal distribution of outside aid and projects (see chapter 8). Entrepreneurial activities such as the ones by the inhabitants of La Gardenia of fixing the road and forcing passing trucks to pay for the service (see chapter 2) were "irregular" in the sense that they constituted an initiative by individual community members rather than a Zapatista project. The fact that the guerrilla movement allowed this type of economic activities to occur can be seen as a concession made by the organization in the light of looming desertions. Cases such as the village that used roadblocks or the ones that pressed for the installation of a water system just like the one their neighbors were receiving (see introduction), show how individual communities can apply leverage from within the organization. The issue of wood exploitation in San Emiliano (chapter 4) serves as an example of how control over a united rebel village can slip from the EZLN community council and end up with individuals who decide to act in their own interest rather than in that of the wider movement.

With the betterment of their economic situation and the growing perception that the guerrilla organization did not live up to expectations, the indigenous campesinos of Chiapas seemed all too willing to try out what they perceived as other options. Frequent shifts of affiliation among the inhabitants of Selva Lacandona and Las Cañadas confirm that they are pragmatic planners of their fate, willing to throw their lot with whomever they trust to help them along the way to fulfilling their aspirations. This, however, does not mean that experiments with communalism, grassroots democracy, communist ideology, and other forms of radical utopias do not leave their mark on the people exposed to them. Indeed, the relative stability of allegiance particularly among the inhabitants of the new Zapatista settlements where revolutionary practice is part of everyday life (more so than in the older and usually divided communities) bears witness to the fact that these people are indeed committed to a cause that transcends their own immediate benefit.

Notes

Notes to Preface

1. Las Cañadas refers to a region of deep river valleys reaching from the high-altitude region of Los Altos in central Chiapas into the vast and low-lying plains covered by the tropical rain forest known as Selva Lacandona on the Mexican side of the border and as El Petén on the Guatemalan side.

2. An Indígena is an indigenous person. I have chosen Indígena instead of Indian, Indio, or indeed Maya, because the native people of Chiapas use this term to refer to themselves.

3. I changed all names of the communities where I personally conducted ethnographic research to protect their inhabitants from police and paramilitary repression. Likewise, the names of all my informants and some of the local NGOs mentioned in this book were altered.

4. The names of all people affiliated with the Zapatista struggle, solidarity activists and people from indigenous communities alike, were changed as a measure of protection.

5. Our visitors were mainly Cipriano's relatives or friends whom I refer to in the text by their pseudonyms of Sergio, Miriam, Griselda, Santos, Yasmin, and Blas.

6. These five "civilian bases" were created after the destruction of the convention center in Guadalupe Tepeyac, the site of the National Democratic Convention (Convención Nacional Democrática, or CND) convoked by the Zapatistas in August 1994. The name Aguascalientes refers to the northern Mexican town that had hosted the meeting of Emiliano Zapata and Francisco Villa in 1914. With the introduction of a regional Zapatista administration, the Aguascalientes were rechristened Caracoles in August 2003.

7. A finca is a landed estate owned by wealthy families and run by way of a feudal system employing the workforce of peons. In the cases covered in this book, most terrains occupied in the course of the 1994 uprising (particularly in the cases of La Gardenia, San Emiliano, and Tierra Nueva) were indeed finca land. Levya Solano (1998), Harvey (1998), and Gledhill (1999), however, have pointed out that a significant portion of the lands taken over by Zapatistas and independent peasant organizations included medium-size farms.

Notes to Introduction

1. Ladino is a term used in Central America and southern Mexico to contrast members of the Spanish-speaking local elites from indigenous peasant farmers.

2. The concept of hegemony is attributed to Antonio Gramsci who defines it as "rule through a combination of coercion and consent" (Mallon 1995). Mallon's own concept of hegemony is more complex, as she defines it both as the "nested continuous processes through which power and meaning are contested, legitimated and redefined at all levels of society," and as the result of such hegemonic processes: a common social and moral project based on a precarious balance among contesting forces. It is this project, which includes elite notions of political culture, that enables those in power to rule through a combination of coercion and consent (4).

3. Compa is a locally used term for *compañero* (comrade) that particularly stresses the bond between the remaining Zapatistas in former united communities, which are often characterized by the existence of several political factions.

4. In the literature, the term "faction" refers to a form of political groupings, which appear in situations of conflict and rival for the control over resources and people (Nicholas 1965). They are usually characterized by patron-client relationships, with a local leader making use of material incentives, debt, and kinship to recruit his followers and keep them in line. I use the term to include political groupings that are not necessarily defined by such vertical ties and the resulting imbalance of power between individual members, but whose cohesion rather stems from shared experiences characterized by poverty, outside repression, and collective organization.

5. Ejido is a common land owned and used by *ejidatarios* forming an association of independent producers with usufructuary rights over individual parcels of land (Chevalier and Buckles 1995).

6. Keck and Sikkink (1998, 4) define the term "framing" (first introduced by Erving Goffman 1974 and adapted by Snow and Benford 1988) as "the conscious strategic efforts by groups of people to fashion shared understandings of the world and of themselves that legitimate and motivate collective action" (McAdam, McCarthy, and Zald 1996, 6).

7. In 1995 and 1996 the highland town of San Andrés Larrainzar hosted a series of dialogues between delegates of the EZLN and the Comission for Concord and Pacification (Comisión de Conrcordia y Pacificación, or COCOPA) from the Mexican parliament, under the mediation of the San Cristóbal diocese, particularly bishop Samuel Ruiz. Out of the five topics covered—Indigenous Rights and Culture, Democracy and Justice, Living Standards and Development, Women's Rights, and Peace with Justice and Dignity—only the first was ever agreed on; it was signed in February 1996 (García de León 2002, 261–63).

8. According to Alvarez, Dagnino, and Escobar (1998) the division between "new" and "old" social movements came about in the 1980s. "New Social

Movements were those for which identity was important, that engaged in 'new forms of doing politics,' and those that contributed to new forms of sociability. Indigenous, ethnic, ecological, women's, gay, and human rights movements were the candidates of choice. Conversely, urban, peasant, labor, and neighborhood movements, among others, were seen as more conventionally struggling for needs and resources" (6).

9. I first noticed the term "the second phase of the revolution," which was later employed both by NGO workers and my indigenous informants, when it was used by delegates taking part in an autonomous municipal assembly in the Zapatista village of 29 de Febrero in December 2001, as they discussed setting up an autonomous production scheme in their region.

10. NGO activist Charlie, conversation, November 2000.

Notes to Chapter 1

1. Campesino is a Mexican term for peasant farmer.

2. For example, Campeche received federal developmental aid during the presidency of Echeverría in 1970–1976 (Gates 1993).

3. The joining of local producer groups in large associations was first encouraged under the presidency of Echeverría (1970–1976) (Fox and Gordillo 1989, 141–42).

4. Chicle is the coagulated milky juice of the sapodilla tree, used as the principal ingredient of chewing gum. *American Heritage Dictionary*, 3rd ed., s.v. "Chicle."

5. A pallacate bandana is a red patterned scarf that has become one of the Zapatistas' insignias. It is worn around the neck by both men and women in the base communities to indicate their membership in the guerrilla movement, and can also be used to cover the face when being photographed.

6. Catequistas are Catholic indigenous lay preachers who act as "cultural mediators between the community and the church" (Leyva Solano 1995, 393).

7. The bolstering of Protestant communities as an important feature of the government's counterinsurgency campaign of the second half of the 1990s can be seen as an answer to the subversive role of the Catholic diocese and the grassroots organizations it had helped to set up. It is worth noting that the percentage of Protestant converts in the regions in question (e.g., Ocosingo had 27 percent in 1990) is proportionally higher than in the rest of Chiapas (16 percent in 1990) (Leyva Solano and Ascencio Franco 1996, 68).

8. State repression culminated in the year of the Olympic Games in Mexico when police and army units perpetrated a massacre among hundreds of students who had gathered for a demonstration on the Plaza de las tres Culturas in Tlatelolco, Mexico City.

9. Tello's book appeared at the same time that the Zedillo government launched its February 1995 offensive against the EZLN's support base in eastern Chiapas, and when arrest orders were issued for dozens of alleged EZLN leaders by the attorney general's office (Procuraduría General de la Rebública, or PGR). Many of them had been "unmasked" in Tello's book, which relies on uncited police and military files and on selective interviews with advisors of peasant organizations (see also Harvey 1998, 9).

10. Leyva Solano (2003a) contends that, particularly for the first significant government projects in 1992, the Unión de Uniones functioned as a political broker with the final say over primary schooling, health campaigns, the building of infrastructure, and the flow of subsidies.

11. Since late 1989 the public face of the EZLN was known as the Emiliano Zapata Peasant Alliance (ACIEZ). In early 1992 it changed its name to ANCIEZ, adding "National" to its title, with member organizations in six central and northern Mexican states (Harvey 1998, 195).

12. Xochitl Leyva Solano, conversation, May 12, 2001; inhabitants of San Emiliano, conversations, 1997; inhabitants of La Gardenia, conversations, 2001.

13. Eyewitnesses, conversations, January 2001.

14. Ronfeldt and Arquilla (1998) define the term "swarming" as the convergence of the dispersed nodes of a network of small forces on a target from multiple directions.

15. Moreover, I question the value of Ronfeldt and Arquilla's unspecific approach (1998) that classifies hackers, the Islamic fundamentalist Hamas, and pro-Zapatista NGOs as part of the same category.

16. In the mid- to late 1990s, an approach to asserting autonomy in Chiapas consisted in the creation of Autonomous Pluriethnic Regions (RAPs) at the initiative of the CEOIC. In their willingness to compromise with the government, their strategy differed from that of the Zapatistas and turned out to be short-lived but effective as they were taken into account in the remunicipalization realized by the Salazar government, who came into power in 2000.

17. The establishment of Zapatista autonomous *municipios* continued over the following years. The strategically important and multiethnic (Tzeltal and Tzotzil) autonomous municipio "Ernesto Che Guevara" with its municipal seat in Moisés Gandhi north of Ocosingo, for example, was inaugurated on September 28, 1997 (Municipio Autónomo Ernesto Che Guevara 1999).

18. Inhabitants of San Emiliano and La Gardenia who were affected by the army raid, conversations, 1996, 1997, 2001, respectively.

19. Other sources mention an increase of federal soldiers and special police units in Chiapas to seventy thousand at the turn of the millennium (Hidalgo Domínguez 1999).

20. According to Hidalgo Domínguez (1997a, 1997b, 1998), between 1995 and 1997 over 5,000 people had been displaced and 120 killed in the four municipalities making up the north of the state. Since then, the highlands had become a focal point of paramilitary activity. Well over 8,000 people were displaced and 78 killed in the space of eight months alone.

21. In the realization of Programa Cañadas some of the same well-tried mechanisms were used that had been key to both the solidarity committees promoted by the Salinas presidency in the late 1980s and the organizing efforts that led to the emergence of the Zapatista movement. Community assemblies were the backbone of the new development program, and they appointed delegates and drafted petitions. The consultancy, however, was taken on by state agents who were based in twenty-seven Centers of Social Attention (Centros de Atención Social), where matters relating to health, education, and the distribution of subsidized goods were coordinated (Jarque 2000, 137).

22. A particularly salient example is the conflict between the Organization of Coffee Growers from Altamirano and Ocosingo (ORCAO) and the Zapatista autonomous municipio of Moisés Gandhi that flared up over a stretch of territory along the road between San Cristóbal and Ocosingo in 2001. The land had originally been squatted on by members of both organizations in the course of the 1994 uprising but large parts of it were confiscated by the Mexican Federal Army, which built a base there in February 1995. The base was removed as a concession to the Zapatistas when President Fox came to power and both ORCAO members and Zapatistas laid claim to the land. This led to several confrontations focusing on the commercial center Arco Iris, which the Zapatista base communities of the region used to market their products (field observations and interviews carried out in Cuxulhá between October 2001 and May 2002).

23. Another explanation for the involvement of the EZLN could be seen in the strong presence of Basque activists in the autonomous municipios who might have asked Marcos for mediation.

24. My translation of an excerpt from the Common Proposals issued by the Mexican Government and the EZLN and later agreed on by the EZLN and the COCOPA as part of the San Andrés Accords on Indigenous Rights and Culture (*Propuestas Conjuntas que el Gobierno Federal y el EZLN se Comprometen a Enviar a las Instancias de Debate y Decisión Nacional*, Correspondientes al Punto 1.4 de las Reglas de Procedimiento, de 16 de enero de 1996, quoted in Hernández Navarro and Vera Herrera 1998, 68).

25. Enlace Civil is the EZLN's "civil link" organization whose San Cristóbal–based office was set up in 1996 to coordinate aid and solidarity projects destined for Zapatista base communities, as well as to accredit human rights observers (see also chapter 5).

26. Convention 169 recognizes indigenous peoples' right to self-determination and autonomy by way of a separate administrative structure and justice system and the right to retain their customs, institutions, and customary laws (Assies,

van der Haar, and Hoekema 2000, 3). Mattiace (2003, 161) sees the convention's principal limitation in the fact that, although it refers to indigenous peoples as "peoples," it does not imply that Indígenas can claim the rights accorded to peoples in international law.

27. The campaign to promote the ratification of the San Andrés Accords was first outlined in the Fifth Declaration of the Selva Lacandona (EZLN 1998) and culminated three years later with the march of twenty-four Zapatista comandantes to Mexico City. They were accompanied by a caravan of supporters, many of them from the Congreso Nacional Indígena (see chapter 9).

28. In the context of a nationwide publicity drive in September 1997, there was a march from Chiapas to Mexico City by 1,111 Zapatistas, each one representing an autonomous village. In a joint communiqué (Autonomomous Communities on Attack against San Juan la Libertad) by thirty-two Zapatista municipalities from June 13, 1998, the following municipios were listed: San Juan de la Libertad, San Pedro Chenalhó, Nuevo Bochil, Jitotol, Ixtapa, Simojovel, Vicente Guerrero, Francisco Villa, Benito Juárez, José María Morelos y Pavón, San Pedro Michoacán, Maya, Ricardo Flores Magón, San Salvador, Miguel Hidalgo y Costilla, Cabanha, Sakamanch'en de los Pobres, Santa Catarina, Magdalena de la Paz, Cancuc, Huitiupan, Sabanilla, Trabajo, Independencia, La Paz, Libertad de los Pueblos Mayas, Tierra y Libertad, Francisco Gómez, San Manuel, 16 de Noviembre, Ernesto Che Guevara, and Primero de Enero.

29. Enlace Civil (2002a) listed the following twenty-two autonomous municipios pertaining to five different zones: 16 de Noviembre, Ernesto Che Guevara, Lucio Cabañas, Miguel Hidalgo y Costilla, Olga Isabel, Primero de Enero, and Vicente Guerrero in the Zona Altamirano; San Andrés Sakamch'en de los Pobres, San Juan de la Libertad, San Pedro Polhó, and Santa Catarina Pantelhó in the Zona Altos; La Paz, El Trabajo, and Vicente Guerrero in the Zona Norte; General Emiliano Zapata, Libertad de los Pueblos Mayas, Tierra y Libertad, and San Pedro de Michoacán in the Zona Selva Tojolabal; and Francisco Villa, Francisco Gómez, Ricardo Flores Magón, and San Manuel in the Zona Selva Tzeltal.

30. The ARIC *independiente* (Independent Association of Collective Interest) resulted from a split in the ARIC Unión de Uniones in July 1994, as some member organizations established parallel leadership structures identified with the EZLN while the elements that subsequently turned into the ARIC *oficial* cooperated with the governing PRI (Harvey 1998, 215).

31. In a December 1994 declaration the EZLN states that legislation in the new rebel municipalities is based both on the Mexican Constitution of 1917 and on the Zapatista revolutionary laws. These laws, first published in *El Despertador Mexicano* (EZLN 1993a), were complemented by local laws set by the respective community assembly (EZLN 1994a).

32. The cargo system, where public offices are taken on by community members for a certain time, is extensively described by Favre (1973) for Tzeltal Highland communities; it still exists in a modified form in the recent settler communities of Las Cañadas and Selva Lacandona.

Notes to Chapter 2

1. The vagueness regarding the location and history of the villages featured in this chapter is intentional. With a heavy heart, I have chosen to omit salient historical and geographical details to protect my informants, who live in a region still marked by factional violence, extrajudicial killings, and repression by army, police, and paramilitaries.

2. Peones are day laborers on finca land working under conditions resembling serfdom.

3. Ampliaciones are extensions in acreage to the total area of ejido land made available to a particular community by the state.

4. The following sections on San Emiliano are mainly based on conversations and interviews with eight men and three women from the village, carried out during my stay as a volunteer human rights observer in 1996 and 1997.

5. The collective management of ejido lands by capacitados was not an invention of modern Zapatistas, for this option had already been laid down in article 27 of the Mexican Constitution. In an article on everyday endeavors by local groups to appropriate the institution of the ejido and use it to their own ends, Sergio Zendejas (1995, 30–31) describes the arrangements in a village in northwestern Michoacán, where the entire local population had access to communal lands, regardless of the individual's legal landholding status. In this setup each nonejidatario household was allowed to clear small plots of stony hillside for cultivation as well as to use the ejido's common hills to hunt and gather firewood and wild fruits.

6. Pozól is coarse dough made solely from boiled maize and lime that is mixed with water and drunk for breakfast. The pozól balls, which are taken along to the milpas as a snack by the men, can be kept for three days. They become increasingly sour as fermentation sets in and are eaten with sugar, salt, and chili, often accompanied by leafy vegetables and tree shoots that grow wild in the mountains.

7. The lime is produced locally by burning rocks for three days in earthen furnaces, a process undertaken twice a year by each family.

8. When I asked whether the procedure in the other two villages had been similar, I was told that the majority of their inhabitants were not Zapatistas and did not understand that the land had been liberated only as a result of armed organization. Instead, they thought the land had finally got into their possession because they had been soliciting it from the government for years. In fact, there had been pending requests by the three communities in question for those very finca lands in an office drawer somewhere in Tuxtla (Cipriano's family and Miriam, interviews conducted in La Gardenia, January 2001).

9. The term insurgentes (insurgents) refers to the full-time guerrillas who are stationed in the mountains and the jungle and only seldom visit their villages of origin. While also constituting part of the EZLN, milicianos (militias), on the

other hand, are usually young men in possession of a firearm who spend most of the time in their villages and are mobilized only in emergencies (see chapter 2, La Organización).

10. At the time of my research, the Mexican peso was valued at about ten pesos to the U.S. dollar. Conversions of peso amounts into U.S. dollars throughout the book can therefore easily be made by dividing the respective numbers by ten. A *sonte* (a sonte being four hundred cobs of corn) was worth about a hundred pesos. When planted with maize on cultivated terrain, the squatted lands yield forty to sixty sonte per hectare but at least twenty-five in a bad year (Sergio, conversations, January 2001).

11. What a fitting compensation could mean in practice was graphically demonstrated to me one day when I witnessed two young men showing up utterly exhausted at San Emiliano's assembly space. They had just arrived from the mountains and were carrying on their backs an incredibly heavy log, which was to serve as a communal bench in the future. The carrying had been prescribed to them as compensation for a missed day of community work.

12. Sergio and Miriam, conversation in San Cristóbal, November 2000.

13. Cipriano, report, August 2003.

14. See Harvey (1998, 167): "Money that had previously been used for religious fiestas was redirected for purchasing arms on the black market. There was no massive or sudden sale of arms to the EZLN. Instead, they gradually and clandestinely built up their own collection of weapons and munitions."

15. Already at the time of my research there were attempts at intensive agriculture on recuperated terrains. To optimize their maize harvests, local farmers used a tractor available for a percentage of the yield at the autonomous municipal seat.

16. The three new Zapatista settlements introduced in this section all had a water system installed at the time of my research, when I worked there volunteering for a local development project (see chapter 7).

17. A mando is a commander or leader and is the local term for the upper echelons of the EZLN, which evokes military top-down hierarchies rather than democratic mechanisms of decision making.

Notes to Chapter 3

1. In the past, *parentesco* relations and the groups of common descent used to have this function. By the 1970s, these had largely dissolved and lost their significance (Favre 1973, 260).

2. Friedrich describes caciquismo as a type of informal politics in Latin America, characterized by the arbitrary control a local leader has over a given group. This core group around a cacique (a cacicazgo), often consisting of his male relatives and his compadres, usually provides all the important functionaries in a given small or medium-size rural community. Such communities are often composed

of various factions tied up in a power struggle over land. Friedrich regards the phenomenon of caciquismo as the direct result of such power struggles (Friedrich 1965).

3. The existence of organizational functionaries pertaining to the military hierarchy of the EZLN at communal, municipal, and regional levels was also explicitly mentioned by Subcomandante Marcos in a series of communiqués issued at the occasion of the creation of new regional Zapatista governments in August 2003 (Marcos 2003).

4. Every Friday while the autoridades convened, San Emiliano's catequistas held a brief church service with the principales and chose the Bible passages for the coming Sunday. In doing this, they took into account the momentary situation in the community. Thus, after a humiliating army encroachment upon the community in January 1997, a passage from the Old Testament was chosen in which the people of Israel, with whom the community identifies strongly, after initial defeat, emerge victorious from a battle with their enemies (Joshua 6:1–27, the destruction of Jericho, Kings James Version).

5. Former insurgente Espártaco, conversations, 2001, 2002.

6. Interestingly, the fine was only ten pesos for women. Is this an indicator of their perceived relative unimportance or rather an acknowledgement of their domestic responsibilities and/or lesser opportunities to get cash?

7. Two women from La Gardenia who attended an artesanía workshop in San Cristóbal, interview, May 2001.

8. The assembly was composed of adults, which in the local context included everyone over the age of fourteen.

9. Obviously, any comparison with former times has to be specific. Cancian (1965, 24–27) for example found that, in 1960s Chiapas, it was not uncommon to have a presidente municipal in his late twenties.

10. This development was finalized under the presidency of Carlos Salinas in 1992, when several modifications to article 27 of the constitution and a new agrarian law were converted into Mexican legislation. The main changes included the right to purchase, sell, or rent the individual plots and communal lands that made up the ejido. Moreover, private companies were allowed to purchase land, associations between private investors and ejidatarios were made possible, and most importantly the sections of article 27 that allowed for campesinos to petition for land redistribution were deleted (Harvey 1998, 186–87).

11. Inhabitants of La Gardenia, conversations, 2001.

12. Such raids took place in Taniperlas (autonomous municipio of Ricardo Flores Magón), Amparo Aguatinta (autonomous municipio of Tierra y Libertad), Nicolas Ruiz (a non-Zapatista independent town in the highlands of Chiapas), San Andrés Larrainzar (autonomous municipio of San Andrés Sacamchen) and El Bosque (autonomous municipio of San Juan de la Libertad), where ten

indigenous Zapatistas and an unaccounted number of soldiers were killed in the attack on the town hall (Enlace Civil 1998).

Notes to Chapter 4

1. As part of a government scheme to bolster subsistence agriculture, an average of two hundred pesos per month and family was given to Mexican campesinos as a subsidy for their crops (see introduction).

2. Exceptions were the relatively few Zapatista villages benefiting from NGO involvement at the time, such as Polhó and Guadalupe Tepeyac, as well as some of the mostly smaller new population centers with road access.

3. This excludes many of the new villages founded by the EZLN on squatted farmland (nuevos centros de población), most of which consisted of fewer than thirty families, all with particularly strong ties to the guerrilla movement.

4. The word rajones, from *rajarse*, to break down or to burst, is the local term for former Zapatistas who have deserted the guerrilla movement. Within Mexican vernacular the term actually means "letting yourself be raped," a signification that dates back to the conquest.

5. Inhabitants of nearby Gardenia, at that time still unanimously Zapatista, spoke of truckloads full of cattle arriving in San Emiliano. They also marveled at the new school and clinic built by the government and wondered aloud how much PROGRESA money the women of San Emiliano were receiving.

6. The government's strategy was particularly apparent in light of the accounts from municipios outside the Zapatista core area where EZLN defectors had been turned away when applying for PROCAMPO aid (inhabitants of 29 de Febrero, interviews, November 2001).

7. Paying the teachers for their work had not been an option due to the fact that the inhabitants of the village were all subsistence farmers with only an occasional income from the sale of pigs or small amounts of coffee.

8. After having been in power for most of the twentieth century, in 2000 the PRI lost both the Mexican presidency and the Chiapas state government to the PAN and to a PAN/PRD alliance, respectively.

9. An ARICista is member of the ARIC, in this case of the ARIC independiente.

10. For example, Blas, the community teacher, was hypocritically denounced by ARICistas for selling them beer, while Zapatistas accused the guerrilla dropouts for secretly selling communal land to logging companies.

11. In its communiqués as well as in the speeches of its local functionaries, the EZLN has regularly referred to the Mexican government as the *mal gobierno*, juxtaposing its own autonomous councils as Juntas de Buen Gobierno (Good Government Councils).

Notes to Chapter 5

1. Information in these paragraphs is from Gaspar Morquecho, a former member of the San Cristóbal–based NGO CHILTAK and a founding member of CONPAZ (interview in San Cristóbal, May 8, 2002).

2. The municipalities in these partnerships were from Italy, Catalonia, and the Basque country (Enlace Civil 2000).

3. The effort to portray the hermanamientos as a two-way partnership shone through in the Zapatistas' public delivery of gasoline to Cuba in 2006 and maize to their partners in Central America (EZLN 2005).

4. The students were mostly from the National Autonomous University of Mexico (Universidad Nacional Autónoma de México, or UNAM), the Autonomous Metropolitan University (Universidad Autónoma Metropolitana, or UAM), and the National School of Anthropology and History (Escuela Nacional de Antropología y Historia, or ENAH).

5. To protect the people who work in what remains a volatile situation, I have changed the names of local organizations that supported development projects in Zapatista villages at the time of my research.

6. When showing movies in Zapatista communities, they were copying the well-tried practice of *cine mecapál* (carry-on cinema). The Austrian filmmaker Thomas Waibel and a crew of local indigenous cinematographers were the first ones to hook projectors to a head-strap harness (mecapál) and carry them on their backs into remote rebel villages in 1996, where they showed home-made documentaries with relevance to the Zapatista struggle as well as cinematic classics.

7. The following excerpts are taken from SFC's online brochure:

   "The Maya peoples of Chiapas, Mexico, dream of building a better life for their children. After centuries of horrific oppression, they chose January 1, 1994, as the day to begin an idealistic insurrection to bring attention to their plight. . . .

   After more than ten years of returning to the roots of Maya culture, rescuing lost ceremonies, and studying democratic community practices, the best women and men of the Tzeltal, Tzotzil, Chol, Tojolabal, Mam and Zoque people made their cry of '*Ya Basta.*' . . . The corporate sector seems to feel that investment in Chiapas, extraordinarily rich in natural resources such as hydroelectric, uranium, copper, and most importantly oil, would be more productive without the presence of the Maya people. . . .

   JOIN THE 'TOURISTS OF CONSCIENCE'

   Live and work in a rebel Maya community in the highlands of Chiapas, MEXICO. Volunteer in a unique cultural and educational exchange working for peace with justice. Help create the first autonomous, indigenous junior high school in the Mexican southeast. Learn Spanish and Tzotzil. Skills required are respect for indigenous culture and acceptance of collective process."

(Schools for Chiapas 2002)

8. CIEPAC stands for Centro de Investigaciones Económicas y Políticas de Acción Comunitaria, or Center for Economic and Political Research of Community Action, a San Cristóbal–based NGO that has been publishing informative bulletins on issues regarding the Zapatista struggle as well as on broader issues of resistance and exploitation in Chiapas. COMPITCH stands for Consejo de Organizaciones de Médicos y Parteras Indígenas Tradicionales de Chiapas, or Council of Organizations of Indigenous Traditional Healers and Midwives of Chiapas.

9. Information from this paragraph is from a SEVA employee (interview, November 2001).

10. The Mut Vitz Collective is an association of primarily Zapatista Tzotzil highland villages. Mut Vitz was initiated by 500 coffee-producing campesinos in 1997, whose number rapidly grew to 1,400 in 2001. The members of the cooperative maintained 0.5 to 1.0 hectares each with an average yield of 460 to 920 kilos of raw coffee, which was refined on location and sold in North America and Europe by the Human Bean Company or the Café Libertad solidarity group as "Zapatista Coffee." Due to fair-trade price policies, the cooperative was able to pay its producers eighteen pesos per kilo instead of the twelve pesos that the *coyotes* (intermediary merchants) were paying (Gallardo Caballero 2001; Café Libertad 2001).

11. The name of this organization is a pseudonym.

12. Mexican students are required to contribute six months of social service as part of their university education, often as teaching assistants in indigenous communities.

13. Allusions to noble Mayan rebels and revolutionary romanticism are particularly salient on the Web sites of the Schools for Chiapas (2002) and Global Exchange (2002).

Notes to Chapter 6

1. That the role of women in the Cañada of Morelia was generally a rather active one came across in the fact that of the twenty-six basketball teams, eleven were made up of women. Players on the eleven football teams, however, were all male except for the one team staffed by internationals.

2. I am grateful to Anne Hild, who conducted her own research on educación autónoma at the time, for arranging the interview.

3. By 2004, educational promoters from the Zona Altamirano associated with the Caracol Morelia had addressed the problem of providing Zapatista children with school lunches in the following way: for every child enlisted in one of the autonomous primary schools, the parents had to donate a hen for the school's chicken run, which the pupils took care of and which supplied the eggs to sustain them (Muñoz Ramírez 2004).

Notes to Chapter 7

1. As this was still prior to the introduction of resistencia policies by the EZLN, that move did not actually represent a transgression of Zapatista law.

2. Gardenia Zapatistas discussed the difficulties to obtain any government aid faced by PRIistas from their own village as well as by those from San Emiliano (interviews, April 2002).

3. Ya Basta is an association of several local groups organized in the context of the autonomous *centri sociali* (social centers) in Italy. The movement emerged in solidarity with the Zapatista struggle at the time of the Intergalactic Meeting in 1996. Beyond solidarity work, Ya Basta has organized local campaigns in support for the free movement of migrants and against capitalist globalization (More about the Italian Ya Basta 2000).

4. See for example the English translation of an article by Gil Olmos (2000) informing of the impending completion of the turbine or the Web site of the local Amnesty International Group in the East German town of Jena that features a German translation of an article by Bellinghausen (2001) announcing the eventual installation of the turbine a year later.

5. Gil Olmos (2000) comes up with a figure of US$250,000, while Avilés (2000), published a few days later in the same newspaper, also provides a figure of US$150,000.

Notes to Chapter 8

1. By that time (January 2001) the community had not yet completely divided and still had one set of autoridades.

2. He actually used the term *forastero* (stranger), which denoted his status as an outsider as well as his landlessness.

3. Coletos is the term for the nonindigenous and often conservative inhabitants of San Cristóbal.

4. This regulation is particularly crucial in the case of fair-trade coffee links such as those the Mut Vitz cooperative was involved in. Part of the "socially friendly" policies of organizations such as the Human Bean Company consisted in awarding bonuses for the producer communities to invest in organic agriculture as well as in community projects.

Notes to Chapter 9

1. During the lengthy strike at the National Autonomous University of Mexico (UNAM) in 1999/2000, the EZLN endured in their solidarity with the students organized in the General Strike Committee (Comité General de Huelga, or CGH) who had become almost completely isolated toward the forced end of the strike.

2. These eleven demands, issued in the first declaration of the Selva Lacandona, are work, land, housing, food, health care, education, independence, freedom, democracy, justice, and peace (EZLN 1993b).

3. The slogans are "Living for the homeland or dying for freedom," "Everything for everyone, nothing (only) for ourselves," and "For a world wherein many worlds fit."

4. Both mailing lists were created to disseminate information on the situation in Chiapas, particularly with regard to the human rights situation, but also on Zapatista issues in general. In September 2003, the Chiapas-95 list archive was situated on the server of the University of Texas, Austin, and maintained by Harry Cleaver. The Chiapas-1 list archive, however, had disappeared along with the BURN! server that hosted it as the University of California, San Diego, had shut down the server in June 2000 (Halleck 2003).

Glossary of Spanish Terms

Definitions of terms are not all-inclusive; they have been selected to reflect the context of this book.

acuerdo	agreement (often based on communal consensus)
agencia	communal police agency
Aguascalientes	Zapatista political and cultural center (1994–2003)
alcalde	mayor
alférez	communal religious official
ampliación	plots of land added to an original ejido area
aricista	militant of the peasant organization ARIC
artesanía	arts and crafts
asamblea	(village) assembly
asesores	(political) advisors
autocrítica	self-critique as part of a group discussion
autoridades	(communal) authorities
base de apoyo	Zapatista support base
cacicazgo	core group around a cacique
cacique	power broker with a patron-client network at his or her disposal
camioneta	pickup truck (regularly used as a means of mass transportation)
campamentistas	(international) human rights observers staffing a peace camp
campamento de paz	peace camp in an indigenous community
campesino	peasant subsistence farmer
caoba	type of mahogany
capacitado	someone in possession of an ejido title
Caracol	conch shell, Zapatista regional government seat (since 2003)
cárcel	(village) prison
cargo	communal office, duty
carta liberada	document certifying undertaken military service or the exemption thereof
catequista	catechist, lay preacher
cecri	member of the CCRI

célula	revolutionary cell (of Zapatista insurgents), a meeting of such a cell
chayote	spiny pear-shaped vegetable endemic to southern Mexico
coleto	nonindigenous inhabitant of San Cristóbal
colonia	settlement
comandancia	central command (of the EZLN)
comandante	military commander
comisariado (ejidal)	ejidal commissariat, highest ejidal authority
comité	committee, also member of the CCRI
comité de educación	education committee
comité de salud	health committee
comité iglesial	church committee
compa	comrade (fellow Zapatista)
comunidad (indígena)	(indigenous) community
consejo	council, also individual member of the council
consejo de vigilancia	ejidal communal council for land control, also supervising institution in Zapatista municipal and regional structures
consulta	consultation of the EZLN's support base or of civil society
cooperación	(monetary) contribution
coyote	intermediary merchant
crítica	critique as part of a group discussion
cumpleaños	celebration of a birthday
delegado	delegate, also Zapatista community teacher
de mojado	to cross the border into the United States without documents
derecho consuetudinario	customary law
dirigente	political leader (of a peasant organization)
educación autónoma	autonomous education, state-independent Zapatista school system
ejidatario	someone in possession of an ejido title
ejido	Mexican agrarian institution, also a village on ejido land
encargado	officeholder, someone in charge of a certain (communal) duty
encuentro	meeting (of Zapatistas and their civil society supporters)
finca	landed estate
finquero	landowner
hermanamiento	partnership between a Zapatista municipality and an (international) solidarity group
Indígena	indigenous person
ingeniero	ejido surveyor
insurgente	insurgent (Zapatista full-time guerrilla)
integración	political education in the context of the Zapatista struggle

Junta de Buen Gobierno	Good Government Council (Zapatista regional Government)
ladino	nonindigenous person, member of the Spanish-speaking elite
libre determinación	self-determination
magrina	female holder of a communal ceremonial church office
mal gobierno	bad government, usually a reference to the Mexican government
mandar obedeciendo	Zapatista principle of "governing by obeying"
mando	military superior
maquiladora	assembly plant for export production
mayor	village police
mayordomo	communal religious official
mazorca	cob of corn
mecapál	a porter's head-strap harness
mesa	panel (of the San Andrés consultations)
miliciano	Zapatista village militia
milpa	traditional maize field
monos blancos	white coveralls, members of the Italian Ya Basta Movement
monte	underbrush, fallow milpa
multa	fine (used for compensation in the context of indigenous law)
nuevo centro de población	new population center (newly founded Zapatista settlement)
organización	the EZLN
padrino	godfather
pallacate	red neckerchief worn by Zapatistas and used to cover the face
panela	raw sugar made from cane
pasamontañas	black, woolen balaclava worn by Zapatistas to protect their identity
patrón	landowner, boss
peón	serf
perredista	militant of the Democratic Revolutionary Party (PRD)
portavoz	spokesperson
pozól	maize gruel eaten for breakfast and on the milpa
preparatoria	Mexican equivalent to high school
presidente	president
PRIista	militant of the Institutional Revolutionary Party (PRI)
principal	ceremonial communal office of church elder
promotor/a	health or educational promoter
pueblos de base	(Zapatista) base communities
Quiptic ta Lecubtesel	Unity Is Strength (name of a local ejidal union)

rajón	quitter (former Zapatista who has broken off guerrilla membership)
regidor	community representative to the municipal government
regional	municipal representative of the EZLN
resistencia	(political practice of) resistance against the Mexican State
responsable	communal representative of the EZLN
robo	abduction and sometimes rape of a woman by a man wanting to marry her
sección	revolutionary cell, fighting unit
secretario	secretary
secretario ejidal	ejidal secretary
secundaria	secondary school, Mexican equivalent to junior high school
síndico	attorney general
solar	plot of land beneath and around an ejidatario's house
solicitante	applicant for a land title
sonte	four hundred cobs of corn
subcomandante	title of Marcos, the military chief of the EZLN
suplente	stand-in official
tesorero	treasurer
tierra recuperada	land taken over in the course of the Zapatista uprising
tortilla	plain maize pancake, staple food for Mexico's indigenous population
tuhunel	indigenous deacon
usos y costumbres	local (legal) customs, traditional ways of administering justice
zacate	a type of reed used for thatching

References

Abrams, Philip. 1988. Some Notes on the Difficulty of Studying the State. *Journal of Historical Sociology* 1 (1): 58–89.

Alta, Virginia, Diego Itturalde, and Hermilo López Bassols, eds. 1998. *Pueblos Indígenas y Estado en América Latina*. Quito, Ecuador: Universidad Andina Simón Bolívar.

Alvarez, Sonia E., Evelina Dagnino, and Arturo Escobar, eds. 1998. *Culture of Politics, Politics of Culture: Revisioning Latin American Social Movements*. Boulder, CO: Westview.

American Heritage Dictionary. 1994. Electronic version, 3rd ed. New York: Bartleby.

Anderson, Benedict. 1983. *Imagined Communities: Reflections on the Origin and Spread of Nationalism*. London: Verso.

Assies, Willem, Gemma van der Haar, and André J. Hoekema, eds. 2000. *The Challenge of Diversity: Indigenous Peoples and Reform of the State in Latin America*. Amsterdam: Thela Thesis.

Aubry, Andrés, and Angélica Inda. 1997. ¿Quienes Son los Paramilitares? *La Jornada*. November 23.

———. 1998. La Vida Cotidiana en Pueblos Paramilitares. *La Jornada*. January 29.

Aufheben Collective. 2000. A Commune in Chiapas? Mexico and the Zapatista Rebellion. *Aufheben* 9 (Autumn): 1–56.

Autonomous Municipios. 1998. Autonomous Communities on Attack against San Juan de la Libertad: Joint Communiqué by Thirty-two Zapatista Municipalities. Trans. irlandesa. *Revolt Collection*. Irish Mexico Group. June 13. http://flag.blackened.net/revolt/mexico/ezln/comm_san_juan_june98.html (accessed July 3, 2002).

Avilés, Jaime. 2000. Llegará Mañana a la Realidad la Turbina Donada por Italianos. *La Jornada*. November 29.

Bailey, Frederick George. 1969. *Stratagems and Spoils: A Social Anthropology of Politics*. Oxford: Blackwell.

Banton, Michael, ed. 1965. *Political Systems and the Distribution of Power*. London: Routledge.

Barmeyer, Niels. 1999. Politische und Soziale Organisation in einem Zapatistischen Rebellendorf in Chiapas, Mexiko. Master's thesis, Freie Universität, Berlin.

———. 2003. The Guerrilla Movement as a Project: An Assessment of Community Involvement in the EZLN. *Latin American Perspectives* 30 (January): 122–38.

Barreda Marín, Andres. 2001. Los Peligros del Plan Puebla Panamá. In *Mesoamérica: Los Ríos Profundos: Alternativas Plebeyas al Plan Puebla Panamá*, ed. Armando Bartra, 133–201. Mexico City: El Atajo.

Barth, Frederic. 1966. Models of Social Organization. *Royal Anthropological Institute Occasional Papers*. No. 23. London: Royal Anthropological Institute.

Bartra, Armando, ed. 2001. *Mesoamérica: Los Rios Profundos; Alternativas Plebeyas al Plan Puebla Panamá*. Mexico City: El Atajo.

Bellinghausen, Hermann. 1999. El Gobierno de Chiapas Engrosa Sus Filas con Base en Desertores. *La Jornada*. April 4.

———. 2001. La Solidaridad Hizo Llegar la Energía Eléctrica a la Realidad. *La Jornada*. October 6.

———. 2003. La Fiesta de los Caracoles: En Marcha, las Juntas de Buen Gobierno. *La Jornada*. August 10.

———. 2004a. Consejos Zapatistas Refrendan la Consigna de Mandar Obedeciendo. *La Jornada*. November 19.

———. 2004b. Con Solemne Sobriedad, las Juntas de Buen Gobierno Entregaron Informe Actual. *La Jornada*. September 18.

Benjamin, Thomas. 1996. *A Rich Land, a Poor People: Politics and Society in Modern Chiapas*. Albuquerque: University of New Mexico Press.

Bierschenk, Thomas, Georg Elwert, and Dirk Kohnert, eds. 1993. *Entwicklungshilfe und ihre Folgen: Ergebnisse empirischer Untersuchungen in Afrika*. Frankfurt: Campus.

Bob, Clifford. 2005. *The Marketing of Rebellion: Insurgents, Media and International Activism*. Cambridge: Cambridge University Press.

Bourdieu, Pierre. 1991. *Language and Symbolic Power*. Cambridge, UK: Polity.

Burbach, Roger. 1994. Roots of Postmodern Rebellion in Chiapas. *New Left Review* 205:113–24.

Burguete Cal y Mayor, Araceli. 2003. The De Facto Autonomous Process. In *Mayan Lives Mayan Utopias: The Indigenous Peoples of Chiapas and the Zapatista Rebellion. Impactos Regionales del Zapatismo en Chiapas*, ed. Jan Rus, Rosalva Aida Hernández Castillo, and Shannan L. Mattiace, 191–218. Latin American Perspectives in the Classroom. Lanham, MD: Rowman and Littlefield.

Cabedo Mallol, Vicente. 2004. *Constitucionalismo y Derecho Indígena en América Latina*. Valencia: Colección Amadís.

Café Libertad Kooperative. 2001. Das Konzept unserer Kooperative. http://www.cafe-libertad.de (accessed November 12, 2001).

Calvert, Paul. 2003. Compost Toilets: Technical Brief. *Intermediate Technology Development Group*. http://www.dwaf.gov.za/dir_ws/tkc/vdFileLoad/file.asp?ID=261 (accessed September 26, 2008).

Cancian, Frank. 1965. *Economics and Prestige in a Maya Community*. Stanford, CA: Stanford University Press.

———. 1992. *The Decline of Community in Zinacantán: Economy, Public Life, and Social Stratification, 1960–1987*. Stanford, CA: Stanford University Press.

Castro Soto, Gustavo. 2003. Para Entender al EZLN. *Chiapas al Día* 381. Center for Economic and Political Research of Community Action (CIEPAC). October 23. http://www.ciepac.org/boletines/chiapasaldia.php?id=381 (accessed September 26, 2008).

Castro Soto, Gustavo, and Onésimo Hidalgo Domínguez. 1998. The Untenable Trivialization of Law: Impunity; Three Months after Acteal. *Chiapas al Día* 108. Center for Economic and Political Research of Community Action (CIEPAC). April 11. http://www.ciepac.org/boletines/chiapasaldia.php?id=108 (accessed September 26, 2008).

Centro de Derechos Humanos. Fray Bartolomé de las Casas. 1998. *La Legalidad de la Injusticia*. San Cristóbal de las Casas, Mexico: CDHFB.

Chevalier, Jaques M., and Daniel Buckles. 1995. *A Land without Gods: Process Theory, Maldevelopment and the Mexican Nahuas*. London: Zed Books.

Cloudforest Initiatives. 2000. Interview with Lucio González Ruíz of the Mut Vitz Café Cooperative. In *Cooperativa Mut Vitz, Chiapas, México: Iniciativas Locales para el Autodesarrollo*, ed. Mario Gallardo Caballero. March 4. http://www.pangea.org/ellokal/chiapas (accessed November 12, 2001).

Collier, George A. 1997. Reaction and Retrenchment in the Highlands of Chiapas in the Wake of the Zapatista Rebellion. *Journal of Latin American Anthropology* 3 (1): 14–31.

Collier, George A., and Elizabeth L. Quaratiello. 1999. *Basta! Land and the Zapatista Rebellion in Chiapas*. Oakland: Food First Books.

Columbia Electronic Encyclopedia. 2005. 6th ed. New York: Columbia University Press. http://www.bartleby.com/65/ (accessed December 12, 2005).

Coordinadoras Regionales de la Sociedad Civil en Resistencia. 2002. *Es; Declaration of Coordinadoras*. Chiapas-95 mailing list archive. Harry Cleaver, University of Texas, Austin. June 7. http://www.eco.utexas.edu/~archive/chiapas95/2002.06/msg00110.html accessed July, 3, 2003).

Cornelius Wayne A., Ann L. Craig, and Jonathan Fox, eds. 1989. *Mexico's Alternative Political Futures*. La Jolla: Center for U.S.-Mexican Studies, University of California, San Diego.

————. 1994. *Transforming State-Society Relations in Mexico: The National Solidarity Strategy*. San Diego: University of California.

CORSAM, Coordinación Suiza de Acompañamiento en México. 2001. Warum Chiapas? January. http://corsam.peacewatch.ch (accessed November 12, 2001).

Cuarto Poder. 1999. Desertan Supuestas Bases de Apoyo del EZLN. In *Melel News Synthesis*, ed. Melel Xojobal. Chiapas-1 mailing list archive. Burn! Student Collective Web site. May 4. http://burn.ucsd.edu/ archives/chiapas-l (accessed May 12, 2000; site discontinued in June 2000).

De la Grange, Bertrand, and Maite Rico. 1997. *Marcos, La Genial Impostura*. Mexico City: Nuevo Siglo Aguilar.

Deler, Jean-Paul, ed. 1998. *ONG et développement: Societé, Économie, Politique.* Paris: Edition Karthala.

De Vos, Jan. 1995. El Lacandón: Una introducción histórica. In *Chiapas: Los Rumbos de Otra Historia*, ed. Juan Pedro Viqueira and Mario Humberto Ruz, 331–61. Mexico City: UNAM.

————, ed. 2003. *Vjajes al Desierto de la Soledad: Un Retrato Hablado de la Selva Lacandona*. Mexico City: CIESAS.

Díaz Polanco, Héctor. 1997. *La Rebelión Zapatista y la Autonomía*. Mexico City: Siglo XXI.

————. 1998. La Autonomía, Demanda Central de los Pueblos Indígenas: Significado e Implicaciones. In *Pueblos Indígenas y Estado en América Latina*, ed. Virginia Alta, Diego Itturalde, and Hermilo López Bassols. Quito, Ecuador: Universidad Andina Simón Bolívar.

Dresser, Denise. 1994. Bringing the Poor Back In: National Solidarity as a Strategy of Regime Legitimacy. In *Transforming State-Society Relations in Mexico: The National Solidarity Strategy*, ed. Wayne A. Cornelius, Ann L. Craig, and Jonathan Fox, 143–66. San Diego: University of California.

Duran Duran, Claudia. 2001. Trabajando con Comunidades Diversas. Paper presented at the annual meeting of the Society of Applied Anthropology, Merida, March.

Eade, Deborah, and Suzanne Williams. 1995. *The Oxfam Handbook of Development and Relief*. Oxford, UK: Oxfam.

Earle, Duncan, and Jeanne Simonelli. 2005. *Uprising of Hope: Sharing the Zapatista Journey to Alternative Development*. Walnut Creek, CA: Alta Mira.

Enlace Civil A. C. 1998. Muncipios Autónomos, Ponencia de Enlace Civil A. C. para el Encuentro de la Sociedad Civil y el EZLN. November 19. http://www.enlacecivil.org.mx (accessed May 18, 2001).

————. 1999. Tres Indígenas Zapatistas Encarcelados con Delitos Fabricados. Chiapas-1 mailing list archive. Burn! Student Collective Web site. June 8.

http://burn.ucsd.edu/ archives/chiapas-l (accessed May 18, 2000; site discontinued in June 2000).

———. 2000. Enlace Civil, Autonomía Indígena en Chiapas, Hermanamientos. February 12. http://www.enlacecivil.org.mx/lm_hermanamientos.html (accessed July 20, 2001).

———. 2001. Salud y Desarrollo Integral Comunitario: San José del Río, Chiapas, México. November 2. http://www.enlacecivil.org.mx/pr_salud.html (accessed August 20, 2002).

———. 2002a. Autonomía Indígena en Chiapas. July 3. http://www.enlacecivil.org. mx (accessed August 20, 2002).

———. 2002b. Programa Educación: Proyecto Semillita del Sol. July 3. http://www. enlacecivil.org.mx/pr_e_semillita.html (accessed August 20, 2002).

———. 2002c. Programa de Producción y Comercialización. July 3. http://www. enlacecivil.org.mx/pr_produccion.html (accessed August 20, 2002).

———. 2002d. Programa de Salud. July 3. http://www.enlacecivil.org.mx/pr_salud. html (accessed August 20, 2002).

Esteva, Gustavo. 2003. The Meaning and Scope of the Struggle for Autonomy. In *Mayan Lives Mayan Utopias: The Indigenous Peoples of Chiapas and the Zapatista Rebellion. Impactos Regionales del Zapatismo en Chiapas*, ed. Jan Rus, Rosalva Aida Hernández Castillo, and Shannan L. Mattiace. Latin American Perspectives in the Classroom. Lanham, MD: Rowman and Littlefield.

Estrada Saavedra, Marco. 2007. *La Comunidad Armada Rebelde y el EZLN: Un Estudio Histórico y Sociológico sobre las Bases de Apoyo Zapatistas en las Cañadas Tojolabales de la Selva Lacandona (1930–2005)*. Mexico City: El Colegio de México, Centro de Estudios Sociológicos.

Excelsior. 1999. Purported Zapatista Deserters in Las Margaritas Ask for Government Aid. In *Melel News Synthesis*, ed. Melel Xojobal. Chiapas-1 mailing list archive. Burn! Student Collective Web site. May 4. http://burn.ucsd.edu/ archives/chiapas-l (accessed May 18, 2000; site discontinued in June 2000).

EZLN. 1993a. El Despertador Mexicano. Irish Mexico Group. December 31. http:// flag.blackened.net/revolt/mexico/ezln/ezln_editoral.html (accessed July 20, 2002).

———. 1993b. Primera Declaración de la Selva Lacandona. *Cartas y Comunicados*. December 31. http://palabra.ezln.org.mx/comunicados/1993/ 201993.html (accessed September 15, 2006).

———. 1994a. Declaración del CCRI-CG del EZLN. *Cartas y Comunicados*. December 19. http://palabra.ezln.org.mx/comunicados/1994/1994_12_19.html (accessed September 15, 2006).

———. 1994b. Discurso del Subcomandante Insurgente Marcos a la Caravana de Caravanas. *Cartas y Comunicados*. June 14. http://palabra.ezln.org.mx/comunicados/1994/1994_06_14.html (accessed September 15, 2006).

———. 1994c. *Documentos y Comunicados*. Vol. 1. Mexico City: Era.

———. 1994d. Mensaje del CCRI-CG del EZLN a los Organizaciones Non-Gubernamentales de México. *La Jornada*. February 1.

———. 1994e. Segunda Declaración de la Selva Lacandona. *Cartas y Comunicados*. June 10. http://palabra.ezln.org.mx/comunicados/1994/1994_06_10_d.html (accessed September 15, 2006).

———. 1996. Comunicado del CCRI-CG del EZLN del 29 de Agosto. *La Jornada*. September 3.

———. 1998. Quinta Declaración de la Selva Lacandona. *Cartas y Comunicados*. July 17. http://palabra.ezln.org.mx/comunicados/1998/1998_07_a.html (accessed September 15, 2006).

———. 1999. Comunicado del CCRI-CG del EZLN al Pueblo de México, a los Pueblos y Gobiernos del Mundo y a la Prensa Nacional e Internacional. Frente Zapatista de Liberación Nacional (FZLN). March 31. http://www.fzln.org.mx/archivo/ezln/1999/showalbores.html (accessed July 12, 2001).

———. 2005. Sexta Declaración de la Selva Lacandona. *Cartas y Comunicados*. June. http://palabra.ezln.org.mx/comunicados/2005/2005_06_SEXTA.html (accessed September 15, 2006).

Favre, Henri. 1973. *Cambio y Continuidad entre los Mayas de México*. Mexico City: Instituto Nacional Indígena.

Foucault, Michel. 1980. *Power/Knowledge: Selected Interviews and Other Writings, 1972–7*. New York: Pantheon Books.

Foweraker, Joe, and Ann L. Craig, eds. 1990. *Popular Movements and Political Change in Mexico*. Boulder, CO: Lynne Riener.

Fox, Jonathan, and Gustavo Gordillo. 1989. Between State and Market: The Campesinos Quest for Autonomy. In *Mexico's Alternative Political Futures*, ed. Wayne A. Cornelius, Ann L. Craig, and Jonathan Fox, 131–72. La Jolla, CA: Center for U.S.-Mexican Studies, University of California, San Diego.

Friedrich, Paul W. 1965. A Mexican Cazicazgo. *Ethnology* 4:190–209.

Gabbert, Karin, Wolfgang Gabbert, Bert Hoffmann, Albrecht Koschützke, Kalus Meschkat, Clarita Müller-Plantenberg, Eleonore von Oertzen, and Juliane Ströbele-Gregor, eds. 1997. *Lateinamerika: Analysen und Berichte*. Vol. 21. Bad Honnef, Germany: Horlemann.

Gabbert, Wolfgang. 1999. Violence and Social Change in Highland Maya Communities, Chiapas, Mexico. *Iberoamerikanisches Archiv* 25 (3/4): 351–74.

Gallardo Caballero, Mario. 2001. Cooperativa Mut Vitz, Chiapas, México: Iniciativas Locales para el Autodesarrollo. May. http://www.pangea.org/ellokal/chiapas.html (accessed September 12, 2002).

García Aguilar, María del Carmen. 1998. Las Organizaciones No-Gubernamentales en Chiapas: Alcances y Limites en su Actuación Política. In *Anuario de Estudios Indígenas*. San Cristóbal, Mexico: CESMECA-UNICACH.

García de León, Antonio. 1994. Prólogo. In *EZLN, Documentos y Comunicados*, 11–29. Vol. 1. Mexico City: Era.

————. 2002. *Fronteras Interiores. Chiapas: Una Modernidad Particular.* Mexico City: Oceano.

Gates, Marilyn. 1993. *In Default: Peasants, the Debt Crisis, and the Agricultural Challenge in Mexico.* Boulder, CO: Westview.

Gellner, Ernest, and John Waterbury, eds. 1977. *Patrons and Clients in Mediterranean Societies.* London: Duckworth.

Gerber, Phillip. 2005. *Das Aroma der Rebellion: Zapatistischer Kaffee, indigener Aufstand und Kooperativen in Chiapas, Mexiko.* Münster, Germany: Unrast Verlag.

Giddens, Anthony. 1985. *The Nation-State and Violence.* Cambridge, UK: Polity.

Gilly, Adolfo. 2005. *The Mexican Revolution.* New York: New Press.

Gil Olmos, José. 2000. Se Instalará un Generador Eléctrico en La Realidad. *La Jornada.* November 24.

Gilsenan, Michael. 1977. Against Patron-Client Relations. In *Patrons and Clients in Mediterranean Societies*, ed. Ernest Gellner and John Waterbury, 167–83. London: Duckworth.

Gledhill, John. 1994. *Power and Its Disguises: Anthropological Perspectives on Politics.* London: Pluto.

————. 1999. Getting New Bearings in the Labyrinth, the Political Consequences of Mexican Neoliberalism. Paper presented to the interdisciplinary Latin American Seminar, Manchester University.

Global Exchange. 2002. Reality Tours in Chiapas. http://globalexchange.org/tours/921.html (accessed February 8, 2002).

Goffman, Erving. 1974. *Frame Analysis: An Essay on the Organization of Experience.* New York: Harper and Row.

González Galván, Jorge A. 1997. *Derecho Indígena.* Mexico City: McGraw-Hill/Interamericana.

Guerrero Chiprés, Salvador. 1996. Decae el EZLN, según Análisis Oficial. *La Jornada.* September 25.

Halleck, Deedee. 1994. Zapatistas On-Line. *NACLA Report on the Americas* 28 (September–October): 31–32.

———. 2003. The Censoring of Burn! July 30. http://www.electronicbookreview. com/thread/technocapitalism/escalating?mode=print (accessed August 24, 2008).

Harvey, Neil. 1994. Rebellion in Chiapas, Rural Reforms, Campesino Radicalism and the Limits to Salinismo. *Transformation of Rural Mexico* 5. La Jolla, CA: Center for U.S.-Mexican Studies, University of California at San Diego.

———. 1998. *The Chiapas Rebellion: The Struggle for Land and Democracy*. Durham, NC: Duke University Press.

Henriquez, Elio. 2004. Revuelta contra CFE en Chiapas. *La Jornada*. August 8.

Hernández Castillo, Rosalva Aída. 2006. The Indigenous Movement in Mexico: Between Electoral Politics and Local Resistance. *Latin American Perspectives* 33 (2): 115–31.

Hernández Navarro, Luis, and Ramón Vera Herrera, eds. 1998. *Acuerdos de San Andrés*. Mexico City: Era.

Hidalgo Domínguez, Onésimo. 1997a. Testimonios de la Matanza. *La Jornada*. December 28. Masiosare supplement.

———. 1997b. El Vuelo de Las Abejas. *La Jornada*. December 28. Masiosare supplement.

———. 1998. La Situación de los Desplazados de Guerra. *Análisis*. Centro de Investigaciones Económicas y Políticas de Acción Comunitaria (CIEPAC). March. http://www.ciepac.org/archivo/analysis/desplazadoscencos.html (accessed September 26, 2008).

———. 1999. En los Albores de la Guerra. *Chiapas al Día* 146. Centro de Investigaciones Económicas y Políticas de Acción Comunitaria (CIEPAC). February 19. http://www.ciepac.org/boletines/chiapasaldia.php?id=146 (accessed September 5, 2008).

———. 2006. Los Acuerdos de San Andrés a Diez Años Después. *Chiapas al Día* 494. Centro de Investigaciones Económicas y Políticas de Acción Comunitaria (CIEPAC). February 15. http://www.ciepac.org/boletines/chiapasaldia. php?id=494 (accessed September 26, 2008).

Higgins, Nicholas. 2004. *Understanding the Chiapas Rebellion: Modernist Visions and the Invisible Indian*. Austin: University of Texas Press.

Hobsbawm, Eric, and Terrence Ranger. 1983. *The Invention of Tradition*. Cambridge: Cambridge University Press.

Husson, Bernard. 1998. Les ONG: Une Légitimité en Question. In *ONG et Développement: Societé, Èconomie, Politique*, ed. Deler Jean-Paul, 545–58. Paris: Edition Karthala.

Intermediate Technology Development Group (ITDG). 2003. Intermediate Technology. http://practicalaction.org/?id=faq#What%20is%20'appropriate'%20 or%20'intermediate'%20technology? (accessed September 26, 2008).

Irish Mexico Group. 1998–2003a. Revolt Collection. http://flag.blackened.net/revolt.

———. 1998–2003b. Struggle Collection. http://www.struggle.ws/mexico.html.

Jarque, Carlos. 2000. *La Política Social del Gobierno de México: Resultados 1995–2000 y Retos Futuros*. Mexico City: Secretaría de Desarrollo Social. http://sedesol2006. sedesol.gob.mx/publicaciones/libros/politica/portada.pdf (accessed July 2, 2006).

Joseph, Gilbert M., and Daniel Nugent, eds. 1994. *Everyday Forms of State Formation: Revolution and the Negotiation of Rule in Modern Mexico*. Durham, NC: Duke University Press.

Judge, Anthony. 1995. NGOs and Civil Society: Some Realities and Distortions: the Challenge of 'Necessary-to-Governance Organizations' (NGOs). *Transnational Associations* 47 (3): 156–80.

Kampwirth, Karen. 2002. *Women and Guerrilla Movements: Nicaragua, El Salvador, Chiapas, Cuba*. University Park, PA: Pennsylvania University Press.

Katzenberger, Elaine, ed. 1995. *First World, Ha Ha Ha! The Zapatista Challenge*. San Francisco: City Lights Books.

Keck, Margaret E., and Kathryn Sikkink. 1998. *Activists beyond Borders: Advocacy Networks in International Politics*. Ithaca, NY: Cornell University Press.

Klandermans, Bert, Hanspeter Kriesi, and Sidney Tarrow, eds. 1988. From Structure to Action: Comparing Social Movement Research across Cultures. In *International Social Movement Research*. Vol. 1. Greenwich, CT: JAI.

Klein, Hilary, and Gustavo Castro. 2001. Autonomy and Health in Zapatista Communities. *Chiapas al Día* 228. Centro de Investigaciones Económicas y Políticas de Acción Comunitaria (CIEPAC). January 17. http://www.ciepac.org/ boletines/chiapasaldia.php?id=228 (accessed December 17, 2002).

Knight, Alan. 1990. Historical Continuities in Social Movement. In *Popular Movements and Political Change in Mexico*, ed. Joe Foweraker and Ann L. Craig, 78–102. Boulder, CO: Lynne Riener.

Krauze, Enrique. 1994. Zapped: The Roots of the Chiapas Revolt. *The New Republic*. January 31.

Land und Freiheit. 1995–1999. *Die Aktion*. Periodical supplements with news and information for solidarity with the Chiapas insurgents. Hamburg, Germany: Nautilus.

Le Bot, Yvon. 1997. *Subcomandante Marcos. El Sueño Zapatista: Entrevistas con el Subcomandante Marcos, el Mayor Moisés y el Comandante Tacho, del Ejército Zapatista de Liberación Nacional*. Mexico City: Plaza y Janés.

Leyva Solano, Xochitl. 1995. Misioneros, Catequistas y Tradiciones. In *Chiapas: Los Rumbos de Otra Historia*, ed. Juan Pedro Viqueira and Mario Humberto Ruz, 375–406. Mexico City: UNAM.

———. 1998. The New Zapatista Movement: Political Levels, Actors and Political Discourse in Contemporary Mexico. In *Encuentros Antropológicos: Politics, Identity and Mobility in Mexican Society*, ed. Valentina Napolitano and Xochitl Leyva Solano, 35–55. London: Institute of Latin American Studies.

———. 1999. Regional, Communal and Organizational Transformations in Las Cañadas. Paper presented at the minisymposium, Chiapas 1994–1999: Five Years of Conflict, Resistance and Negotiation, Princeton University, February 19.

———. 2003a. Neo-Zapatista Advocacy Networks: From Local to Global Experience. Paper presented at the conference on global protest movements and transnational advocacy networks, Another World Is Possible! Development Studies Center-Kimmage, Dublin, March 6.

———. 2003b. Regional, Communal and Organizational Transformations in Las Cañadas. In *Mayan Lives, Mayan Utopias: The Indigenous Peoples of Chiapas and the Zapatista Rebellion. Impactos Regionales del Zapatismo en Chiapas*, ed. Jan Rus, Rosalva Aida Hernández Castillo, and Shannan L. Mattiace, 161–84. Latin American Perspectives in the Classroom. Lanham, MD: Rowman and Littlefield.

Leyva Solano, Xochitl, and Gabriel Ascencio Franco. 1996. *Lacandonia al Filo del Agua*. Mexico City: CIESAS, UNAM, UNICACH, FCE, and CIHMECH.

Libertad Solidarity Group. 2000. Yaxal Chi: Erklärung der Projekte, Projektentwürfe zu Beginn des Jahres. http://www.chiapas.at (accessed November 2, 2001).

———. 2001. Fortschritte der Projekte, ein Zwischenbericht unserer Kontaktperson. http://www.chiapas.at (accessed November 2, 2001).

Lins Ribeiro, Gustavo. 1998. Cybercultural Politics: Political Activism at a Distance in a Transnational World. In *Culture of Politics, Politics of Culture: Revisioning Latin American Social Movements*, ed. Sonia E. Alvarez, Evelina Dagnino, and Arturo Escobar, 325–52. Boulder, CO: Westview.

Lomnitz-Adler, Claudio. 1992. *Exits from the Labyrinth: Culture and Ideology in the Mexican National Space*. Berkeley: University of California Press.

López, Julio César. 1996. Entrevista con Subcomandante Marcos. *Proceso* 1002 (January 15): 30–31.

López Bárcenas, Francisco. 1999. Iniciativas de Reforma Constitucional y Derechos Indígenas en México. In *Memoria*, 199–222. San José, Costa Rica: IIDH.

Lynd, Staughton. 2005. Remarks on Solidarity Unionism. *Solidarity Papers*. Community Labor News. http://www.clnews.org/Solidarity (accessed January 3, 2006).

Mallon, Florencia E. 1995. *Peasant and Nation: The Making of Postcolonial Mexico and Peru*. Berkeley: University of California Press.

Marcos, Subcomandante Insurgente. 1994. Conferencia de Prensa de Marcos. *Cartas y Comunicados*. February 28. http://palabra.ezln.org.mx/comunicados/1994/1994_02_28.html (accessed October 3, 2001).

———. 1999. Carta a Guadalupe Loaeza. *La Reforma*. January 12.

———. 2002. Carta a Baltasar Garzón. *La Jornada*. December 7.

———. 2003. Chiapas: La Treceava Estela. Communiqué in six parts published on the occasion of inaugurating the Juntas de Buen Gobierno. *Cartas y Comunicados*. July 19. http://palabra.ezln.org.mx/comunicados/2003/2003_07_e.html (accessed October 28, 2003).

———. 2004. Leer un Video. *Cartas y Comunicados*. August 21. http://palabra.ezln.org.mx/comunicados/2004/2004_08_22.html (accessed March 2, 2006).

Mattiace, Shannan L. 2001. Regional Renegotiations of Space: Tojolabal Ethnic Identity in Las Margaritas, Chiapas. *Latin American Perspectives* 28 (2): 73–97.

———. 2003. *To See with Two Eyes. Peasant Activism and Indian Autonomy in Chiapas, Mexico*. Albuquerque: University of New Mexico Press.

Mattiace, Shannan L., Rosalva Aida Hernández Castillo, and Jan Rus, eds. 2002. *Tierra, Libertad y Autonomía: Impactos Regionales del Zapatismo en Chiapas*. Mexico City: CIESAS.

McAdam, Doug, John D. McCarthy, and Mayer. N. Zald, eds. 1996. *Comparative Perspectives on Social Movements: Political Opportunities, Mobilizing Structures and Cultural Framings*. Cambridge: Cambridge University Press.

Melel Xojobal. 1999. *Melel News Synthesis*. May 4. Chiapas-1 mailing list archive. Burn! Student Collective Web site. http://burn.ucsd.edu/archives/chiapas-l (accessed May 5, 2000; site discontinued in June 2000).

Middleton, Neil, and Phil O'Keefe. 2001. *Redefining Sustainable Development*. London: Pluto.

Midnight Notes Collective. 2001. *Auroras of the Zapatistas: Local and Global Struggles of the Fourth World War*. New York: Autonomedia.

More about the Italian Ya Basta. 2000. *A-Infos News Service*, December 27. http://www.ainfos.ca/00/dec/ainfos00448.html (accessed March 15, 2003).

Municipio Autónomo Ernesto Che Guevara. 1999. El Municipio Autónomo Ernesto Che Guevara Pide Hermanamiento y Ayuda. January 12. http://www.enlacecivil.org.mx (accessed July 20, 2001).

Muñoz Ramírez, Gloria. 2003. *20 y 10: El Fuego y la Palabra*. Mexico City: Revista Rebeldía.

———. 2004. Chiapas: La Resistencia. *La Jornada*. September 19. Suplemento.

Napolitano, Valentina, and Xochitl Leyva Solano, eds. 1998. *Encuentros Antropológicos: Politics, Identity and Mobility in Mexican Society*. London: Institute of Latin American Studies.

Nash, June. 2001. *Mayan Visions: The Quest for Autonomy in an Age of Globalization*. New York: Routledge.

Nicholas, Ralph W. 1965. Factions: A Comparative Analysis. In *Political Systems and the Distribution of Power*, ed. Michael Banton. London: Tavistock.

Nuijten, Monique. 2003. *Power, Community and the State: The Political Anthropology of Organisation in Mexico*. London: Pluto.

Olesen, Thomas. 2005. *International Zapatismo: The Construction of Solidarity in the Age of Globalization*. London: Zed Books.

Olivera, Mercedes. 1995. Práctica Feminista en el Movimiento Zapatista de Liberación Nacional. In *¿Chiapas y las Mujeres Que?* Vol. 2, ed. Rosa Rojas. Mexico City: Centro de Investigación y Capacitación a la Mujer.

Olivera, Mercedes, Magdalena Gómez, and Diana Damián Palencia. 2004. *Chiapas: Miradas de Mujer*. Bilbao: PTM-Mundubat.

Olivia Pineda, Luz. 1995. Maestros Bilingües: Burocracia y Poder Político en los Altos de Chiapas. In *Chiapas: Los Rumbos de Otra Historia*, ed. Juan Pedro Viqueira and Mario Humberto Ruz, 279–300. Mexico City: UNAM.

Panitch, Leo, and Colin Leys. 2001. *Working Classes: Global Realities; Socialist Register 2001*. New York: Monthly Review.

Paulson, Justin. 2001. Peasant Struggles and International Solidarity: The Case of Chiapas. In *Working Classes: Global Realities; Socialist Register 2001*, ed. Leo Panitch and Colin Leys, 275–88. New York: Monthly Review.

Paz, Octavio. 1994. El Nudo de Chiapas. *La Jornada*. January 6.

Petrich, Blanche. 1998. Parlamento Italiano: Sin Diálogo en Chiapas no se Ratificarán Convenios con México. *La Jornada*. January 28.

Petrich, Blanche, and Elio Henríquez. 1994. First Interview with EZLN CCRI-CG. Trans. irlandesa. *La Jornada*. February 3. Irish Mexico Group. http://flag.blackened.net/revolt/mexico/ezln/ccri_1st_interview.html (accessed October 12, 2002).

Pickard, Miguel. 2002. PPP: Plan Puebla Panamá, or Private Plans for Profit? A Primer on the Development Plan That Would Turn the Region from Southern Mexico to Panamá into a Giant Export Zone. *CorpWatch*. September 19. http://www.corpwatch.org/article.php?id=3953 (accessed May 28, 2003).

Ramírez Cuevas, Jesús. 1997. Chiapas, Mapa de la Contrainsurgencia. *La Jornada*. November 23. Masiosare supplement.

———. 2003. La Fiesta de los Caracoles, la Autonomía Indígena, Basada en los Incumplidos Acuerdos de San Andrés. *La Jornada*. August 9.

Reijne, Miriam E., and Adriaan B. van Rouveroy van Nieuwaal. 1999. Illusion of Power: Actors in Search of Power in a Prefectural Arena in Central Togo. In *Dezentralisierung, Demokratisierung und die zentrale Legitimation des Staates. Theoretische Kontroversen und empirische Forschungen*, ed. Jakob Rösel and Trutz v. Trotha, 176–83. Cologne, Germany: Rüdiger Köppe Verlag.

Rojas, Rosa, ed. 1995. *¿Chiapas y las Mujeres Que?* Vol. 2. Mexico City: Centro de Investigación y Capacitación a la Mujer.

Ronfeldt, David, and John Arquilla. 1998. *The Zapatista "Social Netwar" in Mexico.* Santa Monica, CA: Rand Corporation.

Roper, Montgomery, Thomas Perreault, and Patric C. Wilson. 2003. Introduction. *Latin American Perspectives* 30 (1): 5–22.

Rösel, Jakob, and Trutz v. Trotha, eds. 1999. *Dezentralisierung, Demokratisierung und die Zentrale Legitimation des Staates: Theoretische Kontroversen und empirische Forschungen.* Cologne, Germany: Rüdiger Köppe Verlag.

Ross, John. 1995. *Rebellion from the Roots.* Monroe, ME: Common Courage.

Rovira, Guiomar. 2000. *Women of Maize: Indigenous Women and the Zapatista Rebellion.* London: Latin American Bureau.

Ruiz Hernández, Margarito, and Araceli Burguete Cal y Mayor. 2003. *Derechos y Autonomía Indígena: Veredas y Caminos de un Proceso; Una Década (1988–1998).* Mexico City: Comisión Nacional para el Desarrollo Indígena.

Rus, Jan. 1994. The Comunidad Revolucionaria Institucional: The Subversion of Native Government in Highland Chiapas, 1936–1968. In *Everyday Forms of State Formation: Revolution and the Negotiation of Rule in Modern Mexico*, ed. Gilbert M. Joseph and Daniel Nugent, 265–300. Durham, NC: Duke University.

Rus, Jan, Rosalva Aida Hernández Castillo, and Shannan L. Mattiace, eds. 2003. *Mayan Lives Mayan Utopias: The Indigenous Peoples of Chiapas and the Zapatista Rebellion. Impactos Regionales del Zapatismo en Chiapas.* Latin American Perspectives in the Classroom. Lanham, MD: Rowman and Littlefield.

Sayer, Derek. 1994. Everyday Forms of State Formation: Dissident Remarks on Hegemony. In *Everyday Forms of State Formation: Revolution and the Negotiation of Rule in Modern Mexico*, ed. Gilbert Joseph and Daniel Nugent, 367–78. Durham, NC: Duke University Press.

Schools for Chiapas. 2001. Cooperating with the Maya Peoples' Efforts to Build Dignified Schools while Promoting Social Justice. November. http://www.mexicopeace.org (accessed November 4, 2005).

Schüren, Ute. 1997. 'Land und Freiheit': Mexikos langer Abschied von der Agrarreform. In *Lateinamerika: Analysen und Berichte*, ed. Karin Gabbert, Wolfgang Gabbert, Bert Hoffmann, Albrecht Koschützke, Kalus Meschkat, Clarita Müller-Plantenberg, Eleonore von Oertzen and Juliane Ströbele-Gregor, 33–65. Vol. 21. Bad Honnef, Germany: Horlemann.

SEVA Foundation. 2001. Mission Statement and Financial Information. http://www.seva.org (accessed November 12, 2001).

———. 2002. What Is Appropriate Technology? http://www.seva.org (accessed February 8, 2002).

SIPAZ, International Service for Peace. 2006. Brief History of the Conflict in Chiapas: 1994–2006. http://www.sipaz.org/fini_eng.html (accessed March 19, 2007).

Snow, David A., and Robert D. Benford. 1988. Ideology, Frame Resonance, and Participant Mobilization. In *From Structure to Action: Comparing Social Movement Research across Cultures*, ed. Bert Klandermans, Hanspeter Kriesi, and Sidney Tarrow. *International Social Movement Research*. Vol. 1. Greenwich, CT: JAI.

Speed, Shannon, and Jane Fishburne Collier. 2000. Limiting Indigenous Autonomy in Chiapas, Mexico: The State Government's Use of Human Rights. *Human Rights Quarterly* 22 (November): 877–905.

Stephen, Lynn. 1996. Redefined Nationalism in Building a Movement for Indigenous Autonomy in Mexico. Paper presented at the ninety-fifth annual meeting of the American Anthropological Association, San Francisco, November 29.

———. 2002. *Zapata Lives! Histories and Cultural Politics in Southern Mexico*. Berkeley: University of California Press.

Stephen, Lynn, and George A. Collier. 1997. Reconfiguring Ethnicity, Identity and Citizenship in the Wake of the Zapatista Rebellion. *Journal of Latin American Anthropology* 3 (1): 2–13.

Tatanka. 1998. Progetto di Educazione Attraverso L'Espressione Artistica "La Semillita del Sol." October 8. http://www.geocities.com/CapitolHill/4647 (accessed November 12, 2001).

Tello Díaz, Carlos. 1995. *La Rebelión de las Cañadas*. Mexico City: Cal y Arena.

Terry, Fiona. 2002. *Condemned to Repeat? The Paradox of Humanitarian Action*. Ithaca, NY: Cornell University Press.

Veltmeyer, Henry. 2000. The Dynamics of Social Change and Mexico's EZLN. *Latin American Perspectives* 27 (5): 88–110.

Viqueira, Juan Pedro, and Mario Humberto Ruz, eds. 1995. *Chiapas: Los Rumbos de Otra Historia*. Mexico City: UNAM.

Vogt, Evon Z. 1961. Some Aspects of Zinacantán Settlement Pattern and Ceremonial Organization. *Estudios de Cultura Maya* 1:131–46.

Warman, Arturo. 1994. Chiapas Hoy. *La Jornada*. January 16.

Weber, Max. 1978. *Economy and Society*. 2 vols. Ed. Günther Roth and Klaus Wittich. Berkeley: University of California Press.

Wickham-Crowley, Timothy P. 1991. *Exploring Revolution: Essays on Latin American Insurgency and Revolutionary Theory*. New York: M. E. Sharpe.

Wolf, Eric. 1955. Types of Latin American Peasantry: A Preliminary Discussion. *American Anthropologist* 7 (3): 452–71.

———. 1969. *Peasant Wars of the Twentieth Century.* London: Faber and Faber.

Womack, John. 1999. *Chiapas, a Historical Reader.* New York: New Press.

Yudice, George. 1998. The Globalization of Culture and the New Civil Society. In *Culture of Politics, Politics of Culture: Revisioning Latin American Social Movements,* ed. Sonia E. Alvarez, Evelina Dagnino, and Arturo Escobar, 353–79. Boulder, CO: Westview.

Zapatista Rebels Deny Desertions. 1999. *Cable Network News (CNN),* April 2. http://www.cnn.com (accessed February 12, 2002).

Zendejas, Sergio. 1995. Appropriating Governmental Reforms: The Ejido as an Arena of Confrontation and Negotiation. In *Rural Transformations Seen from Below: Regional and Local Perspectives from Western Mexico,* ed. Sergio Zendejas and Pieter de Vries. Transformations of Rural Mexico. Vol. 8. San Diego: University of California.

Zendejas Sergio, and Pieter de Vries, eds. 1995. *Rural Transformations Seen from Below: Regional and Local Perspectives from Western Mexico.* Transformations of Rural Mexico. Vol. 8. San Diego: University of California.

Web Sites

A-Infos News Service. http://www.ainfos.ca. (accessed March 2003).

Alianza Cívica Chiapas. http://www.laneta.apc.org/alianza (accessed November 2001).

Amnesty International Jena. http://www.amnesty-jena.de (accessed March 2003).

Cable Network News. http//www.cnn.com (accessed February 2002).

Café Libertad Cooperative. http://www.cafe-libertad.de (accessed November 2001).

CAREA Solidarity Group. http://www.epo.de/carea (accessed November 2001).

Cartas y Comunicados del EZLN. http//palabra.ezln.org (accessed 2005–2007).

CIEPAC, Centro de Investigaciones Económicas y Políticas de Acción Comunitaria. http://www.ciepac.org/ (accessed 1999–2007).

Chiapas-1 mailing list archive. http://burn.ucsd.edu/archives/chiapas-1 (accessed 1996–2000).

Chiapas-95 mailing list archive. http://www.eco.utexas.edu/~archive/chiapas95 (accessed 1996–2000).

Cloudforest Initiatives. http://www.pangea.org/ellokal/chiapas (accessed November 2001).

Community Labor News. http://www.clnews.org (accessed January 2006).

CorpWatch. http://www.corpwatch.org (accessed May 2003).

CORSAM, Swiss solidarity group. http://corsam.peacewatch.ch (accessed November 2001).

Enlace Civil A. C. http://www.laneta.apc.org/enlacecivil (accessed 1997–2001); http://www.enlacecivil.org.mx (accessed 2001–2003).

Envirolet Composting Toilet World. http://www.compostingtoilet.org (accessed May 2003).

EZLN, unofficial homepage. http://www.ezln.org/documentos/index.html (accessed 1998–2003).

Frente Zapatista de Liberación Nacional (FZLN). http://www.fzln.org.mx/archivo (accessed 1998–2003).

Global Exchange http://globalexchange.org (accessed November 2001 and February 2002).

Human Bean Company. http://www.thehumanbean.com (accessed November 2001).

Human Rights Center Fray Bartolomé de Las Casas. http://www.laneta.apc.org/cdhbcasas (accessed November 2001).

Independent Media Center, Chiapas. http://www.chiapas.mediosindependientes.org (accessed February 2001–2007).

Irish Mexico Group. Revolt Collection. http://flag.blackened.net/revolt (accessed 1999–2003); Struggle Collection. http://www.struggle.ws/mexico.html (accessed 1999–2003).

ITDG, Intermediate Technology Development Group at the Schumacher Center for Technology and Development. http://www.itdg.org (accessed July 2003).

La Jornada. http://www.jornada.unam.mx (accessed 2001–2007).

Libertad Solidarity Group. http://www.chiapas.at (accessed November 2001).

Melel News Synthesis. http://www.laneta.apc.org/melel (accessed 1998–2003).

Pangea.Org. http://pangea.org (accessed September 2002).

Schools for Chiapas. http://www.mexicopeace.org (accessed November 2001).

SEDESOL, Secretaría de Desarrollo Social. http://www.sedosol.gob.mx (accessed July 2006).

SEVA Foundation. http://www.seva.org (accessed November 2001 and February 2002).

SIPAZ, International Service for Peace. http://www.sipaz.org (accessed March 2007).

Tatanka Solidarity Group. http://www.geocities.com/CapitolHill/4647 (accessed November 2001).

Index

Page numbers in italic type indicate an illustration on that page. The letter *n* following a page number refers to a note. The number following the *n* indicates the number of the note on that page.